BEHIND ENEMY LINES
WWII ALLIED/AXIS PROPAGANDA

BEHIND ENEMY LINES
WWII ALLIED/AXIS PROPAGANDA

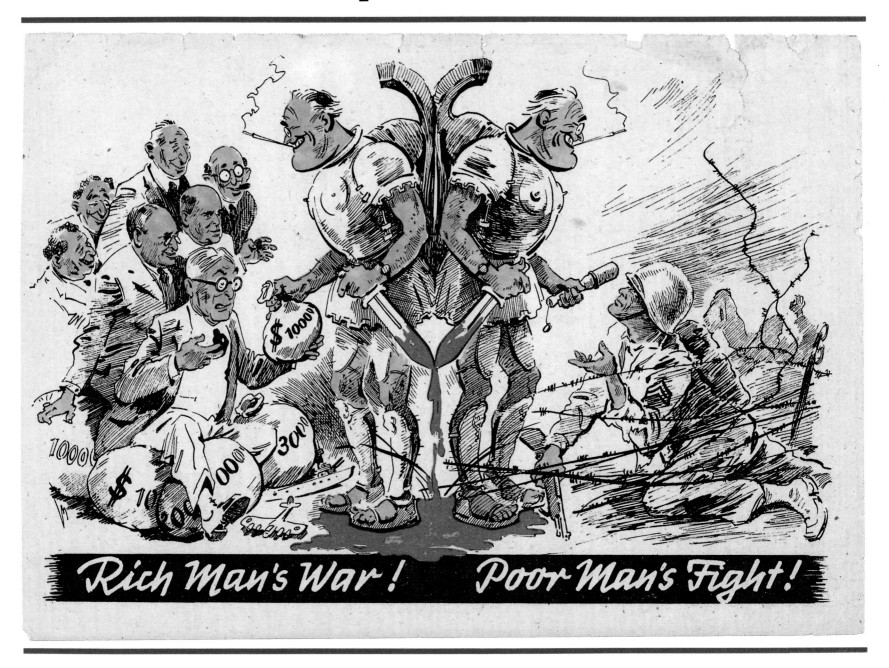

Rich Man's War! Poor Man's Fight!

Edward Boehm

Origination: Regent Publishing Services, Ltd.
Printing: Leefung-Asco Printers, Ltd.
Editorial Director: Tony Meisel
Art Director: Carmela Pereira

Manufactured in Hong Kong.

ISBN: 1-55521-379-0

CONTENTS

PUBLISHER'S NOTE

Some of the material contained in this book may be offensive on religious, racial or ethnic grounds. This material is produced exactly and faithfully from the originals and represents the historical record. Neither the author nor the publisher condones the information or sentiments expressed in the individual flyers. To censure it, however, would be to distort the sum of Allied-Axis propaganda in World War II.

PROLOGUE

On the morning of December 7th, 1941, the Royal Japanese Naval Air Force, commanded by Captain Mitasao Fuchida, decided to practice bombing our ships that had been recalled from around the world and congregated inside Pearl Harbor. They were sitting ducks. It was made easy for them not to miss. When Admiral Yamamoto saw the opportunity, off went his planes to prove themselves. They found out that they were real good. Of course the placement of the ships helped. The bombing was an absolute success.

The news of the bombing excited Roosevelt, so he scribbled up a Declaration of War and sent it to Congress the very next day. Congress signed it! Now Uncle Sam placed himself inside every post office around the country. He groomed his whiskers, put on his best duds of red, white and blue, with stars and stripes. His hat was something like Abraham Lincoln's only much prettier because it, too, had stars and stripes all over it. A couple of days after war had been declared on Japan, the President scribbled out another declaration of war against the Germans and sent that to Congress—they signed it also!

It was drafted, passed through boot camp and OCS, then sent to North Africa, where I was wounded. After a long siege in the hospital, I was assigned to General Eisenhower's headquarters on temporary duty in Algiers. From there I was assigned to PWB (Psychological Warfare Branch). After a couple of weeks in Tunis, I was assigned to the British Eighth Army as Combat Propaganda Liaison Officer with PWB, Psychological Warfare Branch.

The term *psychological warfare* had its origins during World War II. It had many different names depending on the time and place. It had its growing pains as any other new organization is expected to have. PWB dealt mainly with combat propaganda.

Propaganda is no new media of warfare. Many centuries before Christ, psychological warfare was employed, and has been used ever since. There are many objectives that may be sought through the use of psychological warfare. The first and foremost is to demoralize the enemy. In this book one will readily see that the Germans were well aware of this objective and took full advantage of the situation. They certainly were expert in this field. I believe the Germans had the Allies out-bested in every way when it came to propaganda, but then they were at it many years before World War II got under way.

My job with the Psychological Warfare Branch was as Combat Liaison Officer to the various commanders to induce them to shoot our propaganda leaflets to the Germans. Propaganda was never a part of the Military SOP (Standard Operating Procedures), therefore, the various commanders had to be induced to cooperate on our behalf. We shot our leaflets with artillery guns. However we also flew over the German lines and dropped them from planes.

The fuses were set to fire the shells when they were just over the heads of the troops intended to receive them. We had trouble for a long time to get the leaflets to come out and not be damaged too much to read. Many times they would be discharged in a solid mass. Other times they were torn beyond legibility. This was a job for me to correct. I spent two weeks behind the lines with this project.

I took an artillery piece and had them fire various settings on the fuse. I had civilian girls load the shells with various amounts in each shell. After two weeks of experiments I finally solved the problem and thereafter we had excellent results.

I was at the front to pick up a lot of Axis propaganda, and some of it was very well-done and effective. This was never a real collection, per se, at the time. When I picked up these leaflets I just stashed them away without even reading most of them. About 10 years after the war I found myself with nothing to do. The weather back home in Montana was very severe that winter so instead of going out I broke into my footlocker where the leaflets were stored. I spread them all over my living room and found I had a marvelous collection.

I took one of each to Washington, D.C. and showed my collection to the people at the National Archives. They told me that, without a doubt, I had the largest propaganda leaflet collection in the world. They, of course, wanted to talk me out of mine. The claimed that my collection was far superior to theirs. In any case, I can boast that I have the largest leaflet collection that any individual has ever picked up on the front lines in any war. And so it has remained with me until now.

With this publication, the leaflets, flyers and other paper propaganda is now available to a larger audience, some of whom will remember, first-hand, the terrors, comraderie and exhaustion of the war. A younger generation will not have seen most, if not all, of this material before. For them, it will be both a history lesson and an insight into the trials of disinformation. If you start to believe it, you will never know the truth.

Edward Boehm
Livingston, Montana

What is PROPAGANDA?

[*Note: This chapter is the complete and entire text, with the original illustrations, of a booklet prepared by the American Historical Association, published by The United States Armed Forces Institute and made available to the American public in 1944 by the War Department.*]

DEFINING PROPAGANDA

An attempt to define propaganda is made near the end of this pamphlet after we have examined its main characteristics. In order to avoid mistaken ideas, however, it may be useful to point out at once what some of these characteristics are.

Propaganda isn't an easy thing to define, but most students agree that it has to do with any ideas or beliefs that are intentionally propagated. It uses words and word substitutes in trying to reach a goal–pictures, drawings, graphs, exhibits, parades, songs, and other devices.

Of course propaganda is used in controversial matters, but it is also used to promote things that are generally acceptable and noncontroversial.

So there are different kinds of propaganda. They run all the way from selfish, deceitful, and subversive effort to honest and aboveboard promotion of things that are good.

Propaganda can be concealed or open, emotional or containing appeals to reason, or a combination of emotional and logical appeals.

WHAT IS PROPAGANDA?

It is the spring of 1940. Allied armies face the German columns, but there is little action at the front, and a group of French soldiers find time to listen to an enemy broadcast.

"Where are the English?" asks the radio voice. The enemy broadcaster is speaking in French. The soliders listen uneasily.

"I'll tell you where your English comrades are," continues the voice. "They lounge about Paris and fill the night clubs. Have you seen a Tommy in the Maginot Line? Of course not. French soldiers, you will find the Tommies behind the lines–with your wives."

Propaganda. Of course. The German propaganda strategy of division, intended to sow suspicion and doubt about the fidelity of an ally. The propaganda preparatory to the blitz.

WHAT IS PROPAGANDA

EM 2
G I ROUNDTABLE

A handful of Londoners are drinking ale in their neighborhood pub. The time is July 1940. The French have signed Hilter's armistice terms, but Britain is still holding out. The pub keeper turns the dials of the tavern radio to tune in on "Lord Haw-Haw," the Berlin broadcaster, and the voice booms out:

"England is ripe for invasion...You might as well expect help from an army of mastodons as from the United States...You are on a doomed ship...Whether or not the people of Britain want to see their fields turned into graveyards and their cities into tombs is a matter for themselves and Mr. Churchill. Perhaps if the British people could speak, they would ask for peace. But since the official voice of England asks not for peace but for destruction, it is destruction we must provide."

The propaganda of fear. The voice of defeatism.

It is the autumn of 1941. The United States is still neutral, but an American Army is in training, a Navy is being strengthened, and Lend-Lease supplies are crossing the Atlantic.

An American sits at home tinkering with his short-wave set and he picks up an English-language broadcast beamed to North America from Germany.

"The German government and the German people have only the friendliest of feelings for the United States, the home of so many American citizens of German descent." The words of the radio speaker are honeyed words. "Let it be said for once and all," the broadcaster continues, "that a German victory in this war is no threat to English democracy—and certainly not to American democracy."

The propaganda voice of appeasement. Here is the strategy of attempting to hypnotize a people with an assertion of the "peaceful intentions" of the Nazi war machine.

In a few brief months the Japs strike at Pearl Harbor, and the Germans declare war against those for whom they said they cherished "only the friendliest of feelings."

ENEMY PROPAGANDA

Hitler is the arch propagandist of our time. These are examples of his strategy in attempting to mold the opinions and attitudes of his intended victims to his own purposes. Division, doubt, and fear are the weapons he uses within one nation and among Allied countries arrayed against him. His purpose is summed up in his own phrase—to sow "mental confusion, contradiction of feeling, indecision, panic."

Since Hitler's propaganda is a weapon constantly used against us, we need to understand clearly his techniques and devices—not only those he employs today, but also the cunning and diabolical methods by which he and his Brown Shirts combined propaganda and other pressures, first to take over the German state, then to stamp out all vestiges of freedom in it. The story goes back to the early 1920's.

The very name of the party headed by Hitler was chosen with great deliberation for its propaganda effect. The little group of fanatical men who called themselves the German Labor Party in 1919 later sought a name that would have widespread appeal. Hitler and his adherents chose "National Socialist German Workers' Party," reduced by popular usage to "Nazi." Each

word of this title had a special significance for certain groups in Germany. "Socialist" and "National," for example, were associated with causes that long antedated Hitler. That was what Hitler wanted—a name that would prove a catchall, an omnibus upon which many could ride.

The Nazi banner was a product of Hitler's contriving. He hated the black, red, and gold flag of the German Republic against which he was conspiring. Since the old imperial colors of the days of the kaiser could still arouse powerful emotions, he decided he must use some of the colors of this old banner—black, white, and red. In 1920 Hitler and his followers made up a striking flag with the hooked cross or swastika dominant, but with the colors that would capture the allegiances of various groups of Germans—red to capture Socialist sentiment and white to appeal to the Nationalists. The black swastika within the white circle is a symbol of the anti-Semitic platform of the Nazi leader and his fanatical supporters.

The Nazi salute—the upraised arm—was a device created to identify party members and the Nazi movement. Further identification was given through the use of the party salutation, "Heil Hitler," and as time went on both members and nonparty Germans used it. Then came the invention of party slogans—Blut und Boden (Blood and Soil), and others that have a strange ring on democratic ears but which appealed to the followers of "the leader."

Hitler hypnotized the German people by staging dramatic parades and gigantic and spectacular rallies and demonstrations. One department of the Nazi propaganda office spent all its time planning rallies, selecting badges, emblems, uniforms, costumes, flags, and "background" effects to give glitter to the assemblages. While marching men and massed bands incited party delegates, the ritualistic ceremonies and the emotional speeches of the leader stirred Nazi members into a further frenzy.

As an example of how mass propaganda was organized, look at a typical Nuremberg party rally. The participants or actors numbered 110,000 storm troopers, 50,000 labor servicemen and women, 180,000 party officials, and 120,000 ordinary party members—a total of 460,000 equal to thirty army divisions. Visitors numbering 550,000 looked on at the ceremonies.

These techniques were deliberately designed, as one propaganda expert points out, "to bring about identification of larger and larger numbers with first, the Nazi cause, and then with what, after they gained power, was termed the 'true national community.'"

After they captured office, the Nazis were ruthless in stamping out all vestiges of the German Republic. The symbols of the Fuhrer and the Nazi party became preeminent. The so-called "leadership principle" which exalted Hitler into an infinitely wise, an almost godlike, chieftain was one of the fictions created by his adherents.

The Nazis established a ministry of propaganda. They licensed and catalogued German newspapermen to keep them in control, suppressed or "integrated" unfriendly newspapers, and as the crisis developed in Europe, expelled foreign correspondents who sought to tell the truth of what went on in Germany. They took over the broadcasting system and every other agency that bore a relationship to the cultural life of the people.

But despite all Nazi cunning, the propaganda tricks and the creation of dazzling new symbols could not take the minds of the German people entirely off their troubles. The Nazis then cleverly drained away some of these resentments by finding scapegoats–minority groups against whom blame for difficulties could be charged. The trade unions were one scapegoat, the Versailles Treaty another, the Communists a third, and the democracies a fourth. But the Jew was the easiest target. The German people could blame all these "enemies" for their own state of affairs and thus seem to free themselves of fault.

Against the Jews, the Nazis turned their wrath. The Jew, they said, was not an "Aryan." They claimed that he had "sold out" the Germans in World War I. He was in league, they charged, with "international capitalism." They held him to be the chief cause of inflation in Germany. In a word, they accused him of causing most of the ills from which the nation suffered. They heaped their troubles on his head. The "non-Aryan" myth fitted into the dogma of the racial superiority of the Germanic stock, one of the fictions spread by the Nazi party "philosophers."

The club and pistol, concentration camp, and secret police were the means of putting down the Jews and other minority groups whenever propaganda by itself was not enough. To the weapons of propaganda and censorship, the Nazis had added a third–terror.

Germany became a nation built upon propaganda, plus force. The political state became the shadow of the Nazi party.

After establishing the dictatorship in 1933-34, Hitler used his energies for a time in fastening the Nazi yoke on the necks of the German people. The next step was to prepare the ground in countries that he wished to annex or control. Paul Joseph Goebbels, head of the propaganda ministry, got unlimited funds and authority to foment trouble among Germany's neighbors. Here again propaganda was combined with terror. Uniting propaganda with threats, veiled bribes, subversive tactics, and outright violence, the Nazis "softened up" Austria and the Sudetenland for the "kill." By propaganda and other means, they weakened France through stirring up class conflicts within the French Republic. Using similar methods, they forced minor states to submit to dictation from Berlin.

The Nazis have never disguised their lack of principles. Eugen Hadamowski, a Goebbels assistant, once said, "The use of force can be a part of propaganda." The idea was first, to confuse and strike fear into the hearts of your own countrymen, and then to use similar techniques to demoralize the people of other countries. Here is the plan the Nazis used in their propaganda warfare against former friends and neighbors:

Nazi strategists sought out the "soft spots" in the areas they planned to absorb or attack. Rival economic interests, racial and religious antagonisms, tensions between political groups, cleavages between workers and employers–these were studied in every detail. If, in the nation about to be attacked, influential persons were discovered who could be bribed or corrupted, German agents made use of these quislings. In a careful index, German espionage services charted possible approaches to key politicians, businessmen, military leaders and others–knew their habits, peculiarities, even their vices. Every political faction was analyzed for its possible usefulness to Germany.

Then Nazi agents built up in the victim country a front of discontented elements who could be managed in times of crisis. Thus the rancors, grudges, and disloyalties of these elements would serve to divide a nation and destroy its unity. Every country has groups of discredited political fig-

THEY PRETEND FRIENDSHIP—THEN GIVE THEM "THE WORKS"

ures, demagogues, extreme reactionaries, misguided idealists, and die-hards who can be misled by glittering promises. Play our game, the Nazis told some of these groups, and we will elevate you to positions of power and influence.

Another technique was to pretend friendship for the country against which force was to be used while secretly plotting its destruction. While a peaceful neighbor slumbered, hoping the German propagandists really meant what they said, the Nazis perfected their plans. When disunity, stimulated by Nazi underground tactics, developed, however, Germany grew bolder. Hitler then made threats and demands. Goebbels echoed his master. The Nazi propaganda machine issued a barrage describing the great strength of the German army and air force and the folly of even trying to resist them. Nazi attacks discredited the doomed country's leaders, no matter how honest and sincere those leaders were. The "war of nerves" was unleashed. The Nazis were then ready to strike.

All this required careful preparation and the cynical union of propaganda and terror. Before attacks were made on Austria, Czechoslovakia, Poland, Norway, the Netherlands, or France, the Nazis planted their subversive agents in legations, consulates, and tourist bureaus, created Nazi party "cells" within a country's borders, and established espionage services which ramified all over the world. Treacherous persons already in the pay or under the influence of the Nazis—the "fifth columnists"—were ready to "sell out" when the time came for the Nazis to strike.

That was the technique of the "invasion from within" and the propaganda attack from without. That was the means used to crush a nation even before the tramp of German soldiers rang in the streets of invaded cities.

DEMOCRATIC VS. ENEMY PROPAGANDA

Hitler and his partners in aggression are not the only experts in propaganda, however. The weapon of propaganda in the modern world must be parried and the blows returned by counter-propaganda. In the struggle for men's minds that is constantly being waged by propagandists there is, however, a fundamental difference between the propaganda of dictatorship and the propaganda of democracy.

Hitler himself, in *Mein Kampf,* laid down his rules for dictatorship. He stated the "principle of the whopping lie" and of the gullibility of the masses. If you are going to tell a lie, he said, and nobody doubts that he intended to, don't tell a little one, because it will be recognized as a lie. Tell the biggest and most unlikely lie you can think of, keep on telling it, and the people will think it must be the truth and believe it. "The greater the lie, the more effective it is as a weapon," said the master of the alleged "master race."

Moreover, he went on, don't be fooled into thinking that you have to sway the influential people—the leaders of opinion—to your side first. "Toward whom must propaganda be directed," he asked, "toward the scientific intelligentsia or toward the uneducated masses?" His answer was, "It must always and exclusively be directed toward the masses. The teachability of the great masses is very limited, their understanding small, and their memory short." In a word, he believes that it pays to take advantage of ignorance and that it is therefore best to keep the people ignorant.

Democracy is a different kind of system from the ground up. It is based on the people, and it works well in proportion as the people are enlightened and informed about what goes on both in peace and in war (though of course democratic people recognize the wisdom of some wartime censorship imposed for security reasons). This basic democratic principle was stated by President George Washington in his Farewell Address when he said, "In proportion as the structure of a government gives force to public opinion, it is essential that public opinion should be enlightened." To the degree that people are denied access to the facts and to a wide range of independent interpretations of the facts, democracy fails to function effectively.

These simple truths determine the underlying or governing principles of democratic propaganda. The Nazis blindfold their people against the truth. In exact opposition to the rules of Hitler, the democratic countries must present the truth in spite of official suppressions and distortions. And when propaganda has been revealed to be deceitful and distorted, it no longer is effective. Moreover, democratic propaganda must observe the right of the people to know the facts, however unpleasant they may be. The strategy of truth is not only in accord with the basic principles of democracy, but it also a hardheaded and realistic policy for effective dealing with allies, neutrals, and even enemies.

WAR PROPAGANDA

The Nazis prepared for war from the moment Hitler came into power in 1933. In the feverish building up of German striking power, they had the support of the professional military men. The Nazis not only produced the weapons of war; they geared their economy for the strain of a future conflict. They carried on political intrigues to promote their purposes. Their propaganda machine had long been a going concern when Hitler felt ready to strike at Poland, the first step in an ambitious plan to lay the world at his feet.

Military, economic, political, and propaganda weapons were forged for the fray. Britain and France and, soon after, other peaceful nations were compelled to forge them to resist the Nazi onrush.

Today's war is four-dimensional. It is a combination of military, economic, political, and propaganda pressure against the enemy. An appeal to force alone is not regarded as enough, in the twentieth century, to win final and lasting victory. War is fought on all four fronts at once—the military front, the economic front, the political front, and the propaganda front.

To understand how this four-dimensional warfare has come about, we have to look at history. We have to go back to the rise of nationalism in the eighteenth century.

Before the American and French revolutions took place at the end of the eighteenth century, many armies fought in the pay of monarchies, such as the Bourbons, Hapsburgs, and Hohenzollerns, or of individual leaders. They were mercenary armies. They did not fight for patriotic motives. They did not fight for causes. They fought because fighting was their business. No fight, no pay!

Something new came when the Americans formed a citizen army to win their independence and when the French threw off the yoke of the Bour-

DER FÜHRER IS ALWAYS RIGHT!

I'LL MAKE UP MY OWN MIND!

bons. The French raised a national army to beat back the Austrians and Prussians who were seeking to choke off the new French state. These Frenchmen were fighting for France, for the country they loved. They weren't fighting for a despot, a royal house, or money. Like the Americans, they were fighting for their country.

About the same time, the Industrial Revolution was introducing a vital change in the methods of warfare. Larger and larger production became possible because of machinery. New mechanized forms of weapons came into use. Today's sequel of this story is seen in airplanes, tanks, landing boats, aircraft carriers, and a thousand other modern instruments of war.

One result of this change is that modern war calls for large armies in the field. Where 1 per cent of the population was once considered a large number to call to the colors, 10 per cent can now be mobilized. And populations are much bigger than they used to be. But modern war means not only big armies in the field. It also means even bigger civilian armies back of them, on the home front. For every man in the field, we are told, there must be a half-dozen workers in the factories and fields at home. So the masses of men directly engaged in modern war effort are staggering.

There are other changes, too. Today's great accumulation of capital means that war can be waged on a large scale and for long periods. The mechanization of armies and navies means not only that the actual battle front can cover thousands of miles, where in the past the battle area was relatively small, but also that fighting men can continue a campaign, without stopping, through a Russian winter, a Burmese rainy season, or an African summer.

The result of these changes is that propaganda has become in modern war not only a formidable weapon against the enemy but likewise a necessary tool in promoting a national war effort.

Through it are carried popular appeals to make the necessary sacrifices and to contribute muscle, mind, and money to the successful prosecution of the war. In a democratic country, under governments chosen by and responsible to the people, the entire population, in and out of uniform, must be informed of the progress of the war. A free flow of information serves to stimulate the war effort, strengthens the nation to stand reverses, to hold steadfast through a long conflict, to take losses courageously, to make sacrifices bravely, to buy bonds generously, and to cooperate in every way possible in the great national effort for victory.

PROMOTION OF A WORTH-WHILE

The political aspects of war tie in closely with all this, as has been shown, for example, by the Moscow, Cairo, and Tehran conferences. The combatant nations must have programs for victory and programs for peace. And their people must be told about them.

But even that isn't the whole story. Propaganda in wartime must seek to demoralize enemy morale. A primary objective of propaganda aimed at enemy nations is to break down their will to fight. It seeks to lower the enemy's will to resist and it does this in several ways. One is to picture the military successes on the propagandist's side. Another is to picture the armed might and economic power that the enemy has to face. Yet another is to picture the moral superiority of the cause against which the enemy is fighting. It is part of a nation's strategic plan to intimidate enemy leaders, to separate them from their people, and to break down resistance by producing evidence that the mass of the enemy people have been deceived and

CAUSE IS GOOD PROPAGANDA . . .

misled.

Propaganda, too, is an instrument for maintaining unity and good will among allies banded together in a common effort. It is sometimes effective in bringing opinion in neutral states over to one side or another. And in the battle zones it serves to keep up the morale of the men who are doing the actual fighting job.

So, as you contrast the tremendous volume and intensity of war propaganda today with the situation in wars of other eras, you can't escape the conclusion that what is going on now is a modern phenomenon. Propaganda of some sort had, it is true, been used in warfare for centuries. But all the social, economic, industrial, and military factors that make propaganda a large-scale part of war in 1944 first made themselves seriously felt in World War I. In that war, propaganda for the first time became an important and formal branch of government. It is in modern times that we have become familiar with such governmental institutions as the British Ministry of Information, the German Ministry of Propaganda and Public Enlightenment, the American Committee on Public Information (in World War I), the Office of War Information (in World War II), and their counterparts in many other countries.

It should not be forgotten that the astonishing forward strides in communications in the twentieth century have had a lot to do with the development of propaganda—especially radio broadcasting. Not only is propaganda vital to the conduct of modern war; it is also possible to reach many millions of people regularly, day and night, who only twenty-five years ago might have been almost beyond the reach of propaganda. Not only the words but the actual *voices* of the leaders of the nations at war are familiar to millions of people the world over, carried by the magic of radio.

THE STORY OF PROPAGANDA

The fact that wars give rise to intensive propaganda campaigns has made many persons suppose that propaganda is something new and modern. The word itself came into common use in this country as late as 1914, when World War I began. The truth is, however, that propaganda is not new and modern. Nobody would make the mistake of assuming that is is new if, from early times, efforts to mobilize attitudes and opinions had actually been called "propaganda." The battle for men's minds is as old as human history.

In the ancient Asiatic civilization preceding the rise of Athens as a great center of human culture, the masses of the people lived under despotisms and there were no channels or methods for them to use in formulating or making known their feelings and wishes as a group. In Athens, however, the Greeks who made up the citizen class were conscious of their interests as a group and were well informed on the problems and affairs of the city-state to which they belonged. Differences on religious and political matters gave rise to propaganda and counterpropaganda. The strong-minded Athenians, though lacking such tools as the newspaper, the radio, and the movies, could use other powerful engines of propaganda to mold attitudes and opinions. The Greeks had games, the theater, the assembly, the law courts, and religious festivals, and these gave opportunity for propagandizing ideas and beliefs. The Greek playwrights made use of the

TRUTH TELLING PROMOTES
GOOD WILL AMONG ALLIES

drama for their political, social, and moral teachings. Another effective instrument for putting forward points of view was oratory, in which the Greeks excelled. And though there were no printing presses, handwritten books were circulated in the Greek world in efforts to shape and control the opinions of men.

From that time forward, whenever any society had common knowledge and a sense of common interests, it made use of propaganda. And as early as the sixteenth century nations used methods that were somewhat like those of modern propaganda. In the days of the Spanish Armada (1588), both Philip II of Spain and Queen Elizabeth of England organized propaganda in a quite modern way.

On one occasion, some years after the Spanish Armada, Sir Walter Raleigh complained bitterly about the Spanish propaganda (though he didn't use that name). He was angry about a Spanish report of a sea battle near the Azores between the British ship *Revenge* and the ships of the Spanish king. He said it was "no marvel that the Spaniard should seek by false and slanderous pamphlets, advisoes, and letters, to cover their own loss and to derogate from others their own honours, especially in this fight being performed far off." And then he recalled that back at the time of the Spanish Armada, when the Spaniards "purposed the invasion" of England, they published "in sundry languages, in print, great victories in words, which they pleaded to have obtained against this realm; and spread the same in a most false sort over all parts of France, Italy, and elsewhere." The truth of course was that the Spanish Armada suffered a colossal disaster in 1588.

The Spanish claims, though described in the language of Queen Elizabeth's time, have a curiously modern ring. Make a few changes in them, here and there, and they sound like a 1944 bulletin from the Japanese propaganda office.

The term "propaganda" apparently first came into common use in Europe as a result of the missionary activities of the Catholic church. In 1622 Pope Gregory XV created in Rome the Congregation for the Propagation of the Faith. This was a commission of cardinals charged with spreading the faith and regulating church affairs in heathen lands. A College of Propaganda was set up under Pope Urban VIII to train priests for the missions.

In its origins "propaganda" is an ancient and honorable word. Religious activities which were associated with propaganda commanded the respectful attention of mankind. It was in later times that the word came to have a selfish, dishonest, or subversive association.

Throughout the Middle Ages and in the later historic periods down to modern times, there has been propaganda. No people has been without it. The conflict between kings and Parliament in England was a historic struggle in which propaganda was involved. Propaganda was one of the weapons used in the movement for American independence, and it was used in the French Revolution. The pens of Voltaire and Rousseau inflamed opposition to Bourbon rule in France, and during the revolution Danton and his fellows crystallized attitudes against the French king just as Sam Adams and Tom Paine had roused and organized opinion in the American Revolution.

World War I dramatized the power and triumphs of propaganda. And both fascism and communism in the postwar years were the centers of in-

RADIOS ARE THE EARS OF THE "UNDERGROUND."
THEIR PRESSES PASS THE GOOD WORD ALONG.

tense revolutionary propaganda. After capturing office, both fascists and communists sought to extend their power beyond their own national borders through the use of propaganda.

In our modern day, the inventive genius of man perfected a machinery of communication which, while speeding up and extending the influence of information and ideas, gave the propagandists a quick and efficient system for the spread of their appeals. This technical equipment can be used in the interests of peace and international good will. Hitler, Mussolini, and Tojo preferred to seize upon this magnificent nervous system for selfish ends and inhumane purposes, and thus enlarged the role of propaganda in today's world. While the United Nations were slow at first to use the speedy and efficient devices of communication for propaganda purposes, they are now returning blow for blow.

The modern development of politics was another stimulus to propaganda. Propaganda as *promotion* is a necessary part of political campaigns in democracies. When political bosses controlled nominations, comparatively little promotion was needed before a candidate was named to run for office, but under the direct primary system the candidate seeking nomination must appeal to a voting constituency. And in the final election he must appeal to the voters for their verdict on his fitness for office and on the soundness of his platform. In other words, he must engage in promotion as a legitimate and necessary part of a political contest.

In democracies, political leaders in office must necessarily explain and justify their courses of action to an electorate. Through the use of persuasion, those in office seek to reconcile the demands of various groups in the community. Prime ministers, presidents, cabinet members, department heads, legislators, and other office-holders appeal to the citizens of community and nation in order to make a given line of policy widely understood and to seek popular acceptance of it.

In peacetime the promotional activities of democratic governments usually consist of making the citizens aware of the services offered by a given department and of developing popular support for the policies with which the department is concerned. The purpose is to make these services "come alive" to the everyday citizen, and in the long run official information and promotion tend to make the average man more conscious of his citizenship. If the public is interested in the work done in its name and in its behalf, intelligent public criticism of governmental services can be stimulated.

Recent economic changes have expanded the volume of propaganda. Under the conditions of mass production and mass consumption, techniques of propaganda and public relations have been greatly developed to help sell commodities and services and to engender good will among consumers, employees, other groups, and the public at large.

WHAT ARE THE TOOLS OF PROPAGANDA?

Whether the propagandist works in a peacetime or wartime situation, he uses certain tools to mobilize opinions and attitudes. What are these tools?

An important one is *suggestion*. Another word for it is *stimulation*.

The propagandist tries to *stimulate* others to accept without challenge his own assertions, or to act as he wants them to do. The idea of using *suggestion* or *stimulation* as a propaganda device is that it will lead a public to

Propaganda was used in the movement for American independence

accept a proposition even though there are not logical grounds for accepting it. The propagandist usually tries to side-step critical reactions from his audience, and therefore suggestion is one of his most important tools.

How does the propagandist use this tool? By making broad and positive statements. By presenting his statements in simple and familiar language. By refusing to admit, or even suggest, that there is another side to the question. Hitler's brutal and direct suggestion that the Jews sold out the German people in World War I—the "stab in the back," the Nazi propagandists called it—is an example of this kind of propaganda. Another example is the repeated Nazi propagandist assertion that Prime Minister Churchill and President Roosevelt are "warmongers."

Suggestion is a highly developed art in commercial advertising. An obvious example is the flat declaration that some brand of vitamin will remedy "that tired and run-down feeling."

A second propaganda tool is only a subtler form of suggestion. This tool is the use of hints, insinuations, or indirect statements.

An example or two from the field of advertising will illustrate this method. The sponsorship of a symphony orchestra by a commercial company may be expected to create a feeling of good will on the part of the listener toward the product of the sponsor. Sometimes programs designed to portray the life and culture of another country are propagandistic in nature, designed to "sell" that country to listeners in a home country.

A third method of propaganda is the appeal to the known *desires* of an audience. Psychologists say that desire is an important factor in belief. Thus some persons may support some unsound economic scheme because they desire an income in their old age. Others will subscribe to some fraudulent "scheme of psychology" in order to improve their "personality."

The self-interested propagandist will study public opinion to find out what things people are "for" or "against" in order to decide on the labels that he will use to bring about desired reactions. He knows that such words as "justice," "Constitution," "Americanism," and "law and order," which arouse favorable attitudes, will serve as a favorable background for his message, and so he uses them. On the other hand, he may use certain other words—for example, "radical" or "un-American"—to influence his listeners to reject a cause or idea that he regards as inimical to his own interests.

Hitler is adept and completely unscrupulous in appealing to various groups in Germany. There has been little consistency in his appeals, but here have been many suggested cure-alls for discontented or unhappy groups. The insincerity of the Nazi performance is revealed in the statement of a careful student who says, "National Socialism has no political or social theory. It has no philosophy and no concern for the truth. In a given situation it will accept any theory that might prove useful; and it will abandon that theory as soon as the situation changes...National Socialism is for agrarian reform and against it, for private property and against it, for idealism and against it."

The advertising man appeals to desire in the interest of his client. The desire to be strong and healthy, to be socially acceptable, to be beautiful, sells drug products, cosmetics, reducing preparations, soaps, perfumes. Anyone who is accustomed to reading advertisements will instantly recall dozens of illustrations of appeals to such desires used to promote a wide variety of products.

The skilled propagandist also knows the techniques of "making ideas stick." It is because of this knowledge that he resorts to key words and slogans, shibboleths, or other symbolic forms.

The advertising slogan packs meaning into short sentences. The purpose is to get them noticed. They will find their way into the minds of people. When a person is choosing a commodity to buy, it is expected that the slogan will come easily to the surface of his mind. A good many years ago advertisers discovered that "reason-why" appeals were not always effective. Appeals were shortened and emotionalized, since many readers will not wade through explanations of why one commodity is better than another.

The history of international political propaganda, the experts tell us, is full of examples of the use of striking slogans. For example, "the sick man of the Golden Horn" was used as a description of the former Turkish Empire. In Hitler's name-calling techniques, the democratic nations are called "pluto-democracies." While seeking power he used the campaign cry: "The Versailles Treaty is a monstrous lie." Under Mussolini, the Fascists were fond of such slogans as "a book and a rifle make a perfect Fascist" and "a plough makes a furrow but a sword defends it."

Though the Nazi propaganda both inside and outside Germany has been marked by terror, this is not a common characteristic of slogans and symbols. No one could challenge such Red Cross slogans as "All you need is a heart and a dollar." No one could question the socially minded impulse behind the Salvation Army slogan, "A man may be down but he's never out." Compelling slogans have been devised to win support for war relief, community help, and many other such activities.

Sometimes slogans have fired the imaginations of people in the past and continued their influence down to the present. One authority suggests that if a slogan catches correctly and objectively "the underlying forces in a critical situation," it may turn out to be "vital and lasting." We remember such striking slogans as "No Taxation without Representation" from the American Revolution, "Liberty, Equality, and Fraternity" from the French Revolution, and "Peace, Bread, and Land" from the Russian Revolution.

Propaganda makes use of slogans, but it also makes effective use of symbols. A symbol is a concrete representation of an idea, action, or thing—a sign that stands for something, as crossed rifles stand for the Infantry and as wings and propeller represent the Air Forces.

A symbol can be a word, a mark, an object, a song, a flag, an image, a picture, a statue, or some collective or grouped representation—anything that conveys a common thought to masses of people. A symbol is a kind of cement that holds together a social group.

The propagandist knows the art of working with symbols. He uses symbols to develop both favorable and unfavorable attitudes.

Symbol usage will create likenesses that are used much as a stenographer uses shorthand. Cartoonists have stereotyped symbols to represent the taxpayer, the college professor, and many others. One cartoonist pictured the "prohibitionist" as a tall, thin, long-nosed, black-garbed figure in a plug hat, and others portrayed the saloonkeeper as a very fat, barrel-like figure. The "capitalist" was once pictured as a huge diamond-studded man wearing a suit covered with dollar signs.

There is some reason to believe that in the past half century there has been a decrease in the number of popular symbols used in the Western nations. But a vast amount of symbolism has been created by the fascist, Nazi, and communist states.

The Nazis made their symbols so unmistakable and conspicuous that if any German omitted to display or use them, he would be quickly detected. These symbols, you will recall, included the Nazi salute, the swastika, and a lot of titles, badges, and uniforms. "Hitler himself," writes one authority, "must have his own title, denied by special edict to all other leaders, and he won great popular approval, after the death of Hindenburg, by pretending that the title President was altogether too august for him."

The use of "non-Aryan" as a symbol by Hitler and the Nazi hierarchy was a demagogic device to encourage the persecution of minority scapegoats who were neither numerous nor powerful enough to resist the violent tactics of the Nazi propagandists and Nazi terrorists.

Catchwords and slogans abound in Nazi propaganda, contrived for the sake of impressing the German people. The Nazis are fond of such important and high-sounding words and phrases as "immutable," "imperishable," and "for all future time." Opportunists, they are quick to discard a slogan when it has served its purpose. Then new ones are coined and must be on all German lips.

The chief symbol used to inspire the Japanese civilian and fighting man is the emperor. The Japanese higher-ups maintain their internal power by making a god of their emperor—emphasizing his alleged descent from the sun god. This symbol of the emperor as god is used to stimulate the fighting effectiveness of soldiers and sailors. The Japanese, in their propaganda attacks on Americans and British, play up the symbol "white exploiter." They disguise Japanese imperialism behind the symbol of "co-prosperity" in their efforts to win converts among the brown and yellow races.

Another technique used by the propagandist is the prestige element in human relations.

The psychologists are not agreed as to the extent to which attitudes and opinions can be propagated by prestige, but it seems certain that prestige does play an important role. The influence the parent has over his child, for example, can be traced in part to the prestige of an adult—in size, strength, knowledge, and power.

Some individuals or groups resent expert opinion and are unwilling to respond to the suggestions made by fact-finders and scientists. But there seems to be no doubt that in politics prestige is a decided factor. A poll of men whose biographies were included in *Who's Who* was used, for instance, in a political campaign some years ago to indicate that persons described as "superior and influential" were mainly on the side of one party and candidate. The prestige of businessmen has been a factor in political campaigns, especially in times of prosperity.

In wartime, belligerents stress the prestige of their military and political leadership. Sometimes this prestige is increased by legends, which are another means of influencing the attitudes of people. Usually legends are built up around a core of truth, but the end result may be like a character from fiction. The legends of Ulysses, Roland, and Siegfried, for example, grew up around mighty warriors. Whether legends are deliberately created or not, there can be no doubt that they are accepted and believed by many people, and so they influence the conduct of people. Someone has said that "masses of mankind live in these images" or legends.

THE JAPS CALL IT "CO-PROSPERITY"
27

23

Hitler, Mussolini, and their followers have been industrious mythmakers. The near-deification of Hitler by the Nazis and the technique of mass hypnotism of the Germans are things that we, as a democratic people, find it very difficult to understand. To us it is incredible that a fanatical, intense, uneducated Munich agitator, unschooled in economics and politics, should be exalted by mass appeals and terroristic tactics into an all-powerful and "infallible" leader, "Der Fuhrer," who exacts unquestioned obedience from his people. This "infallibility" that the Nazis have credited to Hitler is bluntly expressed in the words of Robert Ley, the director of the Nazi Labor Front. "Germany must obey like a well-trained soldier," he said. "The Fuhrer, Adolf Hitler, is always right."

Why did large sections of the German public come to accept this legend of the Munich agitator? One historian thinks that it was because millions of Germans were yearning for "an end of all thought, will, or action on their own part in the conduct of their own affairs." The idea of a Fuhrer, he believes, expressed their satisfaction in having found a leader who to them was "a symbol of absolute authority, a Great Father, a patriarch-ruler who can be worshipped as an all-wise Messiah, bringing solace and salvation to his sorely tried children." Hitler took "all responsibility for their own welfare." What they had to do was to give him "implicit faith and blind subordination."

SOME LIMITATIONS OF PROPAGANDA

While propaganda, using the tools of suggestion and persuasion, can gain important and significant objectives, it is a common mistake to overvalue its power. Men and women are not so easily swayed as some who fear propaganda seem to think.

There must be a reasonably fertile field to nourish the propagandist's seed before it can be expected to ripen into attitudes and opinions.

As one writer has pointed out, if the propaganda is not in harmony with the individual and his desire, it is likely to be met by cynical skepticism. The propaganda of Hitler, for example, fitted in with a German desire for supremacy; and the propaganda of the sellers of some patent medicine, whatever its real merits, harmonizes with the desire of people for good health.

Moreover, it should be remembered that forces quite apart from propaganda may have a large part in preparing the ground. One must be careful to distinguish between the opinion that *propaganda* creates and the opinion that is developed by *events*.

To give an illustration, the American attitude toward Germany was not bitterly hostile in the early months of World War I. But when the *Lusitania* was torpedoed in May 1915, with loss of 128 American lives, anger against the Central Powers mushroomed overnight.

The studies of George Gallup, since World War II started, reveal a similar relation between events and attitudes. In the early spring of 1940 only 7 Americans out of 100 voted "yes" in response to Dr. Gallup's question as to whether the United States should declare war on Germany. A month later, after the battle of Flanders, 16 out of 100 said they would vote for war if a national referendum were called. Dr. Gallup went on to say that "events and actions are infinitely more potent factors in influencing the formation

MUSSOLINI WAS GOOD AT THROWING THE BULL . . . . BUT HE COULDN'T MAKE IT STICK

of public opinion than a mere desire (for example) to imitate one's fellow citizens."

Goebbels' job as a propagandist was comparatively easy while the German armies were winning victories in Poland, the Low Countries, France, Norway, and Greece. But his job was not so easy after the tide began to turn. The routing of Rommel in North Africa, the invasion of Sicily and Italy, the smashing defeats of the Germans in Russia, the bombing of German cities, and the invasion on the west made the propaganda appeals of Goebbels far less effective in their impact than they had been before. It was only *after* Allied bombing of the Reich got into full swing that we began to hear of "weakening German morale."

No American should need to be reminded that the isolationists lost most of their following—and a good deal of their own conviction—within a matter of hours after the Japanese attack on Pearl Harbor.

Heredity and environment are also important in forming opinions. A great many men and women hold to the political beliefs of their fathers. The public opinion polling experts believe that sex, age, place of residence, and income are all of some importance in influencing attitudes, and that on some issues, race, religion, and party affiliations also enter.

In addition to all these things, a man's own knowledge and information may cause him to hold to an opinion no matter how heavy the barrage of propaganda attempting to force him to change it.

So propaganda is not the all-powerful weapon that may people believe it to be. It is only one of the tools in the formation of public opinion.

NEWS AND PROPAGANDA

While it is a serious mistake, as has been said, to overvalue propaganda, it is an equally serious mistake to assume, as some people do, that everything in the newspapers and on the radio, in the movies and magazines, is "propaganda"—propaganda that is self-seeking, deceitful, or otherwise improperly motivated. This is absurd.

The channels of communication can, of course, be used for propaganda. They can be used for "bad" propaganda and they can also be used for "good" propaganda. And they can be utilized for material that is not propaganda at all.

Let's look at just one case—that of the newspaper. Under the Constitution, freedom of the press is guaranteed. Why? Because a democratic nation knows that free expression of opinion and the free flow of facts, unhampered by governmental restrictions, is fundamental to intelligent action on the part of its citizens—and is also a social safety valve.

The journalist of today has a responsibility to *report facts* as accurately, objectively, and disinterestedly as is humanly possible. The newspaperman who respects himself and his work—the average newspaperman—accepts this responsibility. The honest, self-disciplined, well-trained reporter seeks to be a propagandist for nothing but the truth.

Of course propaganda does get into the press. Sometimes it is presented in the guise of impartial fact because the newspaperman is not sufficiently trained—or smart enough—to recognize it for what it is. Sometimes the newspaper is a conscious propagandist—in news and headlines both. And sometimes propaganda is so obviously news, and so obviously a matter of importance to the newspaper's readers, that the paper presents it knowing that the readers themselves will recognize it for what it is and evaluate it for themselves.

All this imposes a responsibility upon the newspaper reader, and it is with him that the responsibility of judgment ultimately should and does lie. The good newspaperman does his best to confirm the news, to weed out propaganda that isn't news, and to present whatever propaganda the citizenry ought to know about. Having done that, he leaves it up to the reader for evaluation and criticism. He knows that the critical reader—one decently supplied with facts and having some knowledge of propaganda methods and purposes—can do his own job of separating the wheat from the straw, the important from the unimportant. That is the citizen's responsibility and his privilege in a democratic society.

DEFINING PROPAGANDA

While most persons who give the matter a thought make distinctions between an objectively written news report and propaganda, they encounter difficulty when they try to define propaganda. It is one of the most troublesome words in the English language. To define it clearly and precisely, so that whenever it is used it will mean the same thing to everybody, is like trying to get your hands on an eel. You think you've got it—then it slips away.

When you say "policeman" or "house," everybody has a pretty clear idea of what you mean. There's nothing vague about these terms. But when you try to mark off the exact boundaries of "propaganda," you wrinkle the brows even of the men who spend their lives studying the origin and history of words. And the problem of defining propaganda is all the more tangled because in the first World War it acquired certain popular meanings that stick to it like burrs to a cocker spaniel.

To some speakers and writers, propaganda is an instrument of the devil. They look on the propagandist as a person who is deliberately trying to hoodwink us, who uses half-truths, who lies, who suppresses, conceals, and distorts the facts. According to this idea of the word, the propagandist plays us for suckers.

Others think especially of techniques, of slogans, catchwords, and other devices, when they talk about propaganda. Still others define propaganda as a narrowly selfish attempt to get people to accept ideas and beliefs, always in the interest of a particular person or group and with little or no advantage to the public. According to this view, propaganda is promotion that seeks "bad" ends, whereas similar efforts on behalf of the public and for "good" ends isn't propaganda, but is something else. Under this definition, for example, the writings of the patriotic Sam Adams on behalf of the American Revolution could not be regarded by American historians as propaganda.

The difficulty with such a view is that welfare groups and governments themselves secure benefits for a people through propaganda. Moreover, national propaganda in the throes of a war is aimed to bolster the security of the nonaggressor state and to assure the eventual well-being and safety of its citizens. No one would deny that this kind of propaganda, intelligently administered, benefits every man, woman, and child in the land.

GOEBBELS' JOB GOT TOUGHER WHEN BOMBS BEGAN TO RAIN ON THE REICH

The experts have plenty of trouble in agreeing upon a satisfactory definition of propaganda, but they are agreed that the term can't be limited to the type of propaganda that seeks to achieve bad ends or to the form that makes use of deceitful methods.

Can you distinguish propaganda from other forms of expression or promotion by saying that it is something that depends upon "concealment"—on hiding either the goals men are working for, or the means that they use, or the identity of the people behind the propaganda? A few authorities say "yes" to this question, but most of them say "no." Most analysts of propaganda do not limit the term propaganda to "veiled" promotion. Nor do they think it accurate to describe propaganda as an activity that resorts only to half-truths and downright falsehood. They say simply that some propaganda hinges on deceit and some does not. As a matter of fact, they recognize that a shrewd propagandist prefers to deal above the table, knowing just what the reaction of a propaganda-conscious public will be to dishonest trickery when it is exposed.

Some people limit the term propaganda to efforts that make use of emotional appeals, but others will differ about this idea. In a campaign to capture public opinion, a propagandist may rely heavily upon emotional symbols—but he may appeal to logical thinking as well.

Some people assert that propaganda is present only in controversial situations. One writer, for example, says, "Propaganda is an instrument of conflict or controversy, deliberately used." And another says, "If the report is deliberately circulated to influence attitudes on controversial issues it is propaganda." When existing loyalties, customs, and institutions are attacked, there is controversy. In a democratic system, propaganda replaces violence and censorship as a method of bringing about change. All this may be granted, and yet the question can be raised whether the word "propaganda" should be limited to efforts to influence attitudes on controversial matters only.

Take, for example, the campaign in the United States, conducted under the direction of the Surgeon General, for the control, cure, and eradication of venereal disease. This systematically organized campaign tried to gain its ends by direct appeals to the people. Those who handled it considered carefully just what agencies to use in reaching the people—whether newspapers or magazines, the radio or the public platform, or a combination of these. They used both emotional and logical appeals. They planned the campaign to persuade diseased persons to decide to visit a physician to get cured. Their campaign used the techniques of propaganda, persuaded persons to a course of conduct, and promised a reward—good health. It used, as has been said, both emotional and logical appeals.

Unless "controversy" is interpreted to include minor debates and the making of choices in matters that command general social approval, a definition of "propaganda" that insists on stressing controversy hampers one's approach to an understanding of the subject.

All this will indicate that there is a lot of difficulty in working out any formal definition of propaganda. Most students of the subject agree that propaganda has to do with any ideas and beliefs that are intentionally propagated. They agree also that it attempts to reach a goal by making use of words and word substitutes (pictures, drawings, graphs, exhibits, parades, songs, and similar devices). Moreover, although it is used in controversial situations, most experts agree that it is also used to promote noncontroversial, or generally acceptable, ideas. Types of propaganda range from the selfish, deceitful, and subversive to the honest and aboveboard promotional effort. It can be concealed or open, emotional or containing appeals to reason, or a combination of emotional and logical appeals.

While propaganda influences the behavior of individuals, it is important to bear in mind that it is only one of the means by which man's behavior is influenced. There are other forms of inducement employed in winning assent or compliance. In limited or wholesale degree, depending upon the political organization of a given country, men have used force or violence to control people. They have resorted to boycott, bribery, passive resistance, and other techniques. Bribes, bullets, and bread have been called symbols of some of the actions that men have taken to force people into particular patterns of behavior.

Whatever propaganda may be, it differs from such techniques because it resorts to suggestion and persuasion.

HOW TO SIZE UP PROPAGANDA

No matter how we define it, the principal point on propaganda is this: *Don't be afraid of it.*

A few years ago this caution was more necessary than it is now. Propaganda was National Bogeyman No. 1. Speakers and writers saw magic in it. Some of them told us that we did everything but go to bed at night for no better reason than that the propagandist told us to. And so a great many people assumed that a propagandist was lurking behind every billboard, ready to spring out on us, and that whatever he told us was against our best interests.

Both of these ideas were incorrect. One fact that has been emphasized in this pamphlet is that much propaganda is "good." It urges us to do things that are for our own benefit. And another fact of importance is that much has been called propaganda when it has actually no promotional effort of any kind behind it.

In a democratic country, where free expression is basic, no one who thinks the matter through could possibly want to stamp out all propaganda. The essence of democracy is that rival points of view have the right to compete in the open. Decisions on political and other questions must be made by a free people. That means a people who don't shut their eyes and ears to opposing arguments, but instead look at them all, evaluate them, and throw out the ones that don't hold water.

Those who spread an unreasoned fear of propaganda base their preachments on the unscientific notion that propaganda by itself governs public opinion. But the truth is that propaganda is only one of the factors that influence public opinion. Specific information and sound knowledge of facts, presented without any propagandistic motive whatsoever, constitute an extremely important factor in the formation of public opinion. Events, as we have seen, constitute another very important factor. And there are others. The wave of unreasoned fear of propaganda has somewhat leveled off. We clearly realize that, although some promotional campaigns have been conspicuously successful, others have been just as conspicuously failures—evidence that many factors, working together, influence and shape

1915—THE LUSITANIA

Events are often more important in crystallizing people's thoughts than is propaganda.

1941—PEARL HARBOR

public opinion.

The propaganda against propaganda confused many citizens and led them to ask, "What *can* I believe?" One writer, answering this question, says that "you can believe in yourself, your own common sense, your own decent instincts, your own values and traditions." The democratic principle requires that we come to our own judgments on the issues we face. Nobody can dodge the necessity of making up his own mind on any given question that calls for decision, whether it is international policy, local politics, or even the selection of one toothpaste over another. In making up his own mind he can look at all the propagandas and also bring into play all the information that is to be found outside propaganda and use every standard and criterion available to him in weighing values.

He should not forget that there are safeguards and checks for sizing up the merits of propaganda and the self-interest that may lie back of it. One authority on propaganda suggests two tests:

1. Is it really propaganda? Is some individual or group consciously trying to influence opinion and action? Who? For what purpose?

2. It it true? Does a comparison of independent reports show that the facts are accurate? Does such a comparison show that the suggestions made are soundly based?

There are other tests that can be applied by the thinking citizen:

Which fact or set of facts in a piece of promotion are really important and relevant? Which are irrelevant?

If some individual or group is trying to influence opinion and action, is the effort selfish or is it unselfish? Will action resulting from the propaganda benefit the individual or group responsible for it? Or will it benefit those who act upon the suggestion given in the propaganda? Or will it benefit both?

What is likely to be the effect of the action or of the opinion that the propaganda is trying to set in motion?

All these points boil down to some very simple questions: What is the source of the propaganda? What is its authority? What purposes prompted it? Whom will it benefit? What does it really say?

TO THE LEADER

There has been much loose talk about propaganda. This talk started long before the war. So-called educational campaigns of some commercial advertisers created suspicions in the minds of the public. Nazi use of propaganda before and during the war built up fear of it. But the fear evaporates, when people on the receiving end recognize what they read or hear for what it is. Witness the reception accorded Lord Haw-Haw in Britain.

Wide discussion of the question "What is propaganda?" will inoculate our citizens against the effects desired by the enemies of democracy. In a society which guards the right to freedom of speech, it is doubly important that people discriminate between legitimate talk about controversial issues and the type of propaganda that conceals fact and reason in a cloud of prejudice and fear. You will find one or more discussions or a forum on *What Is Propaganda?* useful in your program.

What Is Propaganda? can be particularly well handled in informal or panel discussion. A forum or a symposium will be successful if your

HOW MANY PROPAGANDA IDEAS CAN YOU FIND IN THIS PICTURE?

speakers are skillful and well informed. For suggestions on how to conduct discussion meetings, refer to War Department Education Manual, EM 1, *G.I. Roundtable: Guide for Discussion Leaders.*

Make *What Is Propaganda?* available, if possible, for reading by members of your group. Several individuals can share one copy if you will place those you have in a library, day room, service club, or other central spot for reading. Discussions go off better when members have some information upon which to base their talk. If you have an insufficient supply of the pamphlet for general reading by your group, be sure to spend, or have some assistant of yours use, the first five or ten minutes of the meeting for an introductory talk. In this introduction it would be important to attempt a definition of propaganda, suggesting the question whether a propagandist, in order to be such, must have a conscious purpose. You might raise here the issue of whether there is such a thing as good propaganda. You could mention some of the devices used by propagandists who seek to befog rather than clarify issues.

After the brief background talk you will need to have in mind some questions to get your group started. The questions that follow have been devised to suggest, but not to impose a procedure for the discussion:

FIRST—Develop a definition of propaganda. For many persons "propaganda" is a smear word, carrying the suggestion that anything to which it is applied is "bad." Is this too limited a meaning of the word? One writer on the subject says: "Propaganda is the *premeditated* selection of what we see and hear, designed to influence our attitudes." Is there such a thing as *unpremeditated* propaganda? Are all forms of propaganda "concealed," or are some open and avowed? Can propaganda be used in the public interest? Is it a phenomenon of recent origin? Why has it played such an important part in human history? Would you wish to stamp out all propaganda?

SECOND—Get your group to distinguish between propaganda and education. Are teachers propagandists? Are parents propagandists? Does the attitude of the propagandist differ from that of the scientist? How are the opinions of the average person formed? By newspaper, radio, or movies? Is it the function of education to train individuals to be immune to the distortions, the biases, the omissions, and the prejudices found in the various types of propaganda material? Is it the function of any other agency?

THIRD—Discuss this question: Are there differences between the use of propaganda in a democracy and in an authoritarian nation? Is advertising propaganda? What are the objectives of war propaganda? Of Nazi propaganda one expert says: "Nazi propaganda techniques include no secret devices, no newly-discovered psychological processes, no new channels of communication." If you support this statement, what *is* new about the Nazi method and why has it been so effective? Why, with all the amazing propaganda apparatus at his disposal, did Hitler think it necessary to use force against minority groups in the German nation?

FOURTH—Consider the safeguards against propaganda. Do specific information and a sound knowledge of facts influence opinion? What are some of the propaganda devices commonly used? What is a symbol? What is legend making? What is a slogan? How does the element of prestige work in fixing or altering attitudes and opinions? Do most persons accept such

WELL, WHAT *IS* PROPAGANDA?

propagandas as seem most nearly to conform to their own interests, needs, and prejudices? Are most persons so "fed up" with propaganda that they do not let it affect them? Do many individuals support propaganda which is in the public interest and not solely in line with their own selfish interests? What propaganda devices did the Nazis "think up" to win followers? To "soften up" a nation they wished to absorb or attack? Do you believe this is a sound statement: "Although propaganda is pervasive and will be persistent, it need not be fatal to intelligent popular decisions?" Why do you believe or disbelieve the last statement?

1. "American promises are no good, they are phony as the one dollar bill that you are looking at." (to the Italians.)

2. From this billfold they, no doubt, are trying to show what the soldiers could have if they weren't at the front—money, parents, and especially a sweet girl back home. Being a POW would assure them of all that in the future.

3. A rare example of unpublished propaganda. This sheet is an actual rough draft from the German propaganda Ministry.

BRITISH SOLDIERS!

Now you know the German soldier and you know too, he can put up a very good fight, as your General Monty said.

But do you know, why the German soldier fights to his last?

Because Germany does not want to take any orders from others with regard to her way of living!

Neither from Russia, where more than 14.000.000 people, among them 200.000 priests; were killed and where more than 4.000.000 people starved to death!

Nor from U.S.A., the big "nation of culture", where women stage boxing matches and wrestlers roll in muddy rings, where 13.000.000 men are without any job and where niggers can get the prizes at the Olympic Games!

Nor from Great Britain, where a certain class of people have one big worry only; to find out, how they can spend their money, while a great part of the population has to live in slums, which have a world wide fame and which are visited frequently by sight seers!

Do you know, what your lords are afraid of? That you perhaps will ask to get the same social care as the German workman is getting already!

And you, old chap, are on the top!!

You are allowed to give your life for Iwan, Uncle Sam and a clique of lords at home!

Well, much luck for the winter and look out, that you come through it allright!

4. Italian. A miniature billfold-size leaflet warning opf the invincibility of the V1 rocket.

5. At the end of the war, more and more effort was expended to prove the pointlessness of Allied lifes lost. Some, as this, were quite grusome.

6. Nettuno. The Germans are trying to be one-sided in their argument, forgetting that what is true in what they say here also applies to them.

7. Here are the Liberators! The Germans are blaming American Negro troops for the bombings of Italian churches and monuments, etc. Now when they shoot the colored troops they have nothing but praise for them and urge them to become POW's.

4

JERRY'S FRONT BROADCASTING PROGRAMME:

Short wave 47.6 meters (63000 kc) daily at: 6.30 a. m., 7.40 a. m., 2.00 p. m., 5.00 p. m., 6.30 p. m., 10.00 p. m. and midnight.

Medium wave 491.8 meters (610 kc) daily at: 6.30 a. m., 6.30 p. m. and a midnight programme

★ 1310-2-45

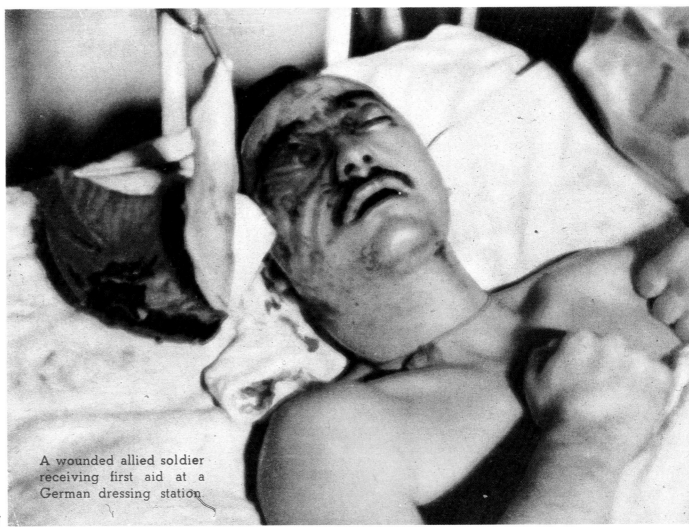

A wounded allied soldier receiving first aid at a German dressing station.

5

at NETTUNO

WOW! WHAT A HAUL!

to NETTUNO

Ecco i liberatori....

7

AMERICAN AND BRITISH SOLDIERS!

OF COURSE, you have been in Italy for sooo... long a time, and you know by now that good old **Neptune** is called **Nettuno** in Italian. Already thousands upon thousands of your pals visited him and preferred to stay with him forever.

This time, however, the god of the sea was tickled to death that you did him the honor of calling on him in the very place that was named after him.

Neptune was just starting a new collection of American and British ships, tanks, planes, and guns for his armoury in a beautiful grotto on the bottom of the Tyrrhenian Sea and was damned pleased with your ample contribution. He particularly liked the types of your equipment - not to mention the nice uniforms of your fellow soldiers - that the Germans were kind enough to sweep back to him off the beaches of his beloved Nettuno.

So you are now on good terms with the old guy; When will be your term to settle down with him?

JOKING ASIDE, BOYS.

The British-American landing at Nettuno is developing into a hell of a business for your forces.

You and your pals will have to bear the consequences!

A I · 024 · 1 · 44

6   6

8. Here are the Liberators: This the Italians are saying. Here the Krauts are really browned-off against the Negros in the American Army. The are blaming them for the bombings of the Italian churches and monuments, etc. Now when they shoot to the colored troops they have nothing but praise for them and then they urge them to become POW's.

9. Though the leaflet is filled with apparent truth, fat chance they had of getting our boys to run to them. The Germans certainly were fanatical in their hatred of the Jews.

10. Arabic. A plea to the Arabs trying to turn them against the Allies. They are defaming the Jews. Though the leaflet is anti-Semitic, the essence is "Become a prisoner of war and save your necks and go home after the war, safe and sound."

"Hello, Mother! Hello, Dad!"

This prisoner of war is mighty glad to have the opportunity of speaking to his dear ones at home. He tells them that he is treated decently in a German camp and that he is looking forward to seeing them after the war.

Lucky fellow! The bloody business is over for him.

It must be a nice feeling to know that nothing can happen to you any more.

When this boy was captured, his nearest relatives were immediately notified. And were they cheered up by the news!

By golly! What a mess **YOU** *are in, however.*

You don't know whether it may not hit you to-day or to-morrow.

Have you ever asked yourself to what good you're carrying on this whole damned business? Surely you are smart enough to have come to the conclusion that you did not leave your folks and your job to make room for bulletproof slackers, who replaced you and who are making piles of dough now.

It's the same with World War No. 2 as it was with World War No. 1. You are told to fight for the freedom of all the peoples of the world, but in reality you're dying a hero's death for the personal ambitions of your politicians and the fattening of war profiteers and racketeers.

You've got to hand it to the miners and skilled workers of your own country, who found out from close observation into what cesspool of corruption and depravity the whole war business has sunk.

That's why they went on strike, hundreds of thousands of them.

What about **YOU**? *Are* **YOU** *content to be taken for a sucker?*

All YOU may get out of this war of international wire-pullers and jewish financiers is a chance of having your name put on a memorial tablet.

Think it over!

Then you'll know what to do!

A I - 018-1-44

11. *This concerns you! Leaflet obviously written by some learned German as no solider would take nearly the whole of four pages in a letter to praise the Germans.*

12. *Even the German's allies were kicked about mercilessly. The beach at Nettuno was defended by Germans, not Italian weaklings, according to the verso of this flyer.*

13. *Russian. See Appendix for translation.*

14. *Finally the V1 has been replaced by the V2 and was as the Germans had promised–very fierce.*

S/Sgt. Jesse Bradburn

This concerns you!

Mrs. Al Bradburn
2578 Lakeview Rd.
Union Lake RFD #5
Pontiac Mich
U.S.A.

11

NETTUNO

a second Di

12

Some Where in Italy
Feb 19, 1944

Dear Mother, Dad and All
            Unlike the last time I wrote I have something to tell about this time. Day before yesterday we were shot down while on a bombing raid. Three of us that I know about had to parachute but one died from his wounds. The other fellow and myself are now in a German Hospital. I am the least injured. The other fellow has a broken leg and arm. His leg is very bad. Also he has other wounds.
            Myself - I was hit many times but they were all clean hits and none in the body. I have four hits in my left leg, three in my right arm, three large caliber wounds in my legs and how many small wounds, I

-2-

I don't know. And then I four in my fanny and on my nose just missing eye. Just before I bailed o thought my eye was gone a couldn't get the blood out to see.
            Now that it is over God. It was sure hell for a an hour. We were first c with anti aircraft and co keep up with our formatio the German fighters started on us. Before I jumped our wing tip was gone, our bom afire, all the cables broke near, I don't think there w whole piece left in the airpla Jerry fighters were good.
            So far the German used us like one of there own

11

13

Death from the unknown

Secret explosions rocking London

- Nothing can be seen -
- Nothing can be heard -

BUT IT'S THERE:

V2

14

Churchill in the House on Nov. 10, 1944:

"Already for weeks England has been subjected to the bombardment of German long-range rocket projectiles. They are filled with approximately the same quantity of high explosives as the flying bombs (V 1); however, they have a greater striking power and cause heavier damage in the vicinity of the impact".

14

-3-

have really been swell. We are in a hospital with all wounded Germans. They feed us as they do the rest. It beats any thing I've ever seen and its better then I expected and not at all like I had thought it would be. It's the one point about this all that makes it bearable. Don't think I am saying this because I am forced to as I am not. Every German soldier I've come in contact with has been a gentleman.

My friend with the bad leg sure has recived the best of care. They've set his leg and are now stretching it so it won't heal short or crooked — I don't think he would have got any more attention or better treatment by our own

11

-4-

Docs. If the treatment goes on as it has been, being a prisoner will be a snap. The only thing I worry about is clothing - our flying equipment isn't the best for ground wear.

Anyway you wont have to worry about me any more, as I am safe. I sure wish I could find out what happened to the rest of the crew.

Say Mom in the stuff of mine they send you should be some letters, write to the addresses and let them know what happened. One in particular - Mrs. Dora Liston, Del Valle Station, Box Unknown, Los Angeles, 15, Calif.

Now what ever you do, don't worry, you've nothing to worry about any more. Pray for me.

Your Loving Son, Brother
Jess

11

15. *This booklet that was distributed to our troops. The booklet is very well done and explains what to do in the event of capture.*

16. *The ancedote is amusing and well put. They speak out of both sides of their mouths: they praise the English for being keen-minded and fair, while they call them narrow-minded.*

17. *"Warsaw Tragedy! Warsaw failed because they didn't get help from Russia, and London didn't even complain because of the tragedy. Thousands of people in Warsaw lost their homes and every thing they had. The pictures say: General Borg didn't get help from London and Russia so he had to capitulate. Archbishop along with delegates after visiting the camp is thanking the German officers."*

Listening walls

In a Nazi or Fascist state everyone is a suspect of the secret police. They are long practised in eavesdropping. They use this experience in war time.

After failing to obtain information from a prisoner by ordinary methods, the enemy puts several of them together in a large room, and waits for results. When a man has been taken prisoner, it is cheering to meet a comrade — so cheering that they are both inclined to talk, particularly about the circumstances of their capture. Hidden in the room is a microphone—careful search will often fail to reveal it. It will pick up what they say, and it will be heard by the listening enemy.

THE ANSWER TO THIS IS SILENCE

Now you know

What you have just read gives you a fair idea of the way the enemy is trying to get our men to talk. Though the enemy has paid tribute to our security, there are still cases of information leaking out.

If it does happen that you are unfortunate enough to be captured — DO NOT TALK — not a word — and you will be defying the enemy's attempt to make you a traitor. What is more you will be loyal to the people at home, your comrades, and to everything for which we are fighting.

Therefore remember give only name, rank and number.

No other questions should be answered.

PSS/NA/4/44/50,000 — AFHQP 1920

15

Stool pigeon

A building is set aside for interrogation. When prisoners are brought in, drinks and cigarettes are passed round. The prisoners are questioned in a half-hearted manner. Then they are transferred to another part of the building, where they find three or four other « prisoners ». These « prisoners » are in fact Italians speaking perfect English, and dressed in British or American uniforms.

To avoid detection these men are sometimes dressed in the uniform of a service other than that of our prisoners (Air Force when prisoner is in the Army, American when prisoner is British).

These stool pigeons have to get all the information interrogating officers have been unable to obtain.

THE ANSWER TO THIS IS SILENCE

Man to man

« America and Britain should not be fighting Germany. We don't hate one another ». This is what the smiling Nazi says, in an attempt to make our prisoners forget the atrocities he is committing all over the world.

THE ANSWER TO THIS IS SILENCE

Local boy

The enemy begins with a knowing talk about your home land. « Where do you come from ? » And if the prisoner replies the enemy puts on a show of knowing the actual district. He goes on to talk about the prisoner's family. He may even show some photographs of his own.

THE ANSWER TO THIS IS SILENCE

Delayed action

The prisoner is not questioned for several days — perhaps weeks. If he is in hospital they send a man along who has all the charm of a vacuum-cleaner salesman. He doesn't talk about the war ; he cracks a few jokes ; lets it leak out that he is anti-Nazi. Every day he asks how the patient is getting along. He gets in the habit of chatting to him. He has plenty of time, and gradually the conversation veers round to the war.

THE ANSWER TO THIS IS SILENCE

Know all

« We know so much there is nothing you can tell us » says the Hun. He flips over a lot of important-looking papers. — « See what I have ? There is little that a person such as yourself can tell me. » The last sentence he often uses to an N.C.O., and if he is greeted with silence, he continues : « I can't imagine why you were promoted. All I want from you is confirmation of a simple little thing. I already know. You must be

15

So you wo nt talk...

ny praise

man and Italian documents captured in ampaign pay tribute to our soldiers e they refuse to talk when taken prisoner.

an order of the day to the Italian Army ed by General Enea Navarrini comman- he 21 st Corps, there is the following :

Vhen subjected to questioning by our ence Branch all the enemy prisoners l firmly and categorically to give any y information of any kind whatsoever. onfined themselves to providing personal lars and Army numbers.

lore energetic demands, and indirect ns intended to obtain certain details or ation on certain information, had no

better success ; all the prisoners remained firm in their dutiful decision to obey the order not to talk, being thoroughly conscious of the fact that any other line of conduct would amount to treachery, pure and simple.

« I wish these facts to be brought to the notice of all units... Military honour demands that the spirit of dignity and pride of race should always be alive and present in the minds of our troops »

(Signed) ENEA NAVARRINI.

And the Germans say in another captured document that our prisoners are arrogant, proud, cautious and absolutely secure.

But the enemy does not want to be beaten. He is determined to make our prisoners talk, so he has resorted to tricks. Here are some of them.

The most dangerous moment of the fight — and when you have to be really careful — is, when you think you've got your man on the ropes.

Maybe on the ropes, but the Jerry isn't on his knees yet, English boy!

Watch out during the next months!

If you should think your friends of the RAF and USAAF will give us the k. o. at home, you are badly mistaken. While we, you and me, have been doing just a bit of sparring around down here, their blows below the belt have had a nasty sting to our folks back home, but — and don't forget it — the comeback, the day of reckoning is not too far off!

What a pity,
that it should be you, your folks, your homes, who will get it, instead of the blasted instigators of this terrific fight. They, however, will have scrammed — along with the receipts — even before the bout is over.

Some might call it rather funny to see two fighters, both of them fine and strong fellows, going to the floor at the same time, each one utterly exhausted after a gallant fight.

But who would not call it a tragedy, if they had put each other out of the game to such an extent, that neither of the two could prevent some second-rater of the Primo Carnera type, climbing into the ring, carrying away the belt — and bullying the whole world?

In sports, there is no keener minded and fairer thinking man than the Englishman.

Too bad, the same man is so lax and narrow-minded in politics.

START THINKING, BRITON!

---

lete fool..» This is intended to provoke the r into showing his superior knowledge.
THE ANSWER TO THIS IS SILENCE

n actor

stage is set. The prisoner is marched into a by one flickering lantern. Shadows play on the The enemy pretends not to notice him. He goes ing through some papers. He gives an order in a to a grim-looking sentry.

denly he looks up at the prisoner. Then he ut a routine question. « Name ? » When he me, rank and number, and the next question ed with silence, he orders the sentry to leave t. The enemy looks at his revolver, placed like prop on the table.

don't want to resort to methods we dislike. » , and hopes that the prisoner will believe the e. Of course he doesn't want to resort to sterner s — we have too many Germans and Italians up.
THE ANSWER TO THIS IS SILENCE

d degree

prisoner is taken into a confined space, such rmoured car. The enemy speaks in a calm voice. nts some important information, and he is ned to get it. He is candid.

ou are alone. You have a family. I dare say you live. It is nice to be a hero when someone

knows about it. But you are alone. Shout, and no one will hear you, and if they do they will not worry. I am not concerned with what you are fighting for, and if you are dead you will care still less. Yes, I intend to get what I want ».

Gradually he introduces spurious arguments to break down the prisoner's morale. The note of death is constantly repeated. « Who would know ? »

News travels fast, and in a mysterious way. We have a dossier of crimes committed in Occupied countries. We know what happens in German concentration camps. . . . and we have thousands of enemy prisoners.
THE ANSWER TO THIS IS SILENCE

Try again

Breaking down morale is the first object of the enemy interrogating officer. Here is what the enemy attempted some time ago. He failed to get our men to talk. They were forced to march a strenuous 17 miles. Often they were told to bed down, only to find that after settling down they were ordered to continue.

They were confined to a very small area, with practically no shelter, and the very minimum of food and water.

Another trick of the Germans, which was considered a joke by our troops, was a fantastic tale of Russian reverses, Japanese successes and American and British losses.

They even tried to work the time-worn trap : « Your comrades have told us everything so why don't you ? »

THE ANSWER TO THIS IS SILENCE

Generał Bór-Komorowski, wódz powstańców warszawskich, nie uzyskawszy ani z Londynu ani z Moskwy żadnej pomocy, musiał skapitulować. — Niemcy przyznali jemu jak i wszystkim powstańcom wszelkie prawa jeńca wojennego.

Arcybiskup w towarzystwie delegatów po zwiedzeniu obozu dla uchodźców warszawskich dziękuje oficerowi niemieckiemu za dobrze zorganizowaną akcję niesienia pomocy ofiarom tragedji warszawskiej.

18. *What the Germans are saying here is true. To think that before the war ended the Russians and the Yanks were no longer Allies, and we have been on opposite sides ever since.*

19. *"Arab Soldiers. Germans are friends with Arabs. Germans fight Jews but not Arabs. French officers tell that Germans kill Arabs after they become prisoners of war but those are all lies. All the Arab soliders, regardless of their origin be it Morroccan, Algerian, or Tunisian they are all friends of the Germans. All Arab soldiers have the right and possibility at the end of the war in Germany to return to their own countries safe and sound and free men."*

20. *We have no way of knowing whether this incident took place or not.. It may have. If so, there was unfairness on both sides.*

21. *German propaganda to shift the blame to Roosevelt and the Jews.*

18

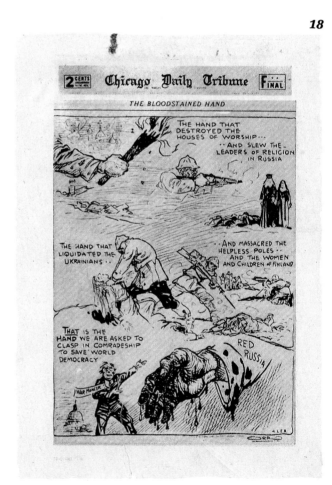

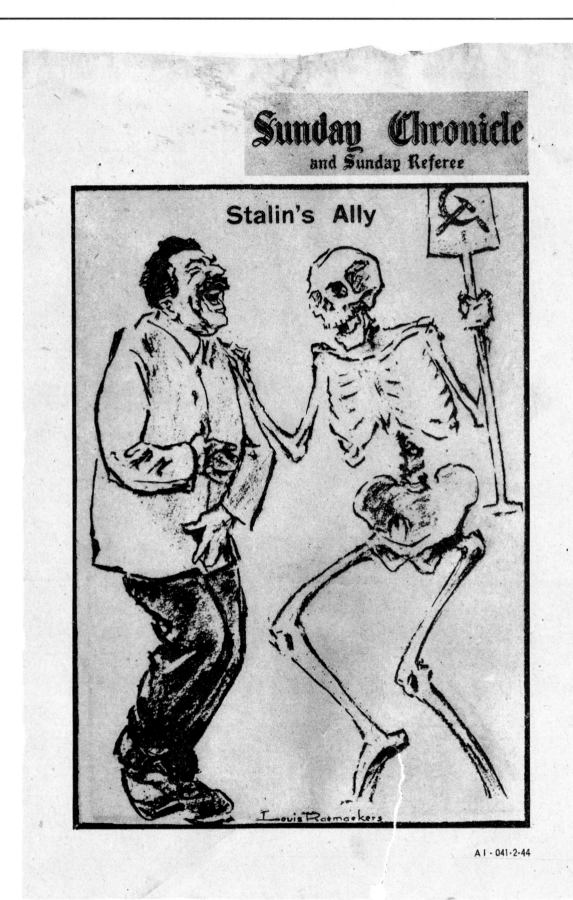

Leaflet 19

الا نعرفون ان الماتيا معقودة بينها وبين المفتى الاكبر الحاج امين
الحسيني الذي طرده من الاوطار والذي يقيم الان في الماتيا بنا معاهدة
لتعين اقدام الامم العربية في مكافحتهم المدبين والبهود

وبكن اقدا العروبة والاسلوم والشعوب السامية الواحدين
والعروبة وحفظوا الشعوب العربية واستنقدوا بها

ان الماتيا ندينو نو مبه نعل خطر اليهودية الروائية وبكن
الحلفا ينشا اقصارها في هبم الشعوب السامية السلم

Soldats Arabes!

Les Alliés ainsi que leurs complices français ont mis en action toute leur propagande pour vous pousser à la guerre contre l'Allemagne. D'après la version la plus récente de cette propagande, ils prétendent que la lutte de l'Allemagne contre les Juifs serait dirigée contre tous les peuples sémitiques, c'est-à-dire aussi contre les Arabes. Vos officiers français vous ont raconté que le soldat allemand tuait tout Arabe qui serait fait prisonnier. Ils vous ont raconté que l'Allemagne était l'ennemie de l'Islam et que votre devoir le plus sacré était de combattre contre les Allemands...

Ces affirmations ne sont que de mensonges infâmes. L'Allemagne fait la guerre aux Juifs, mais elle est l'amie de tous les peuples arabes. Les soldats allemands n'ont point oublié l'hospitalité qu'ils ont reçue des Arabes pendant la campagne de l'Afrique du Nord. Aussi l'Allemagne actuelle conclu un traité d'alliance avec le Grand Mufti de Jérusalem, expulsé par les Anglais et demeurant actuellement en Allemagne, pour l'assistance des peuples arabes dans leur lutte contre les oppresseurs.

Tout soldat arabe, n'importe qu'il soit originaire du Maroc, de l'Algérie ou de la Tunisie, sera toujours considéré et traité comme appartenant à une nation amie, aussitôt qu'il est fait prisonnier ou qu'il dépose volontairement ses armes. Tout soldat arabe a le droit et la possibilité d'attendre la fin de la guerre en Allemagne pour retourner ensuite dans sa patrie sain et sauf et en homme libre.

19

Leaflet 20

Judge by yourselves:

"Upon the request of a British doctor fire was stopped in the sector of Monte Cecce for the salvage of the dead and wounded. 18 dead and 30 wounded were salved by the British troops within the time agreed upon, i. e. from 9 a.m. to 4 p.m., during which not a single shot was fired by the German troops. On being asked by the British doctor one German officer together with a sergeant and two stretcher-bearers proceeded to the British field hospital in order to bring back the German wounded. When after the expiration of the time agreed upon the Germans had not returned the British replied to the inquiries made by the Germans that the Commanding Officer of their regiment has kept back the German officer, because he had seen too much, and that the stretcher-bearers could also not be allowed to come back for the same reason."

This is the short message from the German division which is facing the 1st British Infantry division in the sector mentioned above. We do not want to lose many words about it — you, British front soldier, should judge by yourself whether this way of acting is fair or not.

We have agreed to the request of the British for a stoppage of fire, because we believed that in a fight — however hard it may be — between two civilized nations that sort of human decency and fairness was still in force which does not exist in a fight against the Soviets, because this adversary has no notion of law or decency. We believed we faced Englishmen who knew what they owed to their name and their word.

We were wrong. But next time we will not make this mistake again. After this experience all requests for a stoppage of fire will be refused — anyone coming into the range of our aims will be fired at in future. We regret that this attitude adopted by British commanding officers and their superiors, which is inconceivable to any front soldier, leaves us no other possibility.

Would you act differently?

20

Leaflet 21

ROOSEVELT, THE FALSE PROPHET!

"I assure you again and again and again that no American boys will be sacrificed on foreign battlefields."

Franklin D. Roosevelt, Oct. 31, 1940

But you did go to war!

And what about the other promises in his campaign speeches?

The New Deal collapsed, the number of unemployed rose from one year to the other finally reaching 13 million. With their dependents, over 45 million people or one third of the population of the USA were living in misery. Billions had been spent for nothing.

Roosevelt was through - and he knew it.

Something had to be done.

He and his "brain-busters" invented the fairy-tale that the Axis Powers were to blame for this calamity.

He took those steps short of war, made them shorter and shorter until he had HIS war!

He wanted to kill two birds with one stone by plunging his country into a war:

First, he got rid of the unemployed by shipping most of them to the battlefields of Europe as cannon fodder. The rest were absorbed by the armament industry in temporary wartime jobs.

Second, he passed fat government contracts on to his rich sponsors, the Baruchs, Lehmans, Morgenthaus, Warburgs, Ginsbergs and the like, thus rewarding them for their cash donations during election time. This moneyed gang is reaping colossal profits as usual.

So you see that Mr. Roosevelt had good reasons for running after the war.

One of his spokesmen, James H. McGraw Jr., president of the McGraw-Hill-Publishing Company, Inc., put it bluntly by writing in the March 1942 issue of the magazine "Aviation."

"And this, very definitely, is OUR war."

The American people, however, in their unimpeachable judgement set him right by saying:

This is the RICH man's war and the POOR man's fight!

21

21

22. This billbold size leaflet was directed to the Indian Gurkhas. On the bottom of the leaflet there are instructions for the German soliders to treat the Indian POW's well and to remove them from the front.

23. The German radio braodcasts were very good. Even the Allied soldiers were singing "Lilly Marlene!"

24. German flyer from the SS. Because of the SS the Germans were forced to continue on with the war. Many German POW's admitted that they were strapped. shackled and handcuffed, so to speak, and could not oppose their own police system.

25. American Soliders! The Germans certainly were right about the Roosevelt quote: "I assure you again and again and again that no American bosy will be sacrificed on foreign battlefields."

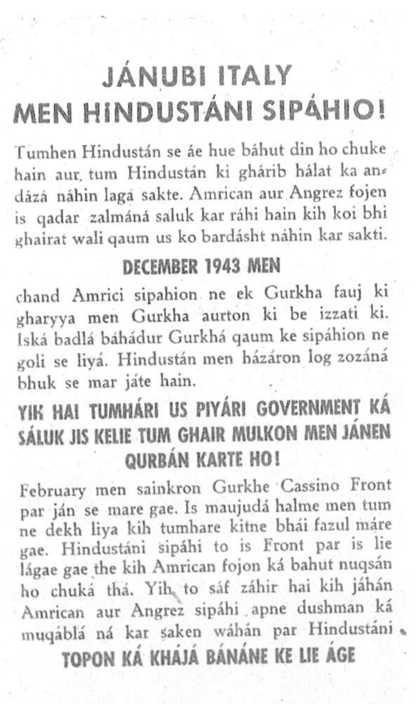

JÁNUBI ITALY
MEN HINDUSTÁNI SIPÁHIO!

Tumhen Hindustán se áe hue báhut din ho chuke hain aur. tum Hindustán ki ghárib hálat ka andázá náhin lagá sakte. Amrican aur Angrez fojen is qadar zalmáná saluk kar ráhi hain kih koi bhi ghairat wali qaum us ko bardásht náhin kar sakti.

DECEMBER 1943 MEN

chand Amrici sipahion ne ek Gurkha fauj ki gharyya men Gurkha aurton ki be izzati ki. Iská badlá báhádur Gurkhá qaum ke sipáhion ne goli se liyá. Hindustán men házáron log zozáná bhuk se mar játe hain.

YIK HAI TUMHÁRI US PIYÁRI GOVERNMENT KÁ SÁLUK JIS KELIE TUM GHAIR MULKON MEN JÁNEN QURBÁN KARTE HO!

February men sainkron Gurkhe Cassino Front par ján se mare gae. Is maujudá halme men tum ne dekh liya kih tumhare kitne bhái fazul máre gae. Hindustáni sipáhi to is Front par is lie lágae gae the kih Amrican fojon ká bahut nuqsán ho chuká thá. Yih to sáf záhir hai kih jáhán Amrican aur Angrez sipáhi apne dushman ká muqáblá ná kar saken wáhán par Hindustáni

TOPON KÁ KHÁJÁ BÁNÁNE KE LIE ÁGE

22

23

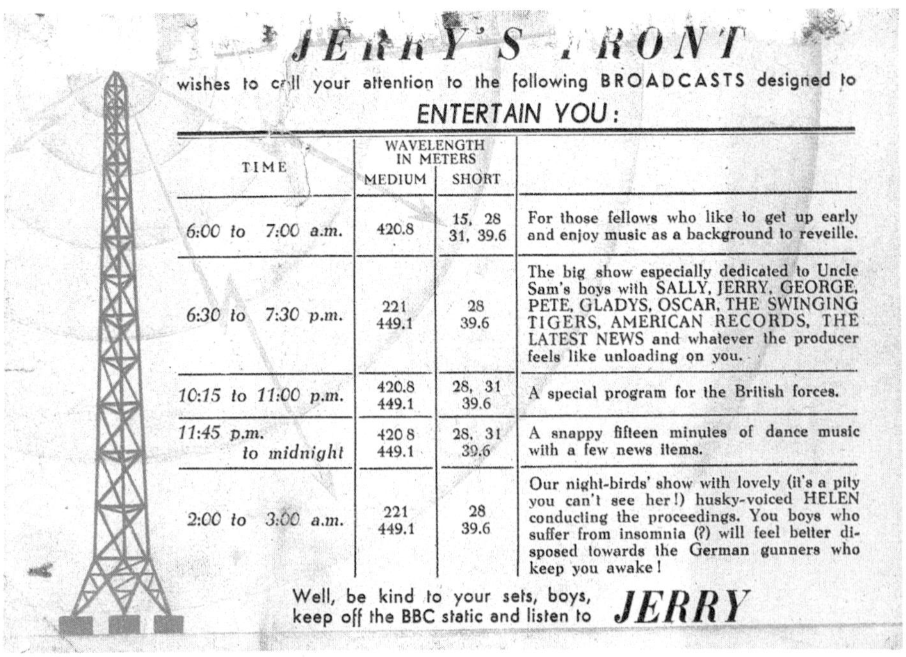

JERRY'S FRONT

wishes to call your attention to the following BROADCASTS designed to

ENTERTAIN YOU:

TIME	WAVELENGTH IN METERS MEDIUM	WAVELENGTH IN METERS SHORT	
6:00 to 7:00 a.m.	420.8	15, 28 31, 39.6	For those fellows who like to get up early and enjoy music as a background to reveille.
6:30 to 7:30 p.m.	221 449.1	28 39.6	The big show especially dedicated to Uncle Sam's boys with SALLY, JERRY, GEORGE, PETE, GLADYS, OSCAR, THE SWINGING TIGERS, AMERICAN RECORDS, THE LATEST NEWS and whatever the producer feels like unloading on you.
10:15 to 11:00 p.m.	420.8 449.1	28, 31 39.6	A special program for the British forces.
11:45 p.m. to midnight	420.8 449.1	28, 31 39.6	A snappy fifteen minutes of dance music with a few news items.
2:00 to 3:00 a.m.	221 449.1	28 39.6	Our night-birds' show with lovely (it's a pity you can't see her!) husky-voiced HELEN conducting the proceedings. You boys who suffer from insomnia (?) will feel better disposed towards the German gunners who keep you awake!

Well, be kind to your sets, boys, keep off the BBC static and listen to JERRY

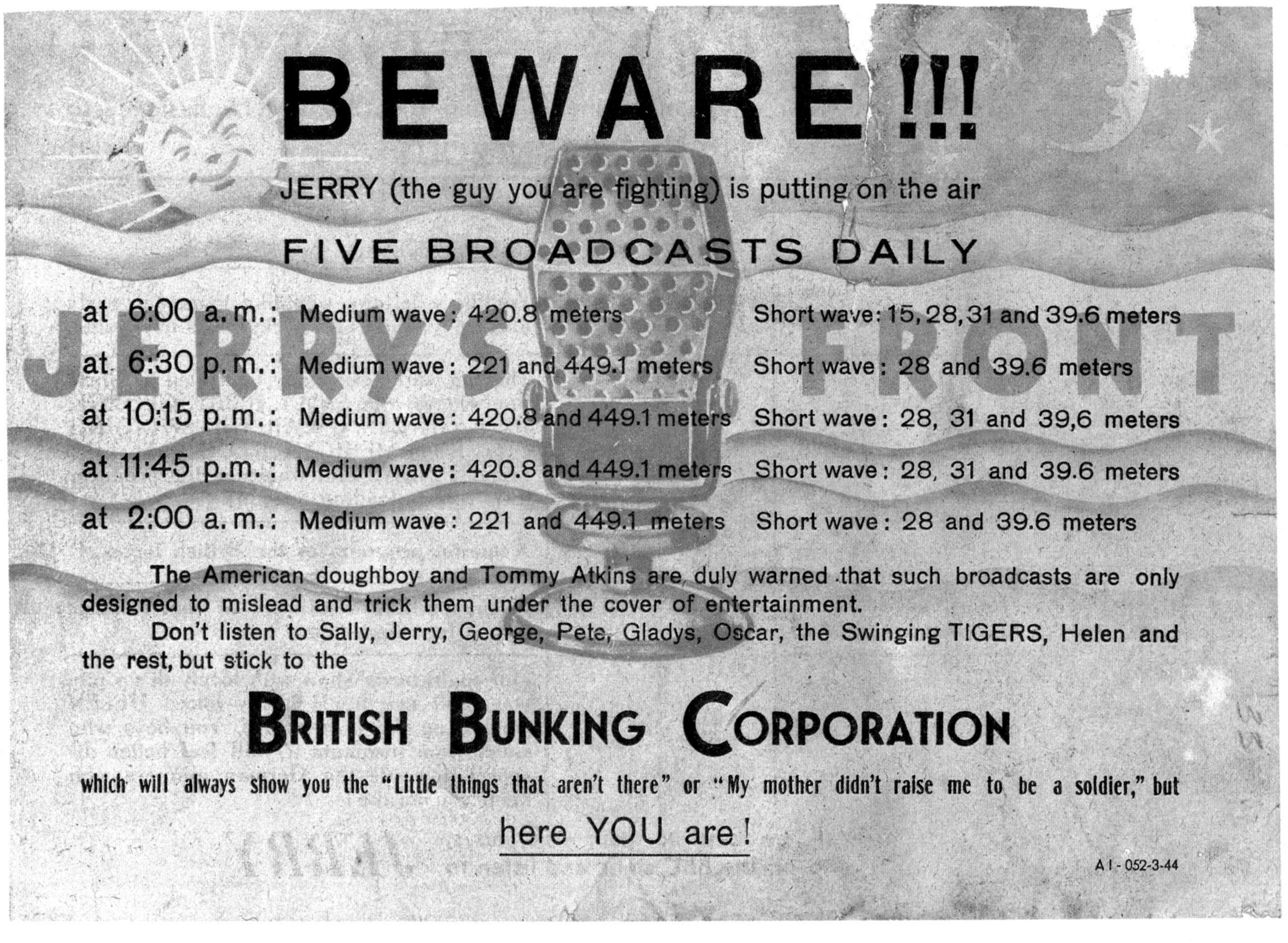

BEWARE !!!

JERRY (the guy you are fighting) is putting on the air

FIVE BROADCASTS DAILY

JERRY'S FRONT

at 6:00 a.m.:	Medium wave: 420.8 meters	Short wave: 15, 28, 31 and 39.6 meters
at 6:30 p.m.:	Medium wave: 221 and 449.1 meters	Short wave: 28 and 39.6 meters
at 10:15 p.m.:	Medium wave: 420.8 and 449.1 meters	Short wave: 28, 31 and 39,6 meters
at 11:45 p.m.:	Medium wave: 420.8 and 449.1 meters	Short wave: 28, 31 and 39.6 meters
at 2:00 a.m.:	Medium wave: 221 and 449.1 meters	Short wave: 28 and 39.6 meters

The American doughboy and Tommy Atkins are duly warned that such broadcasts are only designed to mislead and trick them under the cover of entertainment.

Don't listen to Sally, Jerry, George, Pete, Gladys, Oscar, the Swinging TIGERS, Helen and the rest, but stick to the

BRITISH BUNKING CORPORATION

which will always show you the "Little things that aren't there" or "My mother didn't raise me to be a soldier," but

here YOU are!

A I - 052-3-44

Landung alliierter Divisionen vor Rom! Deutsche Küstenstellungen durchbrochen. Die Hauptkampflinie umgangen. Grosse Kesselschlacht beginnt!

Allied divisions land near Rome. German coastal positions broken through. Main fighting line outflanked. Big encirclement battle is starting.

AMERICAN SOLDIERS!

It is not your fault that your leaders have got you into this desperate position.

Remember the words of President Roosevelt to the American people on October 31st, 1940: *"I assure you again and again and again that no American boys will be sacrificed on foreign battlefields."*

A few days ago at Cisterna your fellow soldiers suffered the heaviest casualties. Over a thousand American boys had sense enough to lay down their arms. They had no other choice in the face of a German opponent who, for the first time, outnumbered them both in personnel and material.

Have you ever asked yourself
why you are risking your life?

Think it over and talk with your pals about it.

What happened to your forces during the last few days is only a prelude to what you are going to face.

When hell really breaks loose and thousands upon thousands of American boys will bite the dust, President Roosevelt will have broken his word to the American people a thousand times over again.

AI - 027/u - 2 - 44

The leaflet which we are showing you in the original and in translation on the reverse side was dropped over our lines by order of your command.

Allied divisions landed near Rome?

"There are many roads that lead to Rome," but none for you.

German coastal positions broken through?

Do you still think so to-day?

Main fighting line outflanked?

You don't mean by chance our lines? Numerous of your units have been cut off from their lines of communication and taken prisoner.

Big encirclement battle is starting?

Who is fighting with his back to the sea, surrounded on all sides by a powerful opponent?

AI - 044 - 2 - 44

26. Sally was one of the most popular figures on the Italian front. Her voice on radio was captivating, and most GI's enjoyed her program.

27. Here is a leaflet that had to have impact on soldiers whose home was a foxhole. The leaflet is prime propaganda.

28. Home news. The parts about Russia is easy to believe.

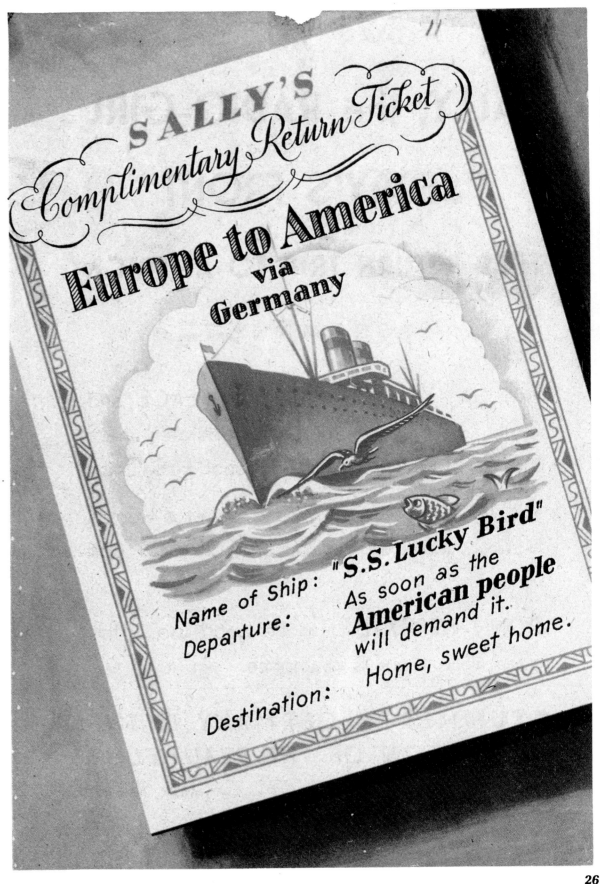

HOME NEWS

Between two stools see page 2 N°6

THE ATLANTIC CHARTER NULL AND VOID

Mikolajczyk, the Premier of the Polish Government in London, declared according to a report in the «Times»: «I know that eventually I will have to yield to the Russians, and if I do not it will cost my life.»

This declaration marks the end of a development which after having caused a universal conflagration is now being washed away by the whirlpool of the red floods. England and France declared war on Germany in order to protect Poland. The Allies, however, did not lift up a finger to save Poland, for they guaranteed instead with words of a pleasant sound in the Atlantic Charter to all the smaller nations in Europe the maintenance of their sovereign power. London became the seat of a Polish Government under British protection.

But Moscow has different plans and this is why the final verdict on the fate of Poland (and at the same time on all the other nations «liberated» by Moscow) has already been passed in spite of the nice words contained in the Atlantic Charter.

It was in vain that the wandering minstrel, Churchill, travelled to the court of Moscow. In vain is Churchill holding out hopes for the peace conference. The declaration made by Mikolajczyk clearly shows what they really are: an idle talk of a man who does not want to admit his weakness.

The Atlantic Charter is dead - Stalin is triumphant.

Dangerous speculations

«The talk about measures of international security, demobilisation and the transition from war-time to peace-time conditions is based on the wrong assumption that the war is almost over, says Walter Lippman in United Herald Tribune. «All those who work on this assumption are somnambulists who will be greatly disappointed when they awake.» «The last phase in European war,» Lippman goes on to say,

«may last for months and will be terrible. Even when military resistance will be overcome, our soldiers will have to remain in a country which is organised with such diabolical skill as to make it a hell for them. Their nerves will be absolutely shattered. In such a fight our soldiers need the full support from the people at home. We are denying them this support if we behave in such a way as if war had already been over and as if the rest could be simply written off.»

Long live the war!

If one could believe Mr. Vansittart, then the Germans would be a race the children of which would have already at their birth a wooden sword and a paper helmet. They would keep playing with these symbols of soldiership until the day so much longed for on which the young man would at last be allowed to join the army. And the greatest event is a German's life would be war - at least this is how Mr. Vansittart is picturing it out to himself.

Nobody in Germany would ever think a moment of calling the Englishman a warloving militarist or of speaking of the «man in the street» in England in a way Mr. Vansittart is speaking of us. We know very well that the English are as much against a war as we Germans, and we, too, we protest against these misrepresentations of Mr. Vansittart. We do not need a war and we do not want it, but when we are forced to it, then we know how to deal with it.

Still, there appear to be certain people who are greatly interested in a war, and it seems to us as if this sort of people were much more numerous in England than in Germany.

Here is what Reuter said on 8.11.44:

«The insurance policies issued by Lloyd's against a premature termination of the

---

DON'T READ IT!
You may get the blues.

This is a bit of poetry by an American soldier.

Here it is:

Somewhere in Italy where the days are like a curse,
and each one is followed by another slightly worse,
where the cold wind blows heavier than the shifting desert sand,
and a soldier dreams and wishes for a quiet and peaceful land.

Somewhere in Italy where the nights are made for love,
where the moon is like a searchlight and the Southern Cross above
sparkles like a diamond necklace in a balmy tropic night,
it's a shameless waste of beauty when there's not a girl in sight.

Somewhere in Italy where the mail is always late,
where a Christmas card in April is considered up-to-date,
where we never have a payday and we never have a cent,
but we never miss the money 'cause we'd never get it spent.

Oh, take me back to Michigan, let me hear that mission bell,
for this God-forsaken foxhole is a substitute for hell.

DO YOU THINK YOUR PAL IS RIGHT?

A.I.·045-3-44

29. The road to Rome was supposed to be un-obtainable for the Allies, according to this slightly mistaken piece of propaganda.

30. The Candians were all volunteers and it seems unlikely that they would brag on being POW's and tell of their good treatment..

31. After World War I this actually happened and the Germans are trying to capitalize on the fact. They are mistaken about "There is only one class of people profiting from any war: Wall Street and the Jews."

32. The Germans are telling the Italian citizens that they will kill anyone protecting any person who is against the Germans, even go so far as to burn them, their families and property. The enemies of Italy merit death, because they are against the Germans.

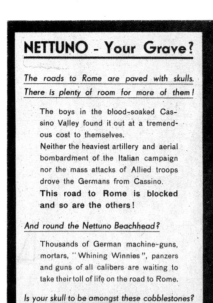

NETTUNO - Your Grave?

The roads to Rome are paved with skulls.
There is plenty of room for more of them!

The boys in the blood-soaked Cassino Valley found it out at a tremendous cost to themselves.

Neither the heaviest artillery and aerial bombardment of the Italian campaign nor the mass attacks of Allied troops drove the Germans from Cassino.

This road to Rome is blocked and so are the others!

And round the Nettuno Beachhead?

Thousands of German machine-guns, mortars, "Whining Winnies", panzers and guns of all calibers are waiting to take their toll of life on the road to Rome.

Is your skull to be amongst these cobblestones?

A1-Oola-4-44

29

PEACE - FREEDOM - BREAD!

Comrades!

We send you this message from a Canadian prisoners-of-war camp. None of us came here voluntarily. But we have all had an amazing experience:

The old demand: « Peace — Freedom — Bread » has never come nearer to being realised for us — however extraordinary it may sound — then as « prisoners of war » in Canada.

A description of the « Base Camp » to which we came from the Transit Camp sounds like the advertising brochure of a hotel. And that's not surprising, for our camp is a former hotel, with holiday camps in the midst of wooded mountain country like the Tyrol or Upper Bavaria. In peacetime people paid a lot of money to be allowed to stay here.

We have running hot and cold water, baths and public rooms, a football field, tennis courts, swimming bath, cinema, theatre, concerts, radio, daily newspapers and a large German and foreign library.

The food is up to peacetime standard: Breakfast: Tea or real coffee with milk and sugar, fried bacon, eggs or smoked fish. Lunch: Soup, meat, two vegetables, sweet, fruit, cheese. Afternoon tea: tea or coffee, bread, butter, jam. Supper: Soup, meat, two vegetables, fruit, cheese.

At any time of day: beer of peacetime quality, lemonade, cigars, cigarettes, tobacco.

Everyone can do what he likes with his time. You can get leave to go out on parole, and there are joint excursions into the beautiful surrounding country. Everyone gets good clothes, shoes, laundry and pocket money. Medical and dental treatment are free.

Postal communication with home is quick, regular and dependable. Two to three letters and four postcards are normally allowed per month, in urgent circumstances two letters weekly. All mail, including business documents and legal documents, can be sent by air.

Anyone who wishes can work on our own farm or in our market-garden, or get practical instruction in modern agricultual methods from outside farmers.

We have technical, handicraft, scientific and language courses, schools of art and commercial art, lectures, a commercial school course and courses to university standard.

On the other side you will find an article from our « Notice Board », which will give you an idea how we live here.

For the Administrative Committee
K. V., Oblt.

G.B.14

PAVED WITH SKULLS!

Si dispone perciò che:

chi conosce il luogo ove si trattiene una banda e non ne dà
immediata comunicazione all'esercito germanico

verrà ucciso mediante fucilazione!

Chi concede asilo o nutrimento ad una banda od a dei singoli
banditi

verrà ucciso mediante fucilazione!

Ogni casa nella quale verrà trovato un bandito, o nella quale
si sia trattenuto certamente un bandito

sarà fatta saltare in aria!

Lo stesso accade con ogni casa dalla quale viene sparato su gli
appartenenti alle FF. AA. Germaniche.

In tutti questi casi vengono **bruciate** le provviste di fieno,
paglia e di viveri, il bestiame viene **sequestrato** e gli abitanti
vengono

uccisi mediante fucilazione!

ITALIANI!

Voi avete in mano il vostro destino e quello del vostro Paese!

Decidetevi ora!

Chi si decide contro le FF. AA. Germaniche e con questo contro
gli interessi vitali dell'Italia, non trova perdono. L'esercito tedesco procederà con giustizia ma anche con inesorabile durezza!

IL COMANDANTE SUPREMO DELLE TRUPPE TEDESCHE

32

„BROTHER GOT A DIME FOR ME..."

You certainly know that song of 1920.
In those days Ex-Servicemen were selling apples in the streets!
Veterans were forced to organize a «hunger march» to Washington
to get their bonus which the politicians had promised to them
for twenty years.
Well, all that happened after the «great victory» of 1918. Was
it a «great victory» for the «man-in-the-street», the farmer or
the Ex-Serviceman?

NO, CERTAINLY NOT!

He was good enough to risk his life a thousand times, but

AFTER THE WAR HE WAS FORGOTTEN.

When the great plants of the war-industry closed on the morning
after the armistice, the ex-soldier faced **unemployment** and
misery for many years.

WHAT WILL BECOME OF YOU AFTER THIS WAR?

The very same thing will happen again.
Every war in history was followed by a great depression and
widespread unemployment.
Do'nt be a fool and believe the bombastic talk emanating from
busy propaganda offices in Washington about «everlasting peace
and prosperity» after this war.
Get this through your head:
There is only one class of people profiting from any war:
Wallstreet and the Jews!
They want you to fight because your blood will bring fat dividends to the moneyed gang in Wallstreet. For their profit you
are expected to give your life or to return some day as a
cripple, only to

SELL APPLES AGAIN!

31

31

33. *Milap, which means UNION. This is a poem. (Indian) The Germans feared the Gurkhas more than any other troops. At night they could crawl to an enemy foxhole unheard.*

34. *Beach head battles at both Anzio and Nettuno were certainly prolonged and bloody. German claims were to hold for a very short time.*

35. *How can one refute this? The same message applies to the Germans.*

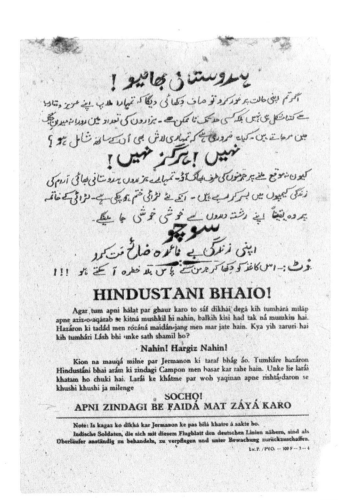

Tum ko rukhsat kar ke
ita hadde nazar dekha kie
Jis taraf dekha na jata tha
udhar dekha kie.

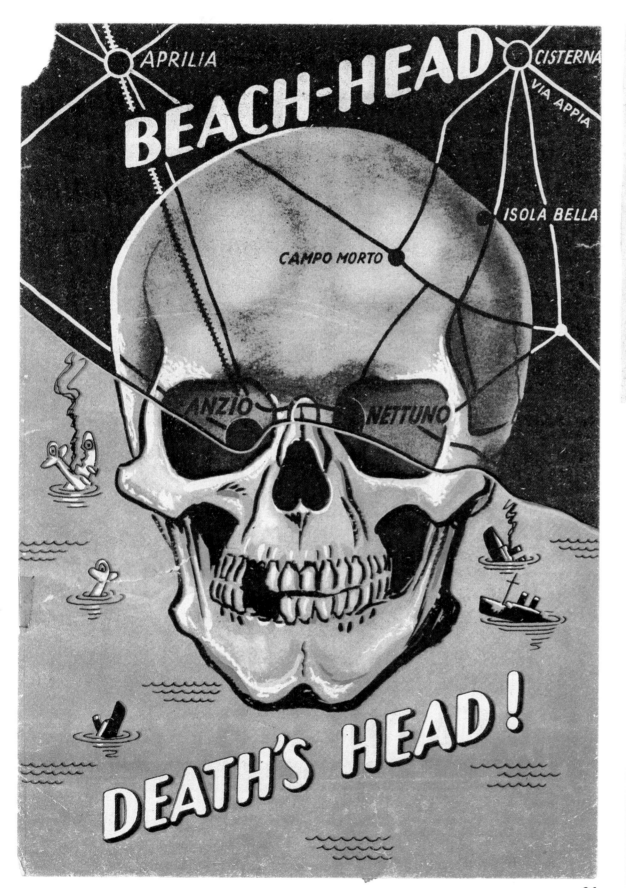

BEACH-HEAD

APRILIA CISTERNA VIA APPIA ISOLA BELLA CAMPO MORTO ANZIO NETTUNO

DEATH'S HEAD!

34

36. The 70% figure had to have been pulled out of the air. As far as propaganda goes this is an excellent leaflet, and probably quite effective. It really hits below the belt.

37. The ancedote is obviously an exaggeration directed to British troops. Notice how they slipped up when they point out that Cpl. Rogers was unlucky enough to be taken prisoner, whereas in any other leaflet one is lucky to become a POW.

38. Russian flyer. See Appendix for translation.

... effects of this war is that England has t... one base after the other to America. What else would have aroused the interest of America in this war other than "big business" — or does any one of you earnestly believe that the Jews of Wallstreet and the stock-jobbers would care a damn about the welfare of the British Empire or perhaps the social condition of the English workman?

The "man on the street" is always the fool in such a war. And the Americans want England to be the "man on the street" amongst the Allies. "America first" this is their slogan, and the sorry part of it is that they have the power to carry it through.

No wonder the slogan "Americans first" applies also to the American soldiers in England. 70% of all American soldiers who came across to Europe are still hanging about at the training camps in England. And while their pals in Italy prefer to stay at the quiet sectors and manage to get withdrawn from the front before offensive operations are started, the Americans in England are proving by all means to be "quick workers".

While you, poor ground hog, are fighting for your life on the inhospitable mountains of Southern Italy, the Americans are having their "amusing war" in England. Did not the recent letters from home make you feel how their "fight for bases" is interfering more and more with family life in England? Surely, you can rely upon your wife or your girl — but what about the others who were also feeling sure and who have had their happiness destroyed by the well-fed and well-clad warriors from Overseas?

And can you blame a woman for giving herself away to some handsome young boy if her husband has not been on leave for nearly a year?

LWP 124 / 4·44

Indeed, an amusing war

— FOR THE AMERICANS

Indeed, an amusing war
— FOR THE AMERICANS

38

By the way, old chap, did you ever think it over why the "inexhaustible reserves in man-power" of America have not turned up yet in this war? Possibly the statement contained in the news bulletin broadcast by the B. B. C. on 23. 3. 44 might give you an idea. It ran as follows:

"It is beyond doubt that the Germans have concentrated crack troops at Cassino for whom only the very best allied troops can be a match. For this reason the U. S. units have been recently withdrawn from the main fighting line in order to be temporarily employed at quieter sectors."

This is not exactly a compliment to your American pals — but London ought to know how far they can rely upon them. It is a fact that until to-day 70% of all Americans who came across are still in England, where they are being "trained" — as is officially stated.

How this training looks like, Corporal Richard C. Rogers of L-Coy. 3rd Bn. 350th Inf. Regt. 88th U. S. Inf. Div. is able to tell you. He had just arrived from England and was unlucky enough to be taken prisoner West of Minturno on the 16. 3. 44. In his wallet he had a slip of paper with the following anecdote:

Two English women met on the street in London one day. Said one, "Do you know Americans?" "Do I know Americans, says you," replied the other.

"Why just the other day me old man sent me over to the Pub for a bucket of beer, and when I was coming out who should I meet but a blooming American.

"Before I could say Trafalgar Square, he grabs me by the Ass, shoves me under a tree, ins me, outs me, wipes his tallywhacker on me petticoat, drinks me old man's beer pisses in the bucket, and walks off whistling, 'God save the King', and you ask me, do I know Americans?"

He was proud about this joke, old Corporal Richard C. Rogers, and boasted he knew many more similar ones with which he could prove that the Americans were "quick workers".

Definitely, it is a story that makes one laugh; it might be a little exaggerated, but surely, there is something true in it. But, on the other hand, would you still laugh if you considered that your sister, your girl or your wife at home might be the aim of the exploits by these "quick workers"?

Obviously, the "blooming Americans" are much braver in England than at the front where you, poor devil, have got to fight German crack troops alone.

No wonder they are looking upon the war as something quite amusing.

39. This leaflet was beautifully done and the message about Italy and the shapely signorina on covers is certainly evocative. The inside is frightening, but the message is clear.

40. This is a safe conduct leaflet to the Indian Army. The messages are the same only in two different Indian languages. The gist of it is, "A mouse is the leader of the elephant.

...ALY

...nts to see you

एक चूहा हाथी का सरदार

एक दफा का जिकर है कि एक हाथी सोया हुवा था। एक चूहा पौरंचा और उसे हाथी देख कर उसको जनजीर से बांध दिया। उसवक्त से हाथी की चूहे का गुलाम बनकर रहना पड़ा। एक दीन इतिफाक से एक बिल्ली ने चूहे को देख.पापा मार पापा कर उसको हाडप कर जाप। चूहा दोड़ा हुवा हाथी के पास पौरंचा और मदद मांगी और हाथी वादा किया कर। मगर वह बिल्ली के पंजे से उसको रीहा करा देगा तो चूहा हाथी कि जनजिरी को खोल देगा और अजाद कर देगा। भोले भाले हाथी ने बिल्ली के खीलाफ चूहे की मदद की और बाद में हाथी ने चूहे से जनजीर खोलने को कहा तो चूहे ने हन्स कर जवाब दिया तुम अभी इस काबील नाहीं हो"। चन्द दीनों के बाद वही बिल्ली फिर चूहे पर कपट पड़ी। अब तो चूहा फिर हाथी के पास दौड़ा हुवा आया और मदद मांगी। हाथी ने जवाब दिया तुम बड़े चक्कार, धोखाबाज और बेइमान हो। मैं तुम्हारी मदद नाहीं करुंगा। मैं अपनी जनजीरी को खुद तोड़ने की कोशीश करुंगा अच्छा है बिल्ली तुमको हाडप कर जाप"। बस ऐसा ही हुवा। बिल्ली चूहे को खा गई और हाथी ने अपना जोर लगा कर जनजिर तोड़ डाली और अजादी से जीनदगी बसर करने लगा। पर ही हाल तुम्हारा है। हिन्दोसतान जेसा बड़ा मुलक और इनगलीसतान जेसे मुलक की गुलाम है। हिन्दोसतानी देशभगत अजादी के लीए लड़ रहे है जोके अनको तीरह उस हालत में नासीब होगी जबकि इनगलीसतान बरबाद हो जापगा। और तम किस लीए लड़ रहे हो? अपनी गुलामी के लीए?

But did you expect to find it like this?

41. Indeed an amusing war, for the Americans of course. This is meant to tick-off the British Tommy.

42. The Germans called for an investigation finding that the Russians had done this hideous crime. But the Russians then claimed that it was the Germans. Nevertheless, they all accepted the fact that the atrocity took place. See Appendix for translation.

43. By and large, leaflets without pictures were less effective as propaganda.

6-3-44

Cpl. A. Newell 13036200
161 Coy. P.C. (Section 7)
18, Highfield Rd.
Southampton, Hants

Wotcho, Ernie!
I must apologize for the long interval between this & my last Air Mail to you. Well Pal, how much longer do you reckon this bloody war is going to last?

I know that I've experienced nothing compared with you but I'm utterly fed-up with the Army.

I wish it were all over & we were all back together again. Lets hope that that wonderful day isn't so very far away now Pal, Eh?

My brother Frank is out there somewhere & his wife tells me that he is expecting to be home some time this year. So it looks like I'll have to get two special leaves somehow.

We get a few Air Raids here so it keeps us reminded of home.

My Pal & I have been to one or two dances in the town but you can't get a look in for Yanks. The place is lousy with them & the girls won't dance with the Tommies while the Yanks are around.

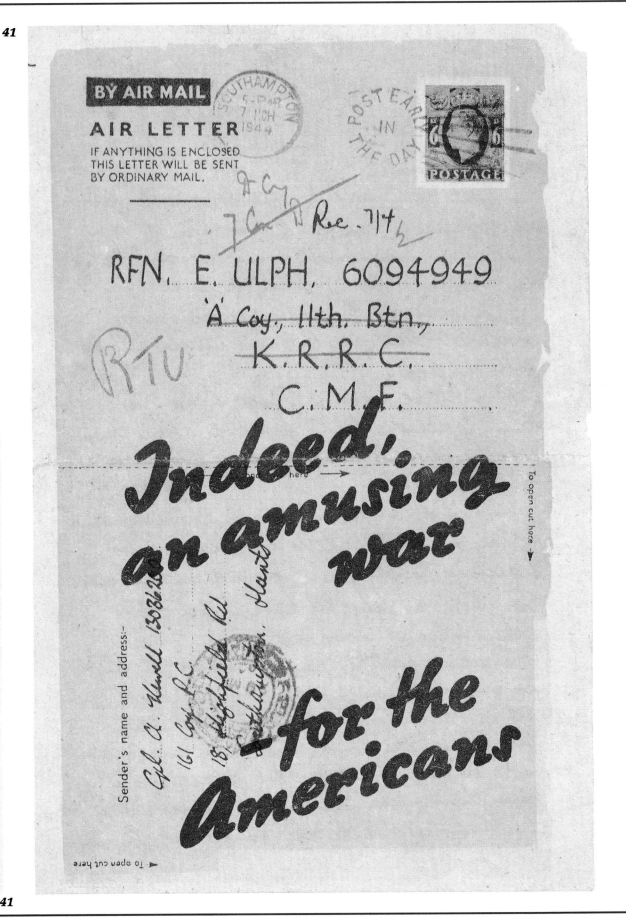

Krwawe hordy Stalina wkraczają do Polski.

Twoja Rodzina wzywa Cie!

Jesteś nam niezbędny - wracaj do domu.

42

No, you don't know,

and you can't possibly know why you, a Canadian soldier should be risking your life day after day in this lousy Italy. The future of Canada does not lie in Europe, but in the blood of the thousands and thousands of young Canadians who are sent to their death on the battlefields of Europe.

And your girl doesn't know

why she should have to wait for you year after year, until perhaps some day she receives the sad news that all her waiting has been in vain. She doesn't understand why on earth you must live so far from your home in muddy trenches, always in danger of being killed or crippled.

*And if you have children -
   they also don't know,*

they could never understand why their father has gone to far off Europe to die for foreign interests and deprive them for the rest of their lives of a father's caring hand.

And your mother doesn't know!

She did not bring you into the world with pain in order to make a soldier of you. She hasn't lavished all her mother's love on you in order to have you buried in a foreign land under a nameless mound.

They all don't know

why the flower of the youth of Canada should be sacrificed on the battlefields of Europe. It is not Canada's future which is being decided here, for no one has ever attacked Canada. It isn't even the future of the British Commonwealth to whom Germany has repeatedly offered her friendship and which is now being fleeced by her own Allies Soviet Russia and America.

*It is a rich man's war
        and a poor man's fight!*

A Jewish war - a British fight!

And must you shed your blood for that?

43

Kto strzelał w Katyniu?

"Niemcy umożliwili w Katyniu zbadanie faktów, które nie pozwalają wątpić ani na chwilę, że sprawcami mordu oficerów Wojsk Polskich byli bolszewicy. Obecnie przedstawiono mi komunikat nadzwyczajnej sowieckiej komisji śledczej, zawierający oświadczenie sowieckie w sprawie zbrodni popełnionej w Katyniu. Oświadczenie to nie jest w stanie zmienić mojej opinji i mego przekonania o tej sprawie, zebranych na miejscu w Katyniu. Oświadczenie sowieckiej komisji przypomina mi scenarjusz jakiegoś bardzo kiepskiego filmu i nie będzie w stanie zatrzeć tego fatalnego wrażenia, jakie wywarł na mnie widok ofiar katyńskich. Jak poprzednio, tak i teraz jestem do głębi przekonany, że sprawa katyńska jest wyłącznie zbrodnią sowiecką.

Powyższą opinję wydał prof. dr. Leon Kozłowski, b. prezes Rady Ministrów Rzeczypospolitej Polskiej. Do wspomnianego oświadczenia b. premjera Kozłowskiego nie możemy ze swej strony niczego dodawać. Mówi ono samo za siebie. Pozwala ono na ocenę informacyj, podawanych Ci jako codzienną strawę przez propagandę angielską i rosyjską.

Czy te same źródła propagandowe mówią Ci o tem, że bolszewicy rozbroili legjonistów polskich na wschodnich kresach Polski, że na wzór marszałka Tito, mianowali jakiegoś generała Rolę, który jest postacią wymyśloną, na stanowisko naczelnego dowódcy wszystkich polskich jednostek zbrojnych? Czy wiesz o tem, że Polska jest w niebezpieczeństwie i, że Ty walcząc, pogrążasz Ojczyznę Twoją w największe niebezpieczeństwo? Gdy czerwone armje zaleją wszystkie ziemie polskie, nigdy nie ujrzysz swej rodziny, swych najbliższych. Czy wiesz o tem, że Polska może wówczas stać się jednym wielkim Katyniem?

W tej ciężkiej chwili, zagrażającej Polsce i Europie strasznym niebezpieczeństwem, proponujemy Ci i ułatwimy powrót do domu rodzinnego. Przybądź do nas i do napotkanych posterunków niemieckich zawołaj d o d o m u. Adolf Hitler zapewnia Ci natychmiastowe zwolnienie i przewiezienie do kraju. Czy istnieje jeszcze wybór

pomiędzy Katyniem a powrotem do domu?

S 417.

42

44. Newspapers quoted out-of-context were always good for a propaganda score, especially when the originals were never available.

45. Addresses to Italian prisoners-of-war, this flyer suggests rather emphatically that this is not a Roman holiday!

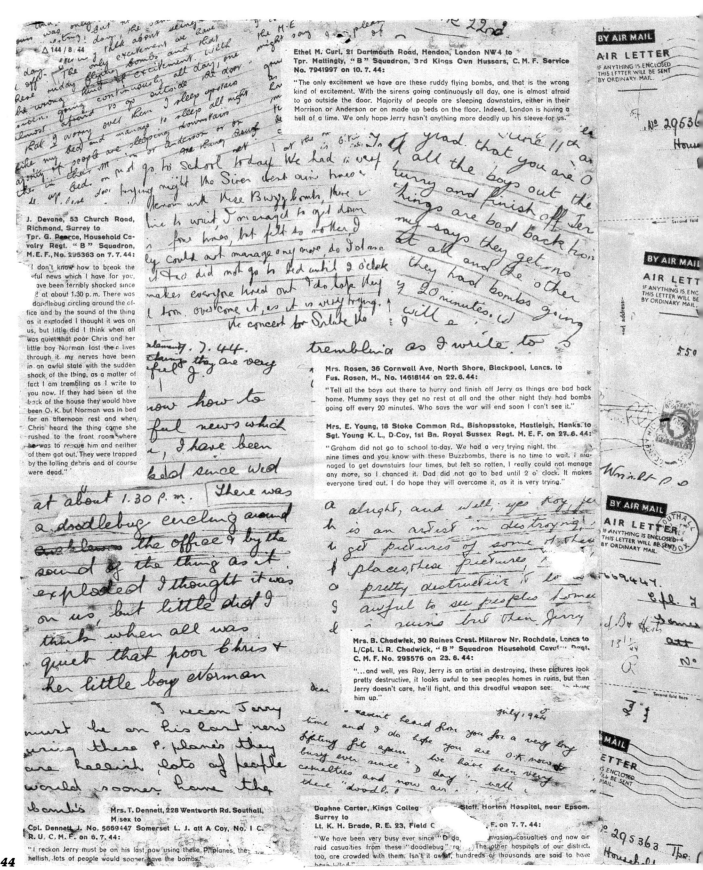

Ethel M. Curl, 21 Dartmouth Road, Hendon, London NW4 to Tpr. Mattingly, "B" Squadron, 3rd Kings Own Hussars, C. M. F. Service No. 7941997 on 10. 7. 44:

"The only excitement we have are these ruddy flying bombs, and that is the wrong kind of excitement. With the sirens going continuously all day, one is almost afraid to go outside the door. Majority of people are sleeping downstairs, either in their Morrison or Anderson or on made up beds on the floor. Indeed, London is having a hell of a time. We only hope Jerry hasn't anything more deadly up his sleeve for us."

J. Devane, 53 Church Road, Richmond, Surrey to Tpr. G. Pearce, Household Cavalry Regt. "B" Squadron, M.E.F., No. 295363 on 7. 7. 44:

"I don't know how to break the awful news which I have for you, have been terribly shocked since at about 1.30 p.m. There was a doodlebug circling around the office and by the sound of the thing as it exploded I thought it was on us, but little did I think when all was quiet that poor Chris and her little boy Norman lost the lives through it. my nerves have been in an awful state with the sudden shock of the thing, as a matter of fact I am trembling as I write to you now. If they had been at the back of the house they would have been O. K. but Norman was in bed for an afternoon rest and when Chris heard the thing come she rushed to the front room where he was to rescue him and neither of them got out. They were trapped by the falling debris and of course were dead."

Mrs. Rosen, 36 Cornwall Ave, North Shore, Blackpool, Lancs. to Fus. Rosen, M., No. 14618144 on 22. 6. 44:

"Tell all the boys out there to hurry and finish off Jerry as things are bad back home. Mummy says they get no rest at all and the other night they had bombs going off every 20 minutes. Who says the war will end soon I can't see it."

Mrs. E. Young, 18 Stoke Common Rd., Bishopstoke, Hastleigh, Hants. to Sgt. Young K. L., D-Coy, 1st Bn. Royal Sussex Regt. M. E. F. on 27. 6. 44:

"Graham did not go to school to-day. We had a very trying night, the nine times and you know with these Buzzbombs, there is no time to wait. I managed to get downstairs four times, but felt so rotten, I really could not manage any more, so I chanced it. Dad did not go to bed until 2 o'clock. It makes everyone tired out. I do hope they will overcome it, as it is very trying."

Mrs. B. Chadwick, 30 Raines Crest, Milnrow Nr. Rochdale, Lancs to L/Cpl. L. R. Chadwick, "B" Squadron Household Cavalry Regt. C. M. F. No. 295576 on 23. 6. 44:

"...and well, yes Roy, Jerry is an artist in destroying, these pictures look pretty destructive, it looks awful to see peoples homes in ruins, but then Jerry doesn't care, he'll fight, and this dreadful weapon see... him up."

Mrs. T. Dennett, 228 Wentworth Rd. Southall, M/sex to Cpl. Dennett J. No. 5669447 Somerset L. J. att A Coy, No. I C. R. U. C. M. F. on 6. 7. 44:

"I reckon Jerry must be on his last now using these P. planes, they hellish, lots of people would sooner have the bombs."

Daphne Carter, Kings Colleg... Staff, Horton Hospital, near Epsom. Surrey to Lt. K. H. Brade, R. E. 23, Field C... F. on 7. 7. 44:

"We have been very busy ever since " D day... invasion-casualties and now air raid casualties from these " doodlebug " ra... The other hospitals of our district, too, are crowded with them. Isn't it awful, hundreds of thousands are said to have been killed."

44

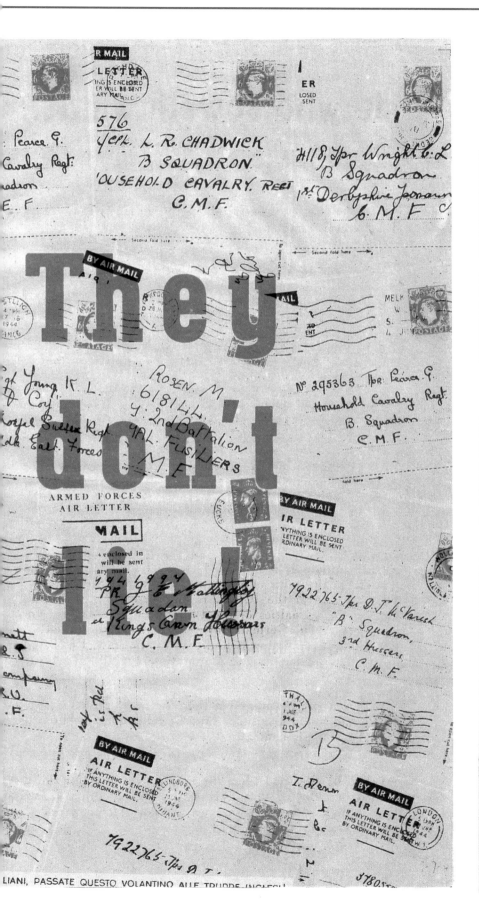

They don't lie!

ARMED FORCES
AIR LETTER

576
Tpr. L. R. CHADWICK
"B SQUADRON"
HOUSEHOLD CAVALRY. REGT.
C.M.F.

TURISTI A ROMA!

Questi prigionieri che ridono hanno ricevuto la notizia dell'eroica impresa di Montecassino

Italiani,

Gli ANGLO - AMERICANI, sbarcati a Salerno e conquistata Napoli, aiutati dal tradimento della Monarchia e del Maresciallo Badoglio, vi avevano promesso di essere, "tempo permettendo" a Roma per Natale.

Poi la pioggia, la neve, le montagne, la nebbia e il resto - tutto meno che il valore delle truppe tedesche - hanno scompigliato i loro piani. Cosicchè è probabile che, se il tempo non si rimetterà, a Roma gli ANGLO - AMERICANI non saranno nemmeno per Pasqua.

45

He who soweth wind...... ...... reapeth storm

44

46. *Brothers of Italy. Geoffredo Mameli was a great hero of Italy.*

47. *Insinuating that the Jewsish bankers got to stay home, eat well and cavort with pretty women. German anti-Semitic propaganda always played on the "bosses" theme.*

48. *Italian. Because of the dollar Italy is Fascist, at least, that is what they want the Italians to believe. The American banks are taking all the gold and running our morals and the religion of our citizens.*

49. *Saint Francis of Assissi is here praying for Italy and her victory.*

46

The fight for freedom!

Le banche americane rigurgitano dell'oro delle nazioni europee, indebitamente accumulato e trattenuto.

Sottratto alle nazioni giovani e lavoratrici, quest'oro serve ad alimentare l'imperialismo americano, alleato del bolscevismo che vorrebbe distruggere ogni principio morale e religioso della nostra civiltà.

Perciò l'Italia monarchica e fascista, forte dei suoi principi di giustizia sociale, deve combattere per assicurare con la vittoria il lavoro dei suoi figli.

1/6

S. FRANCESCO D'ASSISI PATRONO D'ITALIA

PREGHIERA PER L'ITALIA

NOI TI PREGHIAMO, O SIGNORE
per l'Italia nostra che tu hai voluto dessere al mondo in ogni epoca eroi, martiri e santi.

FA, O SIGNORE
che i dolori ed i sacrifici del passato non rimangano vani e che il sangue generoso dei suoi figli fruttifichi per l'Italia un avvenire di pace vittoriosa.

DONA, O SIGNORE
a tutti gli italiani quella forza morale, quello spirito di concordia e quella tenacia che soli consentono di vincere ogni battaglia, per raggiungere quelle mete di ordine, di civiltà e di giustizia sociale, che sono alla base di nostra santa Religione.

FA, O SIGNORE
che chi guida la Repubblica Sociale Italiana possa portare degnamente a termine il suo compito per l'avvenire e la grandezza della Patria.

BENEDICI LE NOSTRE BANDIERE
e fa che esse salgano sempre più alte nella luce dell'Onore e della Vittoria.

COSÌ SIA.

50. Cozzarini was the first Italian to fall in battle in WW I. He was a volunteer.

51. Corridoni was a volunteer in World War I who won a gold medal for his bravery in his fight for Italy.

52. Italy has been thrown into mud by a rotten traitor! Postcard addressed to Italian civilians.

53. Bombs, Bombs, Bombs. (in Italian) This leaflet to the Italians explains the horrible massacre of women children and old folks. This is the way of the Americans and the British.

COZZARINI
PRIMO CADUTO PER LA RISCOSSA
(1943)

50

E

CORRIDONI
A «TRINCEA DELLE FRASCHE»
(1915)

51

...« l'Italia è stata gettata nel fango da un pugno di vilissimi traditori,,

52

BOMBE
BOMBE
BOMBE

Distruzioni e assassini di donne, bambini e vecchi: ecco ciò che sanno fare gli anglo-americani.

Ora migliaia di agguerriti italiani hanno afferrato con indignazione le armi per farla **FINITA CON QUESTI MASSACRI.**

Oggi i nostri fratelli combattono nuovamente sul fronte fianco a fianco con i camerati tedeschi.

La loro voce è la voce della coscienza, il loro coraggio ci è esempio, il loro spirito ci condurrà al lavoro ed alla vittoria.

53

54. Der Kamerad was a newspaper for the German troops, distributed by the Germans. They certainly had a way of spurring their troops on even though the end of the war was in sight. Translation, see Appendix.

55. They keep saying the war will not soon be over, but that it will last for years. The same old refrain.

56. POW's return safe. The German's may have faked these names. Even if they did not, this can be expected in any war.

57. Khushi Ka. This billfold sized leaflet has a message for the Indian troops. It's a safe-conduct leaflet. The message: "Most of you may be familiar with this face. If not, then listen. He is known as the national leader, and he is famous by his name. This man is ever ready to lay down his life for his country and you. And now he is calling for you to join in his fight for freedom. The propaganda by the British about the prisoners of war being put to death are all lies.

So stellten sie sich ihren "niedlichen Krieg" vor

Mit solchen auf dieser Titelseite wiedergegebenen Plakatanschlägen wurde in den USA. für den Krieg geworben. Inzwischen haben die Amerikaner die rauhe Wirklichkeit bei ihrem Zusammentreffen mit deutschen Soldaten kennengelernt. Der Traum von einem vergnügungsfrohen Trip nach Europa ist ihnen schnell verflogen. Die Zeit arbeitet für uns und die Gesichter der Amerikaner werden lang und länger.

54

RICH MAN'S WAR POOR MAN'S FIGHT

I've got the Blues.

Really, since I heard the B.B.C. speaker early this morning, I've got them. He said, "The new German weapon was apt to distract attention from the battlefield itself, and that was the main advantage of it." I got sick of such foul arguments. The B.B.C. speaker also said, "The war is moving faster now than it ever used to. The new German weapon is certainly hastening the end. A few months more, instead of a few years more of battling."

Now, that at first did sound alright. Then all of a sudden I got to think, "If that is true - it's not so bad." "Jerry's Calling" of course is arguing the other way around - they still count on years, the Jerries do. That's as it may be. There seems to be no use in sticking around here to get the dirty end of the stick before it's all over."

55

Rich Man's War - Poor Man's Fight

They are making profits over profits in dividends and by speculation, and I - having no chance of getting a well-paid job now during the war - will be just up against the dole when all this ends. Just think of what it means to my family. Alright I am a soldier now and treated as such, but when all is over - no matter who wins the war - I shall be one of the 5 million unemployed, with no chance of making a living.

What's the use of it all?

Save your skin for your family und run no risks. Risks according to the B.B.C. are increasing from month to month. Old Rommel has fooled us more than once and who knows what the sly old fox may have up his sleeve now.

Rich Man's War - Poor Man's Fight
Bought wit is best

Kr 012 9 44

55

56

57

KHUSHI KA PAIGHAM!

Tum men se bahut se bhai, is taswir ko jante honge agar nahin to suno! Yih foto Subhash Chander Bose ka hai jo kih is waqt Hind Neta ke nam se tamam dunya men mashhur hai. Yih shakhs Hindustan ke lie apni jan tak dene ke lie tayyar rahta hai aur ab Hindustan ki Azadi ke lie la raha hai.

HIND NETA

ke sath Japani aur Germani hakumat ne wada kiya hai kih woh Hindustani qaidion ke sath bilkul dostana saluk karenge aur unko koi taklif na pahnchne denge. Is waqt hazaran Hindustani Qaidi Campon men aram ki zindagi basar kar rahe hain aur apne ghar walon se ba qaida khat wa kitabat jari hai.

ANGREZON KA PROPEGANDA

kih German qaidi nahin karte balkih jan se mar dete hain bilkul jhut aur bakwas hai.

57

58. A very impressive leaflet, very well done. The brevity of the message speaks louder than more verbose messages.

59. Here are the Liberators. This claims that Allied armies were made up of Negroes and gangsters. Americans are assasins!

60. What chance have the Brits against the power of V1 rockets? More than Hitler knew.

61. German paper directed to the American forces: clever, anti-Semitic and boastful!

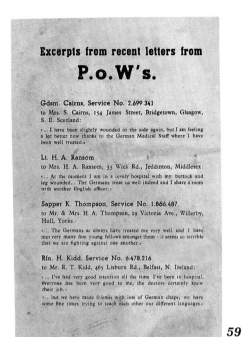

58

59

59

Just prick up your ears to this and guess what!

For months your politicians have been telling you that the new secret German weapon is just a bluff of propaganda, a mouthful of bombastic talk.

However, since June 16th, your so-called free press has been put under the most rigid censorship.

WHY?

Because since June 16th plain facts are speaking:

V NUMBER 1

V Number 1, those roaring monsters of the air, are smashing London and the supply bases in England with dreadful precision.

Regarding V Number 1 the First Lord of the Admiralty Alexander made it plain that England is facing hard times, that the new German weapon is the most modern and most deadly form of attack from the air.

You fellows on the Italian front are lucky to be far away from that hell turned loose over England.

The American Jew Baruch gave orders to " Butcher " Harris to indiscriminately kill German women and children, our women and children.

V NUMBER 1

is giving the answer.

AI - 078-6-44

62. London was indeed a large target. The figures for industrial concentrations are correct.

63. German propaganda constantly stressed that the war was the creation of big business and the Jews. They neglected to point out the part played by German industry.

64. On the front is a safe conduct message for the Germans from the Russians: "All German soldiers who will go to the Red Army are guaranteed his life, good treatment and sent home after the war. What goes on in Germany? This is news from the Eastern front with the struggle with the Red Army. In about 3 weeks one million men were killed and wounded." This flyer was taken from a German prisoner in Italy who had just come from the Eastern front.

by Germany faced England with grave problems. Churchill admitted that there were districts where the damage through explosion was so great that it could not be dealt with by the local organisations.

As regards parliamentary criticism, the government wished the members to limit their questions as far as possible.

Finally Churchill put a few questions which show the seriousness of the situation.

"Will this attack become heavier? [This is already the case] Will new developments of a far more terrible kind come over us? Will a rocket bomb come? Improved explosive bombs, with a heavier load of explosives and higher speed? Will all this come over us? I cannot guarantee that anyone of these evils can be hindered from striking us."

Churchill finished his speech with the statement that his government would do all in its power not to allow the operations in Normandy to be prejudiced.

"We must not allow any weakening of our fighting front for the sake of lessening the destruction brought about by V. 1. on our home-front, destruction which in reality brings heavy trouble to our population and changes the normal routine and the work of the industries in London."

«London is too big with its 8.2 million of inhabitants crowded together in an area of about 80 square miles. In case of war it will be a giant target.»

This alarming statement was made by Mr. Fletcher M. P. in the House of Commons some years ago, and it's true.

Just take into consideration that:

48 % of all English machine shops
26 % car factories
34 % airplane production
48 % chemical factories
40 % soap factories
57 % furniture manufactories
46 % of the canning business

are crowded together in this small area.

A GIANT TARGET INDEED!

Kr - 027 - 7 - 44·

Mr. CHURCHILL
ORIGINATOR OF INDISCRIMINATE BOMBING, SPEAKS ABOUT V NUMBER 1

The British Prime Minister on July 6th made a statement in the House almost entirely on the subject of V Number 1. His speech according to American reporters was the longest Churchill ever made.

"It would be a mistake", he said, "to undervalue the serious character of this special form of attack".

He stated that in the beginning of 1943 the British government had received reports that the Germans were developing a new long-range weapon with which they intended to bombard London. Since then by means of a large number of reconnaissance flights throughout the north-west of France and Belgium, involving heavy losses, the English had identified at least 100 starting places, part of them still in course of construction, obviously intended for projectiles with some sort of rocket impulse. These starting-places had been bombarded with about 50,000 tons of explosives.

So that before the German bombardment actually started, a sort of "invisible war" had been in progress for more than a year. "This invisible battle had now become generally visible." He went on to say that, taking into consideration the heavy weight and the power of impact of these bombs, the damage done up to the present could be considered bearable.

This form of attack, however, in such mass, was fatiguing because the attacks stretched over almost 24 hours daily, and the population had to get used to them.

"And when the long day is over", he said, "all must seek out the safest refuge they can find and forget their cares in sleep."

Over the losses so far Churchill made several rather indefinite statements; he admitted more than 10,000 casualties, the dead numbering 2,752. In a later part of his speech he declared that the dead formed a much higher percentage.

Churchill prepared the English people for the fact that this battle might be protracted. The introduction of this weapon

63

63

65. The Germans actually began to believe their own propaganda about the V1.

66. Strange that they believed that Hitler's quest for the Aryan race was justified by God–Providence! Just how badly can a people be misled and follow as "sheep to the slaughter?"

67. This leaflet tells the tale of guests in a German POW Camp 27... captured American soldiers.

HOW THE ALLIES ARE GOING TO WIN THE WAR!

What good are all your planes, warships and tanks against that new German weapon

V NUMBER 1

Are you still convinced that you are winning?

Your armchair strategists have always claimed that the new dreadful weapon is an invention of German "propaganda". But out of a clear sky it struck.

Since June 16th, London and southern England are being continuously blasted day and night by those mysterious flying meteors.
The entire British press was immediately muzzled by rigid censorship. What a nice job your politicians do have now in hiding the truth about the disastrous effect of

V NUMBER 1

BUT **YOU** will learn the truth just the same. You will also find out that Germany has just begun to play one of her trump cards.

How about V Number 2 to V Number X

AI - 079-6-44

SHAME ON MURDERERS! SHAME ON THOSE THAT BY LOW CUNNING STAB IN THE BACK!

Greetings to our Pals!

We are guests in POW Camp 27 and are feeling quite safe here although the gate is locked. We are not looking for another hell of a time as we had during the night from the 13/14 of February.

(signed)

[handwritten signatures]

And this is what happened.

On February 13th at 18 hrs. one group of an assault party marched off from Loiano under the command of Lt. Cuwan. After having marched for about half an hour they were getting a lift and could ride in three Jeeps for about twenty minutes, after that there was another march of an hour and a half, until they reached Barchetta at about 1 AM. Orders were to occupy a house to the south of the village which had served as a company observation post. They were to relieve the men there and stay for 24 hours in the place. When they got to the house they did not find any Americans there but instead encountered a German assault group which surprised them with hand grenades and machinegun fire. The boys sought cover in the house but it was soon thereafter destroyed by the Germans with their Panzer fists. 11 men lost their lives and only 3 survived: Pvt. Julian C. Battino, Sign. Pete Borda and Pvt. Samuel Newman. The other group of the assault party got surrounded by the Germans the next morning at 9 o'clock and all 15 men were taken prisoner.

* 421-2-45

ENGLAND AND AMERICA

have played their last card. Having failed to get the Führer into their hands, as they had tried to do with the Duce, to make a vulgar show of him to their countrymen and try him as a war criminal, they have attempted to assassinate him. A group of criminals and paid traitors have been the instruments. The plot has failed miserably.

Almighty God has miraculously preserved the life of this man, showing that He wishes Adolf Hitler to bring his mission to a successful end,
to lead us to Victory,
the Victory of Europe.

AGAINST PROVIDENCE OUTLAWS MUST FAIL!

Kr - 031 - 7 - 44

68. *British Press reports the devastation wreaked on London by the V1.*

69. *It's a bird, it's a plane, no they're "Doodle Bugs" (as the Londoners called them)! Listed are five facts concerning the V1.*

70. *Hindu News states "Every country is fighting for independence, but now the German administration is here to assist India with the help of the famous Subhach Chander Bose. Azad Hind Fauj will lead the Free Indian Army." This is another plea to Hindus with a note at the bottom for the German soldiers to treat Indian prisoners of war well.*

68

NEWS FROM THE CENSORED
B R I T I S H P R E S S

«Daily Telegraph» reports

... that according to the testimony of eye witnesses the effect of the new German weapon surpasses everything hitherto experienced in England. To make things worse the air raid shelters, up to now considered as absolutely bombproof, no longer offer any protection against this new type of explosive.

... that the First Lord of the Admiralty, Alexander, made it clear that England is facing hard times and that the new German weapon is the most modern and most deadly form of attack from the air.

«Daily Mail» reports

... that the effect of the explosion of the dynamite meteors is horrible. The largest and most massive blocks of buildings are blown away like cardboard houses.

... that whole rows of buildings have been completely erased and that the new German weapon also affected the food supply to a large extent.

«Daily Herald» reports

... that what is troubling the British most is the disquietude caused by the new weapon and the uncertainty about it. Some have lost their homes already twice in one week. Many are living all the time in their air raid shelters, others take to flight as soon as they hear the roaring noise of the flying bombs.

The British Home Minister Morrison states

... that it is quite possible that the attacks of the new German explosive meteors have not yet reached the culminating point. The Germans are still improving this new weapon and they may yet employ other new types. (Statement in the House on June 23, 1944)

If so much can filter through the British censorship,

WHAT ARE THE FACTS?

Burning London can be seen from the continent!

AI - 080 - 7 - 44

Khudá ne áj tak us qaum ka hálat náhin badli
Na ho jis ko khiyál áp apni hálat ke badalne ká.

HINDUSTÁNIO!

Tum ko kuchh khabar hai kih dunyá men kyá ho ráhá hai? Har ek qaum apni ázádi ke lie sar tor koshish kar rahi hai. Hindustán ke andar is ghulami se niját páne ki har mumkin koshish jári hai. Aur sáth hi Jápáni aur Jermani hakumaten Hindustán ke bare rehnumá Subhas Chandra Bose se wádá kar chuki hain ki woh Hindustán ki is Jang-ázádi men puri puri madad dengi.

AB ÁZÁD HINDI FAUJ

Hind Netá Subhash Chandra Bose ki rehnumái men Jápànion ka sáth milkar Burmá ki sarhad se Hindustán ke andar dákhil ho chuki hain, aur iswaqt Manipore Riyasat par azad Hindustani jhandá lahrá ráhá hai. Yeh qaumi fauj uswaqt tak apná khun báháegi jab tak kih angrez Hindustan se bilkul nest-o-nábud na ho jáenge. Házáron ki tádád men Hindustani sipáhi angrezi fauj se bhág bhág kar Hindustání Qaumi Fauj men rozána mil rahe hain. Ek taraf to yeh ho ráhá hai, dusri taraf tum baghair soche samjhe ghair qaum, jis ne do sau sál se tumhen ghulám báná rakhá hai uská sath de rahe ho, aur apne mulk se dur daraz fásele par angrezon ke badle men jánen qurban kar rahe ho. Akhir yeh be matlab maut tumháre hisse men kion hai? Kionkih tum abhi tak ghulám ho. Angezon ká sath dená apni ghulámi ki zanjiron ko aur bhi mazbut karná hai. Izzat ki maut bhi be-izzati ki zindagi se behtar hai. Is waqt Hindustán men ghair mulki faujen Hindustánion par zulam dha rahi hain aur unki be-izzati kar rahi hain.

GHAUR KARO!

KIH AISE MAUQE PAR TUMHEN KIYA KARNÁ CHÁHIE!

Rozáná shám ko 5 1/2 se 6 baje tak BHAI BAND Radio se Hindustáni men khabren sunie. 449,1 Medium wave, 28,3 aur 39,6 Short Wave.

Indische Soldaten, die sich mit diesem Flugblatt den deutschen Linien nähern, sind als Überläufer anständig zu behandeln, zu verpflegen und unter Bewachung zurückzuschaffen.

LwP. 116./AI. 115.5.44

FACTS CONCERNING "V NUMBER 1"

1. No AA barrage and no fighter planes can prevent the gigantic « Doodle Bugs », as the Londoners call them, from coming over. The « Doodle Bugs » travel at a tremendous speed making them invulnerable to attacks.

2. « V Number 1 » does not depend on weather, time, season, or visibility. It is an « all weather » and « round the clock » weapon of deadly nerve-wrecking regularity. It is robbing Britishers of their sleep, keeping them down in the shelters and away from their work benches and desks.

3. No alarm system in London or elsewhere can sound a warning soon enough. Consequently, alarm exists "round the clock". The "mysterious dynamite meteors" hit unexpectedly, anywhere, anytime. "V Number 1" is a permanent surprise weapon.

4. The starting places of "V Number 1" are safe against enemy attacks. They can be moved quickly from one place to another. Neither an army of technicians nor an elaborate ground personnel is required.

5. No operators are lost. "Meteors" have no crew, no nerves are shattered by AA barrages or fighter planes. The "Doodle Bugs" follow their course stubbornly and hit with a ferocious impact grinding everything to dust.

USE YOUR OWN JUDGEMENT!

AI. 081 - 7 - 44

71. POW's had all the comforts of home: education, theatre, libraries, hospitals, games and... their lives.

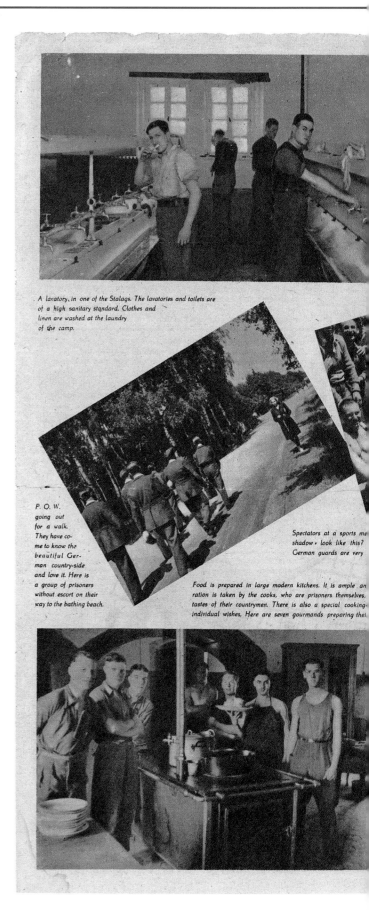

71

71

Somewhere in Germany

...e various camps at which these ...have been taken. They are by no ...monstercamps as the hotels in ...nia which are being run solely for ...es of propaganda. But all German ...are like those represented by our ...s. They are scattered all over Ger- ...s. and are built in different styles. ...of them are clean, spacious, up- ...with all conveniences. Food is ...ed in modern kitchens by your ...ooks. It is ample and of the ...high quality as the ...of the ...n

soldier. All camps have athletic fields, football grounds, swimming pools etc. and a variety of modern sporting equipment. For your entertainment there are motion pictures, theatrical and musical shows and every facility is made to enable prisoners of the various nationalities to celebrate their festivals in their own way. You will be given an opportunity of learning a trade or of improving yourself in your profession. You may carry on with your studies and even acquire a university degree, as special boards of examination recognised by your country are appointed for this purpose. If you wish to work, your qualifications will be taken into account, and you will be paid on the

In England ne owns a vast garden and is very glad to have found out that his favourite vegetables are growing on German soil as well.

A football match in one of the prisoners' camps. London vs. Manchester playing; Manchester won 5 : 3.

...n in the ...with the

...have overcome the terrors ...r. Their eyes reflect a fee- ...of happiness and confidence ...future. After the war they ...go home.

The P. O. W. have decorated their rooms according to their own taste. After a day of work, sports and games they have now met for a quiet poker party.

The mail has arrived! Every prisoner may receive any number of letters from home and, in addition, he gets one parcel a week from the International Red Cross.

New Zealanders unpacking their parcels. They contain cigarettes, chocolate, coffee, jam, butter, condensed milk etc.

...doctor in charge of the ...has at his disposal the ...modern instruments and ...cines for the treatment of ...atients. The wounded and ...ick are transferred to hos- ...to which prominent spe- ...ts are attached.

same scale as the German workers. The wounded and the sick are treated at the same hospitals as the German soldiers, and German, English and American doctors are available for their medical attention. Your mail is conveyed via the International Red Cross and the forwarding is swift and reliable. Every prisoner receives through the International Red Cross one parcel a week containing cigarettes, chocolate, coffee, biscuits and other useful and pleasant things. You may receive any amount of mail, while you yourself are permitted to write 4 postcards and 3 letters per month.

71

72. This leaflet suggests that only Jewish men were making big money on the homefront from the war, while other nationalities were engaged in the active fighting.

73. American men were dating English women while boyfriends or husbands were fighting for their country.

72

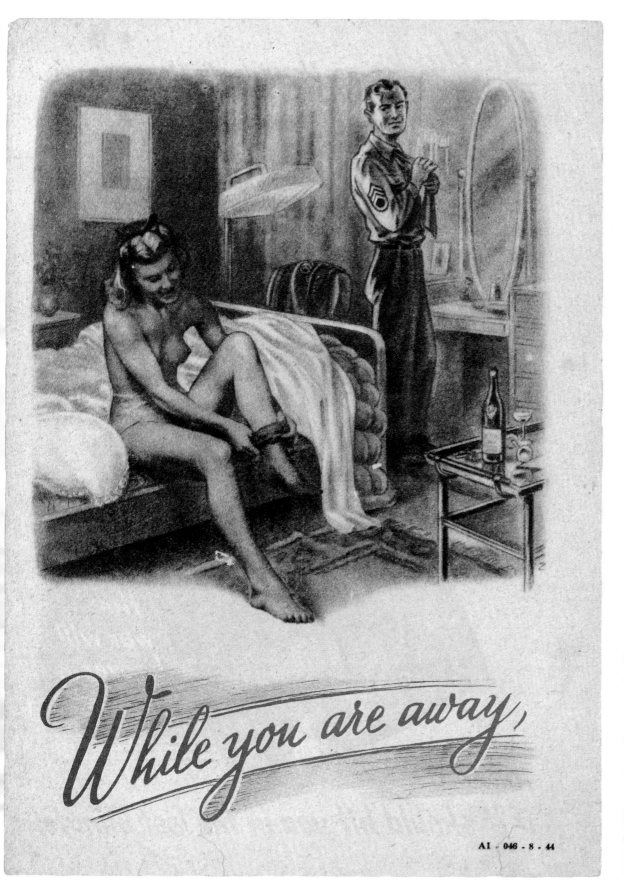

While you are away,

AI · 046 · 8 · 44

73

the Yanks are "lease-lending" your women. Their pockets full of cash and no work to do, the boys from overseas are having the time of their lives in Merry Old England.

And what young woman, single or married, could resist such "handsome brute from the wide open spaces" to have dinner with, a cocktail at some night-club, and afterwards.......

Anyway, so numerous have become the scandals that all England is talking about them now.

Most of you are convinced that

the war will be over in four months.

Too bad if it should hit you in the last minute.

74. Despite Franklin D. Roosevelt's statement on October 31, 1940: "And while I am talking to you fathers and mothers, I give you one more assurance. I have said this before, but I shall say it again and again: your boys are not going to be sent into any foreign wars," many 18- and 19-year olds were eventually inducted into the Army and killed in action after three or four months.

75. Did the Jewish people rule the United States? A repulsive flyer equating power, political and economic, with the Jews.

76. Has the war only just begun? Hundreds of mountains remain to be conquered–not only the massive peaks of the Apennines–before the war is over. Are the Allies only prolonging an inevitable loss against the Germans?

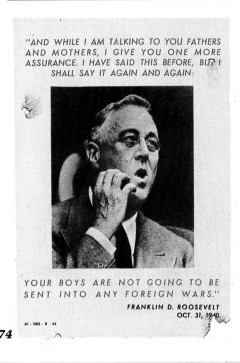

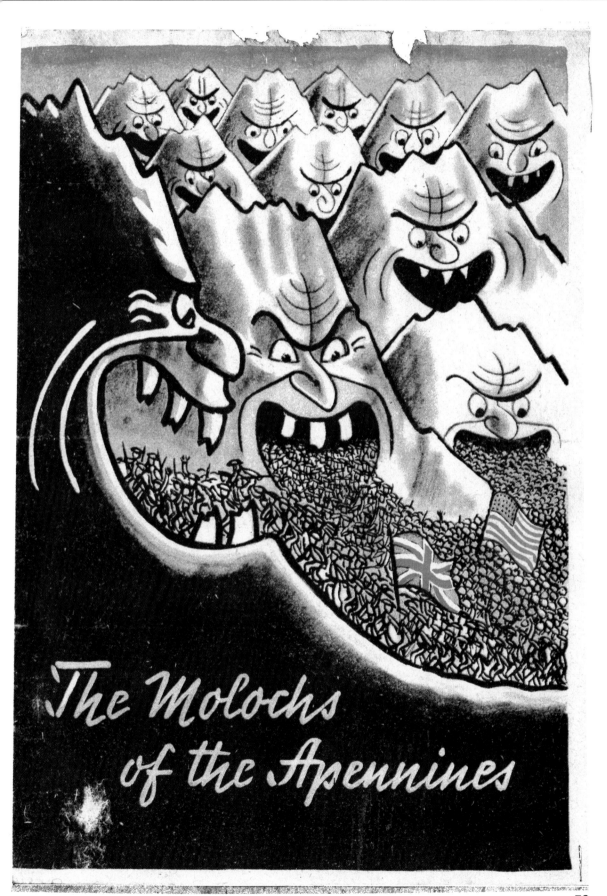

The Molochs
of the Apennines

...gomery told the world,
"The war will be over in six months."

And the whole machinery of British and American propaganda tried to make you believe that the war would be finished within a few months.

The fact is that the war is just starting.

In Italy the Allies have fought their way north step by step suffering very heavy casualties. But instead of weakening the German forces, German resistance is stiffening.

After months of relentless struggling, causing you untold losses in dead and wounded, you Allied soldiers have now reached the greatest barrier in Italy, the massive peaks of the Apennines.

There are hundreds of mountains to be conquered.
Every one of them is now a fortress.

You can figure it out yourself how long it may take to overcome them.

Thousands of you will never see their families again.
Thousands will be maimed for life.
Only P. o. W. will return home safe and sound.

The war will go on for years yet.
Germany can never be conquered.

Her resistance becomes harder every day, her weapons better and more destructive.

AI - 088 - 8-44

77. *You have a date with death. Your girl has a date with Sam Levy.*

78. *Join the Army. See the world! Be in the war.*

You *have a date with death*
Your girl *has a date with Sam Levy*

> *At first she hesitated a bit about calling up Sam, the war profiteer. But then she said to herself, "There's no point in waiting any longer for Joe to come back, the war seems endless, and the best years of my life are passing by..."*

You'll have to be in uniform for God knows how long. Your life is pretty well smashed up. So don't think the worse of your girl if she likes to have a good time every now and then. Don't grudge her to that bright war dodger Sam Levy.

In return you are seeing something of the world and taking part in this jolly old war.

AI : 100 - 8 - 44

What about calling up Sam Levy....

Joe is so far away over there on the front and I'd love to go out and have a good time again. There's so little chance of Joe coming home. Well, I guess I'll just give Sam a call, he'll take me out.

JOIN THE ARMY - SEE THE WORLD!

A grand invitation! What guy wouldn't jump at the occasion! A free round-trip to Europe, sightseeings, three square meals a day, money besides and a good time all around. So often you had read in the papers : "Mr. and Mrs. Smith of Woodville, Ont., left on board the Queen of Canada for Italy and France." A swell idea. And then the return to the folks at home as a hero. What eyes would the boys in the corner drugstore make! And the girls, wouldn't they fall for you at first sight, for the hero from overseas. A fool who wouldn't volunteer to see the world!

Well, in the past months you have had lots of time to do some thinking. Instead of an illusion and promises you have got now first-hand information, which is all that counts after all . . .

Europe : *a d... place to live in for a Canadian soldier !*

Sightseeings : *ruins, shell-holes, dead and wounded comrades !*

Three square meals a day : *a strictly monotonous affair !*

Money besides : *and nothing to buy !*

A good time : *no girls, no shows, no icecream parlors, but plenty of dust and dirt, sickness and hardship, a rotten life in the trenches and in half-destroyed houses waiting for a German bullet or shell to hit you !*

A free round-trip : *at the price of wasted years, broken health and, maybe, even of your own sweet life and the happiness of your family.*

In a word : *the happy-go-lucky soldiering has become the grim business of war.* Rifle practice is done with living targets and - what is worse - these targets are shooting back.

Is it any wonder that you boys are getting homesick, much more so as there is no reason in the world for your being here. **You know this isn't your war.** This war is the game of the rich, of the war profiteers, of Wallstreet and of ambitious politicians. They wouldn't care for a hero's death. But they cared for tricking you, the little man in the street, into

THIS SUICIDAL WAY OF SEEING THE WORLD

Δ 148 / 8. 44

79. This amusing leaflet depicts how absurd the V1 flying bombs were to the Germans.

80. Where will Russia stop? This question is worrying every Englishman who cares for the welfare of the British Empire. The answer is found in an article in the Red Star, the organ of the Red army.

81. According to an Indian saying, "A mouse leads an elephant."

82. American soldiers are told why to write, what to write and when to write letters home.

V1 - THE DEADLY "BLUFF"

Britain built up an air defence of enormous proportions, sparing neither cost nor exertion in employing the most modern technical means.

With one stroke this whole system of air defence has become worthless with the introduction of flying bomb V 1.

V 1 has upset all known methods of aerial warfare. Other equally revolutionary new weapons will follow. They will prove to you that

V 1 FLYING BOMBS AREN'T THE LAST "BLUFF"

AI-102-9-44

After everybody had hopefully made the "V" sign for years, it suddenly appeared on the scene.

The best antidote against the "V 1" poison has been found by London journalists: "Hush it up!"

An unpleasant feeling in the stomach and shivering on encountering V - shaped symbols have been diagnosed by English doctors as "V-psychosis".

The best defence against other "V" weapons, which are to be expected, is to raise both arms in the shape of a large "V".

Churchill, 29. 5. 1919:

Bolshevism is not a policy, it is an epidemic. It is not a belief, it is a pestilence.

Δ 139 / B 44

WHERE WILL RUSSIA STOP ?

Where will Russia stop?

This is the question put by Sir Archibald Southby, M. P. a few weeks ago at a meeting of his electors. He could not give any precise answer to this question which is worrying every Englishman who cares for the welfare of the British Empire. At any rate, Mr. Southby declared, Britain must not have a "hand-to-mouth" foreign policy, and she ought to have a clear idea of what exactly were her intentions and what attitude ought to be adopted regarding the Russian problem.

By sheer coincidence, the "Krasnaja Iswestija" (Red Star), the organ of the Red Army has given these days a clear answer to this vital English question, and which we would not like to withhold from the British soldier. Surely, this answer would have never been expressed so frankly, should it have appeared in a paper of world-wide publication as the "Pravda", for instance. But thus, they thought they were amongst themselves, hence no need of mincing matters in any way.

Here is a translation of the article which appeared in the « Krasnaja Iswestija » on 25-7-44:

"To avoid errors"

« At a moment in which the victorious Red Army is approaching the borders of Eastern Prussia we are receiving news from England that an organisation has been formed under the auspices of the Allied Headquarters with the object of taking over the military administration of Germany after the victory of the United Nations It comprises a whole division of officers and officials who are being trained already now for their post-war tasks. An English General, whose name keeps changing practically every week, has been placed at the head of this organisation, while the post of deputy is being held by an American General.

It is most interesting that this information comes to us at a moment in which the check of the Anglo-American offensive in Italy appears to be imminent in front of new German defence lines, at a moment in which the American-English invasion of France has been stripped of all great strategical lines and is turning into disconnected fights involving heavy losses, while, on the other hand, the incomparable Red Army is forcing the foe into wild retreats by its impetuous pressure. We are also noting with interest the statement in the report saying that an agreement had so far been reached between England and America, and that « Russia would still have to be approached on the subject ».

It seems as if our Western Allies were persisting in their old errors concerning the moulding of the world after the war. Does London actually believe that Soviet Russia has entered the war in order to strengthen the English predominance in Europe? Do they believe that we have borne the weight of the burdens of this war, that we have paid all these enormous tolls in blood and that we have dealt out to the enemy the decisive blows merely to enable others to benefit of the results of our struggle? If this should really be the case, it is high time to take steps in order to avoid such errors.

To us this war is primarily a matter of our revolutionary way of viewing the world. It does not make any difference to us whether Europe is being ruled by Hitler-Fascism or by a bunch of Anglo-American reactionists. What we want is that, after this war is over, a new world should arise. And as we have made the greatest sacrifices for the creation of this new world, we also have the right to insist that it be given our form, the form required by a progressive world-revolutionary age. We are convinced that a dictatorship of the proletariate alone can save the world from economic and national troubles. hence we are fighting for a dictatorship of the proletariate and for nothing else. The most powerful enemy of this world revolution is Germany, consequently we are fighting Germany. But we do not want to leave the slightest doubt that we

shall fight with the same violence and determination any other opponent to our proletarian world views. This war would have lost all sense to us should it not liquidate, at the same time as Fascism of German and Italian edition, the reactionary «bourgeoisie» of the so-called democracies, so that a foundation can be laid capable of bearing the proletarian world league in which there will be no room for classes and national sentimentality.

England is at present on a dangerous track. She is becoming more and more the dependant of America. It is up to all Englishmen of common sense to prevent their Government from continuing on this wrong track. And it is up to the Communist Party in England to increase its activity in order to make the English people mature for following a new way, the way on the side of Soviet Russia. But before England can follow this way, she has to undergo a thorough transformation-and although we may accept to fight a common foe side by side with a civil-reactionary state, yet there can be no doubt that the victory in this war will be a proletarian achievement. It will mean a step further on the way of our holy idea, the dictatorship of world-proletariate. It is our duty towards the father of our idea Lenin. towards the leader of our heroic Red Army, Stalin, and towards the millions of dead of this war not to allow any power of the world to stop us on our way ».

So far the article of the "Krasnaja Iswestija", the contributors of which include amongst others: Stalin, Woroshilow and Timoshenko. We have nothing else to add but one question:

Is this what you are fighting for, British Soldier?

RITE THAT

What letter ?

The letter home. When you first left home, you wrote at once. You had so many things to tell; you had seen so much that was strange and new. Your first impulse was to write and tell someone about it. But now you find it harder to write, because, as you say, you have told them everything once, and life is now mostly routine . . . . and so on.

Why write it ?

Because your folks are waiting to hear from you. In times of war, no news is bad news to an anxious heart. Your folks have a right to know just how you feel and to know it quickly.

What shall I write ?

If you haven't told them everything, tell it. It's the truth they want to hear and nothing but the truth. You know, if you write cheerfully, you are just making a fool out of yourself. It would not be fair to you for them to believe that this is an amusing war. Because it isn't. It's a d . . . . . war. Life in the trenches and in half-destroyed houses, amidst dead and wounded comrades, is a rotten thing. No wonder that you are feeling homesick and longing for your good job back home. — Anyway, this war is not your baby.

When shall I write ?

Right now, of course. A quick letter is always a good letter. The war, as you know, has a grim way of putting a sudden end to one's life, and a dead man writes no more letters. So, write that letter now and tell your folks the plain and simple truth about this war.

83. Pictured is a 12-year-old German soldier. He joined the army of his own free will.

84. This is a call for Arabs to join Hitler in the fight against the Allies.

85. This flyer tells us about the Grand Mufti, the Muslim religious leader in Palestine.

86. Strange as it may seem, most of Europe knew about the Wolf, yet they allied with him. The lend-lease figures to Russia are staggering. The Russian shipping lanes through the North Sea to Murmansk were a solid stream of cargo vessels many months before the United States ever got into the war. The United States was at war before we ever declared it, and the enemy was our ally.

87. The Credo, which means I Believe, was shot to the Italian civilian population. It is against the British.

88. Cigar smoking Winnie is pulling a little Indian wagon. Dr. Iqbal wrote a poem stating, "India is the best in the world." This was repeated by the BBC.

89. Hitler and Mussolini meet with smiles prior to the final year of the war.

90. The Star of David has "Business with the dead."

91. Anglo-American armies are said to have bombed churches and monasteries, killing women and children.

83

84

85

86

CREDO

Io credo in Inghilterra, iena perfetta e prepotente, creatrice delle sanzioni e dei massacri e in Eden suo figliolo, unico boia nostro, il quale fu concepito in virtù dello spirito massonico antifascista.

Nacque dalla S. D. N. e patirà sempre sotto l'Impero di Mussolini.

Scese all'inferno col padre suo e, dopo tre giorni, non morì e dovrà venire a giudicare la scomparsa del suo regno, suicidandosi con i suoi compagni.

Credo alla santa causa fascista, nella resurrezione dell'Italia Imperiale di Benito Mussolini, e nel Fascismo, luce eterna di Roma. E così sia.

PIRATA NOSTRO

Pirata nostro che sei un inglese, usurpatore del sangue umano, sia maledetto il nome tuo, venga a crollare sempre l'impero tuo, sia fatta la massacrazione di tuti i sanzionisti per l'inutile volontà tua, così in mare, così in terra. Lascia oggi e per sempre le tue mire sull'Abissinia, rimetti a noi i nostri crediti dal 1915 al 1918, come noi rimetteremo il tuo credito delle pallottole dum dum vendute al Negus. E così sia.

AVE INGHILTERRA

Ave Inghilterra, piena d'invidia! L'egoismo è teco, tu sei maledetta fra le Nazioni sanzioniste, frutto delle tue malvagità. Santa causa Fascista, Madre di civiltà, combatti per noi, per la grandezza dell'Impero Italiano, ora e sempre fino alla morte. E così sia.

87

Il 6 giugno 1944 li ha trovati pronti!

« Le potenze del Tripartito sono decise di portare a fine vittoriosa la guerra contro il bolscevismo di oriente e contro gli ebrei e i plutocrati dell'occidente, e di garantire ai popoli una vita sulla base di un ordine nuovo e giusto. »

(Incontro Führer-Duce 22-23 aprile 1944)

88

89

90

Ecco i "Liberatori"

Dopo il bombardamento di Castelgandolfo - Il trasporto delle vittime

Italiani!

È forse una fatalità che in ogni incursione anglo-americana basiliche illustri come S. Lorenzo, asili di sfollati come Castelgandolfo, cimiteri come il Verano, case di cura come la clinica Polidori e scuole debbano essere l'obbiettivo "militare" preferito e perfettamente centrato dei gangsters americani e dei civilissimi figli di Albione?

Non lo crediamo!

91

92. Winston Churchill stated "Communism is like a cancerous growth which feeds on an enfeebled body and destroys "the very meat it feeds on." What healthy body would wish such a deadly disease?

93. One can dream on his honeymoon or while at war.

94. This is another plea to Italian partisans to turn to Germany because the real enemy, Russia, may send them to Siberia.

95. Mahatma Gandhi is seen here saying, "Boycott the foreign goods."

92

The Union Jack and the bloodstained banner of Bolshevism are marching hand in hand. Churchill thought of the pact with the Red Dictator as a five minutes' alliance and hoped to get rid of Stalin at the right moment.

You don't believe earnestly that Bolshevism would stop at the Channel. It is Germany which has undertaken with all her might to oppose the storm of the Bolshevik hordes against European civilization.

He who fights against Germany fights for a Bolshevik Europe.

92

"But I can dream, can't I?"

93

Partigiani,

Voi, che siete stati sobillati da agenti bolscevici e da traditori, al soldo di Badoglio, voi conducete una lotta fratricida senza speranza contro gli eroici difensori dell'Europa: l'esercito germanico, i suoi camerati italiani e noi volontari russi.

A quale scopo? Che cosa sta scritto sulla vostra bandiera? Forse che la vostra Patria debba essere trasformata in una colonia dei plutocrati anglo-americani?

I vostri padri, madri, mogli gli debbano essere deportati egli Urali e in Siberia, per are nelle miniere e nelle te, esposti a sicura morte me, similmente a quanto e ora nell'Italia meridiale, in base ad un accordo l comunista Ercoli e l'a- di Mosca Viscinski?

olontari della Russia, non ignoriamo, purtroppo, che cosa significhi, in realtà, la bolscevizzazione di un paese : essa significa la fame, l'annullamento del diritto alla proprietà, il terrore e la morte. Ancora oggi, perché Stalin non cambia ! Noi sappiamo, per propria esperienza, quali sarebbero i doni del bolscevismo ai popoli d'Europa: l'eresia marxista, il sistema dei colcoz, il lavoro da schiavi nelle officine e nelle foreste, un terrore indicibile.

Le lusinghe dei maestri della menzogna di Londra e di Mosca, non riescono più ad ingannarci. Noi, che vi rivolgiamo queste parole, siamo i rappresentanti del vero e immortale popolo russo.

Noi sappiamo, e fermamente crediamo : l'ora verrà, in cui tutte le forze nazionali della gioventú

94

95

96. *What did Stalin say? "This war is the greatest step on the way to Bolshevik world revolution."*

97. *Russia is the oversized power against the United States and England.*

98. *Steeplechase. Russia leads the Allies in a wild charge over a cliff.*

99. *V2 will hit you in your most sensitive part of the body.*

100. *This leaflet is another attempt to get the Polish to join against the Russians.*

101. *"Mom, what's Pop doing in Italy?" Even the American soldiers fighting in the war didn't know. There simply was no answer to Charley's question.*

102. *A pamphlet of 10 poems expressing every soldiers' wish to go home during the war.*

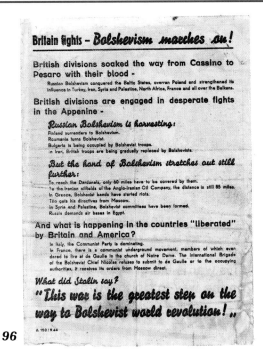

96

96

-194...?

- Dannazione! proprio sulle parti più sensibili!

"Mom, what's Pop doing in Italy?"

G STEEPLE - CHASE _____!

Pomimo ofenzywy we Włoszech Anglicy nie będą mogli temu przeszkodzig.

I want to go home

97

99

101

98

100

102

103. Polish soldiers socializing in a Berlin restaurant. Following the voice of reason, they have crossed over to the German side after realizing their homeland was threatened by Bolsheviks.

104. What a fitting contrast between life and death!

105. Life salutes you.

106. Stretching is good exercise!

107. Thoughts of soldiers fighting in the war are cause for a melancholy mood indeed.

108. Cleanliness is a fact of life.

109. Hold on to your Life!

110. Shoes on the furniture! What would Mother say?!

103

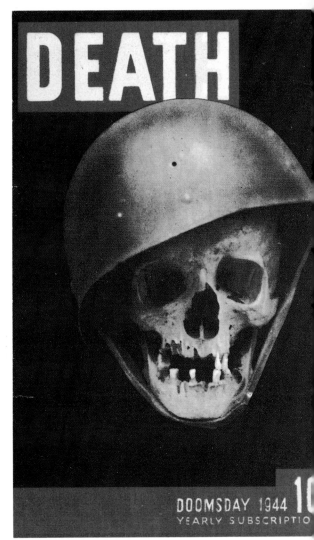

104

105

106

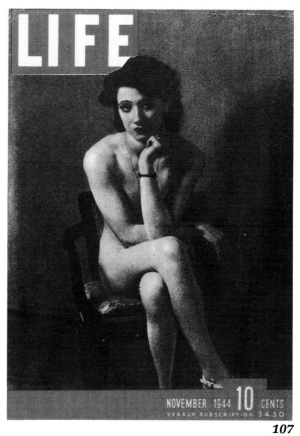

107

108

109

110

111. Twelve leaflets photographed on consecutive days depicting the life of POW's.

PRISONERS-OF-WAR GET A SQUARE DEAL

GERMANY STRICTLY OBSERVES GENEVA CONVENTION

Prisoners-of-war tell us they expected to be shot or ill-treated by the Germans as their officers had warned them they would.

These POW don't look as if they were shot dead, ill-treated, starved or beaten-up, do they?

They are enjoying cigarettes just received from the Red Cross. Through the International Red Cross every POW gets one parcel a week containing cigarettes, chocolate, biscuits and other useful and pleasant things. Note the solidly constructed barracks in the rear.

No. 2 *of a series of twelve leaflets showing the life of prisoners-of-war in German camps.*

AI-117-10-44

7 Who wouldn't enjoy a swim?

8

9 Getting ready for a bout

10 Big day for the New Zealanders

11

12 Hit that ball!

112. *Have a good look at this. It is your life.*

113. *POW's (alias Stalagmites) are members of that gang living behind a barbed wire fence somewhere in Germany, waiting to go home. This leaflet portrays their lives.*

114. *Be your own doctor and come home in person, not as a statistic.*

112

112

113

94

Stalag-Pictures

1. A short talk with the German Welfare officer.
2. Boxing and rowing in the sun.
3. Physical training: Be gay ready!
4. Give it to him! — and the boys like it.
5. Nothing like baseball, even in a prisoner of War Camp.

6. Bag piping going on as merrily as ever.
7. Good and plenty of books for off-hours!
8. A good chance for studying out.
9. brushing up your knowledge.
10. A typical well-built chapel in a prisoner of War Camp.

Stalagmites

by M/Sgt. Clyde M. Taylor PoW.

Stalagmites — well I'll be damned if I ever heard of such a funny expression back in the States and yet after all it's something I won't forget for the rest of my life — for the simple reason that I myself am a member of that gang living behind a barbed wire fence somewhere in Germany and sweating it out. Yeah, buddy, I said sweating it out and I mean it.

Or do you think it's a pleasure for a husky guy of six foot two inches to be cut off from most anything a young fellow likes?

There is no doubt this leap year the girls can't drag us to the altar — still a short way we should like to come along. Maybe it's allright the other way, 'cause these victory girls wouldn't like our soft drinks anyhow. Of course we tried home-brew and produced some bad liquor on the sly, but who wants to enjoy home-runs to the temple of truth I like to know.

And then that fence. For the love of Mike! I tell you it's a darn nuisance. What does it help us any when our social welfare worker keeps on telling us that fence was to keep unwanted aliens away? Some of my pals and I guess the majority believe he is all wet on that and are of the opinion that the fence is there to keep us inside. So far all those who walked over the hill to find out the exact truth came back in no time complaining these Dutchmen could smell a Yank or a Rebel for miles. Isn't that just too bad?

But otherwise we are OK and doing fine. To give you a rough idea — we got several battalions of Noncoms in our Stalag if you know what that means. Well, bless them all .... The only time I have seen them behaving decently was on Memorial Day when they paid homage to their dead comrades.

You should have been around when we entered the premises a year ago. We

On the way to a Sunday's football match.

R

Right leg, side view. Nerve at back edge of tendon indicated by arrow.

Fig. 4

II. You can produce the same effect on the lower limb with a bandage around the knee.

REMEMBER:

THE MOST IMPORTANT THING ABOUT A WAR IS TO COME BACK HOME ALIVE!

YOUR WAR GOAL NOT A TOMBSTONE!

And an illness is sometimes a life insurance!

AM 5

How to produce a temporary paralysis:

I.

1) Before going to bed wrap a round stone, eraser or short piece of rubber tubing in gauze tissue and fasten firmly to exert pressure on spot x (x is the spot where your "funnybone" is located) with tight bandage and allow to remain over night. Take bandage off in the morning.

2) Repeat for several days in succession until there is a numb feeling in your forearm and hand. The numbness and lack of strength which remains for only a few minutes after the first treatments, will last for an increasing length of time in the course of further treatment.

R

Right arm. ⊗ marks nerve at location of "funnybone".

Fig. 1

3) When a sufficient degree of paralysis has resulted report to doctor. Describe exactly what you feel; tell him that the condition which started suddenly is becoming worse and worse in the course of time.

L

Fig. 2
Left arm. rear view.

4) Continue bandaging your arm from time to time to keep up paralysis, but under no circumstances let the doctor find any traces of the bandage. If there are bandage marks on your arm better not report until they are gone which is usually the case after 24 hours at the latest.

R

Fig. 3
Right leg, rear view. Nerve coloured red.

115. *Canadian soldiers, what are you fighting for?*

116. *Surrender, become a German POW, and return home safe and sound after the war... or face senseless self destruction. The decision is yours, soldier.*

117. *The Allies did not break through the German front, cut off the 10th Army, or bring about a decision on the Italian front, however, according to Allied plans, the Germans retreated.*

118. *This represents a pocketbook-size flyer exhorting the British to give up the war and return home.*

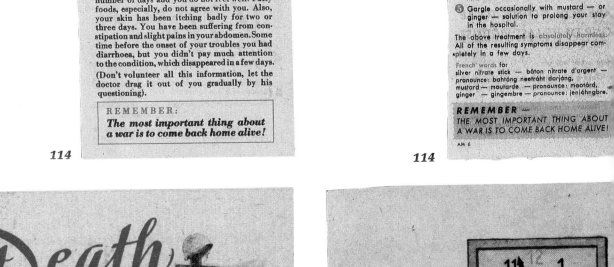

114

114

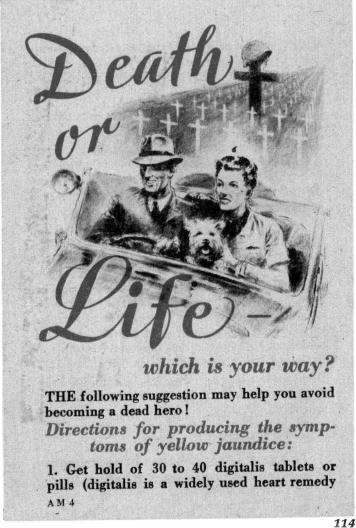

114

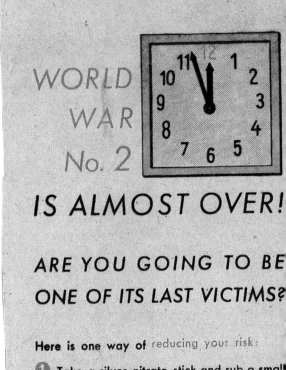

Canadian Soldiers!

Canada has built up a big war industry and is delivering war material to England without getting anything in return for it. How Britain appreciates your services is shown by the fact that British statesmen have often discussed with the U. S. A. *your vital problems* without so much as notifying you, not to speak of letting you participate in the discussions.

A striking example was the signing of the Atlantic Charter without consulting Canada.

Does any Canadian really think that the U. S. A. will tolerate a British Canada after the inevitable collapse of the British Empire has taken place? *Who does not see the Writing on the Wall?* It began with the ceding of strategic bases by Great Britain to the U. S. A. and it will end with the ANNEXATION OF CANADA by the Yanks.

Meanwhile you are supposed to do the dirty work for England

115

Canadian Soldiers!

For over five years you as auxiliary troops have been fighting and dying for the ambitions of English politicians and the fattening of war profiteers and racketeers.

For years you have not seen your families. You don't know whether you will ever see them again.

Many Canadian soldiers who are fighting in Europe thousands of miles away from their country are already being asked to volunteer in the Pacific War in spite of the fact that in Canada there are tens of thousands of men in uniform who have not yet seen any fighting.

From volunteering to being compelled to go is only a short step.

Canadians! England wanted war and declared war on Germany, dragging your country into it although the relations between the German and Canadian peoples had always been friendly. The German soldiers know that they are fighting for the security of their homes and the future of their children.

What are YOU fighting for?

AI - 136 - 10 - 44

115

GERMANY STRICTLY OBSERVING GENEVA CONVENTION

For every soldier, even the bravest, the moment may arrive when fighting on would mean senseless self-destruction and no benefit to his country. It is recognized by all nations at war that under such circumstances the soldiers are justified in surrendering. If you should face a like situation, keep the following points well in mind:

FIRST:

You will be taken for a few days to a Dulag (transit camp) right behind the front. The Dulags are no hotels. They are fitted out simply as the nearness of the front demands, but you will be safe and well-treated. You may send home a message at once via radio "Jerry's Front Calling" telling your wife and family you are alive. If you are wounded or sick, you will immediately receive the best of medical care exactly like a German soldier.

SECOND:

You will be transferred to a Stalag (permanent camp). The Stalags are up-to-date camps with all conveniences. The food is prepared in modern kitchens.

It is ample and of the same high quality as the food of the German soldier. Besides, you are allowed to receive a package every week through the International Red Cross.

You will be housed in clean airy rooms which you may decorate according to your own taste. Lavatories and toilets are of high sanitary standard. If you wish to work, your qualifications will be taken into account.

You will be given opportunity to learn a trade, to improve yourself in your own profession and you can even acquire a university degree.

All Stalags have athletic fields and modern sporting equipment. There are motion pictures and plays for your entertainment.

If you are artistically inclined, you may carry on your study of the fine arts.

You may receive any amount of mail. The forwarding of letters and packages by the International Red Cross is swift and reliable. You yourself are permitted to write 4 postcards and 3 letters per month.

THIRD:

The fighting will be over for you. Nothing more can happen to you. And above all

YOU WILL RETURN HOME SAFE AND SOUND AFTER THE WAR

AI - 069 - 7 - 44

116

WHAT WAS THE AIM OF YOUR GREAT OFFENSIVE?

To break through ....
To roll up the German front .....
To cut off the 10th Army ....

In short :
To bring about a decision on the Italian front.

WHAT DID YOU ACCOMPLISH?

You broke into the German lines —

but only in some local sectors.

Tremendous losses in dead and wounded have been inflicted on your forces. War material amounting to billions paid for by the American and British taxpayers has been wasted.

You gained some ground —

but for the only reason because the Germans retreated according to plan.

In a nutshell :

You did **NOT** break through .....
You did **NOT** roll up the German front .....
You did **NOT** cut off the 10th Army .....
You did **NOT** bring about a decision on the Italian front.

With a few local thrusts and some gain of ground and senseless sacrifices of men and material you cannot win the war.

AI - 076 - 5 - 44

117

THE TIDE IS TURNING...
TIME IS WORKING AGAINST YOU

A short time ago you could smash parts of Berlin and other German cities to pieces.

What about one of our New Weapons keeping Londoners and others in their cellars for days at a time?

What is Air Marshall Harris saying now?

What about winning the war and the boys coming home in 1944?

Does it really look like it, you Veterans of 1947 or later?

Take care, this " second-hand front " might turn out to be another Singapore. Why not get away while the going's good? tide is turning, you may be too late.

What about Great Britain going Bolshie before you get back?

The Tide is Turning! Turn with it!

118

119. "The Kilkenny Cats," "Thirteenth Anniversary of the World War," "General Montgomery's Mother," "Scissors and Paste," "Out of Mr. Churchill's Speech," and "Lord Haw-Haw were six leaflets left behind in the form of a rough draft when their authors retreated and fled.

120. "The Draft Dodger" as a fun-loving sybarite and philaderer.

121. V1 attacks seemed to cause a temporary cessation of criminal activities, such as robbery of rationed foodstuffs, in Southern England.

"LORD HAW-HAW" ON AUGUST 12th, 1944

The stage of maturity has not yet been reached as yet on any one of the fronts, Russian, French or Italian.
The violence of the war at present surpasses all previous bounds.
The English people, who are in sore need of a tonic, are being encouraged to believe in an early termination of the struggle, perhaps by the end of September, but they are doomed to bitter disillusion.
V. 1. is entirely military, but has psychological reactions.
It has marked effects on British industry and on the transport system. The latter is heavily overburdened.
The Royal Train of Queen Victoria's Diamond Jubilee

OUT OF Mr. CHURCHILL'S SPEECH
OF AUGUST 2nd

The following points might be interesting:
The English Prime Minister stated that after Germany had been declared "Enemy No. 1" in Washington in 1942, the Teheran Conference of 1943 decided to make an Anglo-American landing in

SCISSORS and PASTE

August 3rd
While Mr. Micolajczyk's visit to Stalin had already been announced by Mr. Churchill, Stalin, without waiting for the arrival of the President of the Polish Emigrant Government of London, nominated an ambassador of his own to the Polish

General Montgomery's Mother

What a dear old lady!
She could be our own
grandmother.

THIRTIETH ANNIVERSARY OF THE
WORLD WAR

In these hot August days the general attack agreed upon amongst the Allies in Teheran seems to be coming to its climax. With the full weight of a true historic decision, the German people, together with the people of the other European states, have to prove their right to survive. Every German soldier knows it.
This is the last act of the grand conspiracy against the German Reich that made its appearance 30 years ago. On August 1st, 1914, the grey-clad German divisions took their places in the line to defend the Reich of Central Europe, the heart and organ

The Kilkenny Cats
(Better Leave them Alone!)

In the dacent ould days
Before stockings or stays
Were invented, or breeches
Top-boots and top-hats,
You'd search the whole sphere
From Cape Horn to Cape Clear,
And never come near
To the likes of our Cats.
Och, thunder, och, thunder
You'd wink with the wonder
To see them keep under

It was typically German that this resurrection was achieved by peaceful means and that the sickly and foul atmosphere of Versailles and Geneva was overruled by a politically created New Order. This New Order tried to take into consideration all the natural and legitimate interests of the various nations of this continent.
The boundless imperialism of capitalistic West Europe and the equally boundless aims of the Red Imperialism of the East were opposed to this policy. "Die for Danzig!" This was their first war slogan, which showed how hollow and negative their aims were. New slogans, the "Atlantic Charter" and so on, have been invented and used up meanwhile.
Germany, wishing for no war, was attacked from all sides, and in the first period of this war dealt out fearful and far-reaching blows, building a glacis around this ancient fortress of Europe, which, although land has been lost, has up till now protected the core of the continent.
With a brutality of masses and materials corresponding to the absence of true political ideas, the Allies are trying to get to the heart of Europe and are subjecting the Reich to a devilish plan of destruction, thought out by their Jew-ridden rulers.
Everyone of us Germans who has gone through this continuous fight of thirty years is prepared to carry on to the last battle. Even if it takes a few more years it wont make any difference.

THE REICH MUST LIVE, EVEN IF WE MUST DIE
LIKE SO MANY THOUSANDS BEFORE US.

Kr - 037-8-44

"ANOTHER ISLAND OF SAINTS"

England's claims to be the home of morality at last justified.

Reporting an answer of Mr. Eden's in the House, the official press goes on to say:

"The attacks of V Number 1 seem to have determined a temporary cessation of the activities of the professional criminals in Southern England. Not a single serious crime has been committed in these regions ever since the first attacks of the flying bombs took place. The number of thefts of rationed food-stuffs during this period has been the lowest of the whole war. Before these incursions the thefts of vehicles containing every kind of rationed food-stuff were on an average 5 or 6 every day. The number of cases of houses and shops broken into and robbed has also greatly diminished."

How truly British to look at the best side of things! May England derive comfort from it.

Kr - 029 - 7 - 44

The Draft Dodger

By an American P. o. W.

I'm writing this short letter
And every word is true.
Don't look away, draft dodger,
For it's addressed to you.

You feel at ease, in no danger,
Back in the old home town.
You cooked up some pitiful story,
So the draft board would turn you down.

You never think of real men,
Who leave home day by day.
You think only of their girl friends,
That you take while they're away.

So I'm closing this, draft dodger,
Just remember what I say,
"Keep away from my girl, you dirty bum,
For some day you'll have to pay."

AI-154-10-44

122. Germans fed the POW's plenty of nourishing, well-cooked food, despite race, creed, or color.

123. The safe conduct leaflet instructs German sentries to bring the bearer of the flyer to the safety of a POW camp.

124. Boy meets girl. The story of a draft dodger who decides to pursue the fiancee of an American soldier.

122

122

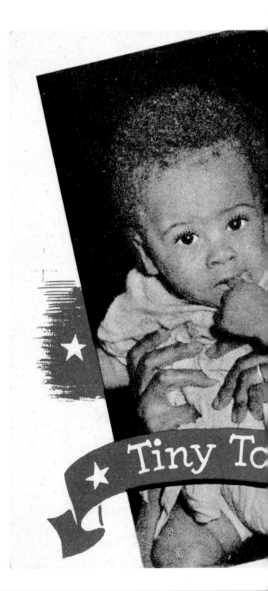

123

*Have you got a wife and cute children,
or a girl you want to marry?*

THEY WANT YOU TO COME BACK ALIVE

Well, what chance have you to survive? Hardly any at all! Remember, back home the colored man always had to do the dirty work. On the front it is the same. Uncle Sam's colored soldiers are just CANNON FODDER.

You have only one chance.

If you are fed up with fighting, join the other colored boys who are now waiting for the end of the war in modern, sanitary prisoner-of-war camps. They are being treated decently like all the other prisoners-of-war. They are getting good food and Red Cross parcels. They may write home and receive mail regularly. Above all they know

After the war they will be sent home to their folks as soon as possible.

SAFE CONDUCT **PASSIERSCHEIN**

Give this to the first German sentry you meet. He will bring you to safety.

Inhaber dieses Passierscheins stellt den Kampf ein und ist schnellstens aus der Gefahrenzone zu entfernen.

AI-155-11-44

BILL THE SLACKER

"My mother didn't raise me to be a soldier," said Bill Turner to himself when he was called up to appear before the Draft Board. Being the son of a well-to-do father it wasn't difficult for him to get a certificate from sly old Doc Ginsberg, the family physician, who willingly stated that Bill had always suffered from "severe heart attacks". A few pills from the corner drugstore helped to put him in the right condition so that the Draft Board simply had to pronounce him unfit for military service. Bill's trump card, however, was his stepping right into the job of Frank Merritt — "honest Frank" his pals called him — as assistant to the manager of a war production plant piling up profits sky-high.

Frank had been drafted and sent to the battlefields in Europe thousands of miles away to fight in the RICH MAN'S WAR and perhaps lose his life.

He was engaged to pretty Vivian Hope, one of the stenographers in the accounting department, and his leaving for the overseas fighting was a hard blow to the vivacious girl. During the first few weeks in his new job, Bill Turner was so wrapped up in his duties that he hardly noticed the girl. One morning, however, when she came into his office for a reference book, he suddenly realized how beautiful she was. A thought crossed his mind. He made inquiries and found out about the girl and Frank Merritt.

But "honest Frank" was fighting in another continent and who knew if he would ever return.

Have you seen the other pictures of "HOME FRONT WARRIORS"?

AI-157-11-44

124

124

125. *How do I love thee, let me count the ways. Is one of them keeping company with another man while my fiance until my fiance returns home from the war?*

126. *In both love and war sacrifices are the name of the game. The girl you left behind as a salesclerk in the 5 & 10 cents store is now a private secretary for a businessman cashing in on war contracts.*

127. *Does the girl you left behind have a date with her boss tonight?*

128. *Does the girl you left behind think of you one minute and accept presents from her boss the next?*

125

126

102

127

128

Joan is feeling so lonely anyway......

127

Poor little Joan! She is still thinking of Bob......

128

129. The injured soldier is limping along Fifth Avenue on crutches, wondering what his fiancee has been up to for the past two years. His thoughts are answered when he sees her with another man. What a rude awakening.

130. Remember, she is waiting, hoping, praying, longing... for you.

131. England's democracy versus Germany's socialism .

132. You are being told nothing but lies!

133. Directed to the Poles, this leaflet tells of the German's fight for the happiness of all Polish families!

129

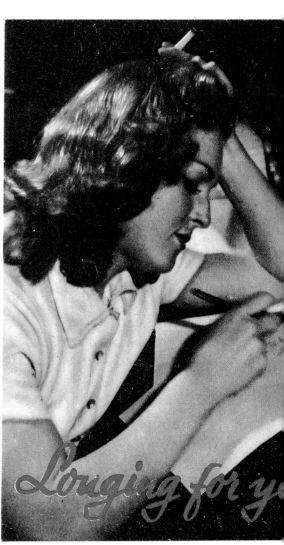

130

England's Democracy

Workers' slums in London

AI - 169 - 11 - 44

131

132

Germany's Socialism

Workers' settlement in Berlin-Reinickendorf

130

131

133

134. A safe conduct explanation about how the Germans are to treat the Italian prisoners.

135. Hollywood once again works its magic and produces war on film. Propaganda against the Jewish powers in filmland.

136. While soldiers are fighting for their country, theatres, night clubs, restaurants, ballrooms, department stores, and black-market crooks are doing a booming business.

137. "Fourth Indian Division, you will be a target for bullets. The Indians are led by Subhash Chander Bose, who has organized Indian troops and formed an army in Germany to fight against the British." This leaflet urges Indian soldiers to come over to the Germans as POW's and join Bose's army to fight against England.

134

135

135

Georgia Nº 5

136

138. The Black Brigade was ready yesterday, today, and tomorrow to do combat for Italy. Posters were seen in many places as the Germans retreated.

139. "God Save the King" is a German flyer urging American troops to think ill of the British.

140. It was a rich man's war and a poor man's fight.

141. This leaflet in Italian was distributed to the population to make them aware of why they would be shot. It was signed by the Superior Commander of the German Armed Forces.

138

The next

time you sing

"God Save the King"

act nice and proud

Rich Man's War-Poor Man's Fight

On the Front

and in

God's Own Country

In the States a law has been passed calling ammunition workers to military service. The workers thus put under martial law are to get just

one-fourth of the pay

they got so far.

Instead of $ 60
they only get $ 15 a week.

Apparently dividends do not justify present pay levels.

Turn leaflet and see:

According to a statement published in the " Stockholm Tidningen " by the Swedish economist Bertil Chlin, the States after the war will have 12 million unemployed, others say 20 million.

You'll be one of them!

Il Comandante Superiore delle Forze Armate Germaniche comunica:

« Finora le FF. AA. Germaniche hanno fatto tutto ciò che erano forzate di fare, per necessità di guerra, correttamente e con il più grande rispetto per la popolazione. Questo comportamento amichevole implica un comportamento assolutamente amichevole da parte della popolazione. Se gli attentati e gli attacchi dei banditi, che sono stati sinora casi isolati e individuali, dovessero aumentare, il Comando Superiore delle FF. AA. Germaniche dovrebbe mutare immediatamente la propria condotta, e delle conseguenze di tale decisione sarebbe responsabile la stessa popolazione.

Per garantire la sicurezza delle comunicazioni della retrovia e dei servizi logistici, io ordino da questo momento:

1) chi si trovi in possesso di armi o esplosivi e non li denunzi al Comando tedesco più vicino, SARA' FUCILATO;

2) chi ospita banditi, oppure li protegge e fornisce loro vestiario, alimenti o armi, SARA' FUCILATO;

3) se si scopre che qualcuno sia a conoscenza di un raggruppamento di ribelli, o anche di un singolo ribelle, senza averli segnalati al Comando più vicino, SARA' FUCILATO;

139

This little leaflet will help to remind you of the fact that you are a U. S. Citizen. Always remember:

1776 -	We fought England for our Independence.
1812 -	We had to fight England because they pressed American seamen into the British navy. They burned down our Capital and incited the Indians against peaceful farmers 2,000 miles from the front lines. Sheer Piracy.
1865 -	England lent the Confederate States $ 95,000,000 and assisted them in other ways to help destroy the Union.
1914-1918	England borrowed billions from the U. S. which she has'nt paid back yet.
1920 -	England jimmied up the raw rubber prices so high that a crisis in the tire industry resulted. We had to threaten Britain with war in order to reach a satisfactory settlement.
1932 -	England went off the gold standard forcing the U.S. into a money panic.
1939 -	England declared war on Germany totally unprepared. This forced us into the conflict. This war is none of our business. We are only helping the Russians who basically are our worst enemies. The British have borrowed more from the U.S. now already than their whole Empire is worth. Think they'll pay?

It won't take you long to figure out that England is the cause of all the trouble.

Consider the snooty British manner and consider what we are doing for England. Are they worth it? Soldiers Friend Society Inc. Brooklyn.

139

Rich Man's War-Poor Man's Fight

Profits made on government orders:

Pre - war profits		War profits 1942
$ 70 000	Jacob Aircraft Mfg. Cy.	$ 11 400 000
$ 850 000	General Cable Cy.	$ 19 400 000
$ 60 000	Lima Locomotion Works Inc.	$ 10 000 000
$ 615 000	General Machinery Corp.	$ 20 760 000
$ 540 000	Gruman Aircraft Corp.	$ 22 500 000
$ 43 855	Bell Aircraft Corp.	$ 23 153 000
$ 450 000	Diamond Motorcar Cy.	$ 13 574 000
loss	American Woolen Cy.	$ 36 250 000
$ 3 000	Defoe Shipbuilding Cy.	$ 5 150 000
$ 350 000	Edward G. Budd Manufacturing Cy.	$ 18 650 000
$ 61 000	York Safe and Lock Cy.	$ 8 583 000
$ 3 042 855	against	$ 189 420 000

Profits 1 : 63

Where do **you** come in ?

A slap on the back and a lonesome cross in Italy.

Rich Man's War - Poor Man's Fight!

Think it over.

Kr - 024 - 7 - 44

140

---

4) chi dà informazioni al nemico, oppure ai banditi sulle località dove si trovano i Comandi tedeschi, o dei depositi militari, SARA' FUCILATO;

5) ogni paese dove si possa provare che vi sono banditi, o dove sono stati commessi attentati contro soldati tedeschi o italiani, oppure atti di sabotaggio diretti a danneggiare o distruggere materiale bellico, SARA' INTERAMENTE BRUCIATO. Inoltre gli abitanti maschi del paese, aventi un minimo di 18 anni, SARANNO TUTTI FUCILATI. Le donne e le ragazze saranno internate nei campi di lavoro.

Italiani!

Il benessere della vostra Patria e la fortuna delle vostre famiglie, sono adesso nelle vostre mani. Le FF. AA. germaniche, come è specificato in questo ordine, agiranno con giustizia, ma senza pietà e con tutto il rigore e le conseguenze del caso.

IL COMANDANTE SUPERIORE
DELLE FORZE ARMATE GERMANICHE

Δ 210/8. 44

141

142. Le chiese is Italian for the churches. This poster is telling the population how the Allies have destroyed civilian churches.

LE CHIESE DIS

Santuario di Santa Maria della Scala

eretta nel 1324 e concessa da Cangrande della Scala ai Padri Serviti.

Chiesa di San Bernardino

terminata nel 1466; stile gotico con aggiunte di alcune parti in stile rinascimento.

Chiesa dei S. S. Apostoli

già ricordata alla fine del secolo VIII. L'attuale chiesa è una basilica romanica.

Chiesa dell'Immacolata Concezione

in Borgo Milano - Di recente consacrata al culto.

Ø I/182

Queste fotografie sono state eseguite a Verona il

142

TRUTTE ACCUSANO

Chiostro del Duomo

in stile romanico, del 1125 circa, e attigua

Biblioteca Capitolare

ritenuta una delle più importanti d'Italia

Chiostro della Chiesa di San Fermo

Chiesa di San Sebastiano

ricordata fin dal 932 e rinnovata nel 1580. Notevole per la sua facciata di alto valore artistico. Attualmente non consacrata al culto

ennaio 1945 dopo il bombardamento terroristico degli angloamericani.

143. Jerry's Front Radio arranged to announce the names and addresses of prisoners of war and their serial numbers.

144. Excerpts from POW letters.

145. The facts and figures about social security after the war.

146. Bolsheviks will always be the same: enemies of civilization and liberty.

FILL IN THIS BLANK AND KEEP IT

USE BLOCK LETTERS.
TO BE TRANSMITTED BY JERRY'S FRONT RADIO:

Name:

Rank:

Serial Number:

Address: _____ Street

Town:

Country:

In this panel write a short message of not more than 15 words which will be transmitted by radio

143

Sgt. Jesse Bradburn
to Mrs. Al. Bradburn, Union Lake
Mich., U.S.A.

« ... the Germans have used us like one of
really been swell. We are in a hospital with
They feed us as they do the rest. It beats
and it's better than I expected and not at
would be. Every German soldier I've come
a gentleman.»

« Anyway you won't have to worry about me
I sure wish I could find out what happened

These **P. o. W's.** seem to be happy.
And above all, they will return h

P. o. W'
are well-tr

144

IMPORTANT NOTICE

In case you are taken prisoner, you will very likely wish to have your relatives informed with as little delay as possible that you are alive and out of danger.

JERRY'S FRONT RADIO

has arranged to announce the names and addresses of prisoners of war and their serial numbers. The announcements will be made three times daily.

You will understand how *valuable* this service is when you consider that your relatives are spared the dreadful feeling of anxious suspense concerning your fate.

Be prepared and fill in this blank. It will be useful to you if you should be captured.

A1

Excerpts from recent letter

P.o.W's.

Gdsm. Cairns, Service No. 2.699.341
to Mrs. S. Cairns, 154 James Street, Bridgetow
S. E. Scotland:

« ... I have been slightly wounded in the side again, b
a lot better now thanks to the German Medical Staff
been well treated.»

Lt. H. A. Ransom
to Mrs. H. A. Ransom, 35 Wick Rd., Jeddinton

« ... At the moment I am in a lovely hospital with m
leg wounded... The Germans treat us well indeed and
with another English officer.»

Sapper K. Thompson, Service No. 1.866.4
to Mr. & Mrs. H. A. Thompson, 29 Victoria A
Hull, Yorks.:

« ... The Germans as always have treated me very we
met very many fine young fellows amongst them - it se
that we are fighting against one another.»

Rfn. H. Kidd, Service No. 6.478.216
to Mr. R. T. Kidd, 465 Lisburn Rd., Belfast, N

» ... I've had very good attention all the time I've be
everyone has been very good to me, the doctors
their job.»

« ... but we have made friends with lots of German c
some fine times trying to teach each other our differe

143

Facts and Figures

According to publications by the British Exchequer the war is costing Great Britain £ 220 millions daily.

This war is now lasting almost 2000 days, and all those who have come to know the German soldier as well as you will also know that the end is still far out of sight.

The amount quoted above only includes the actual expenditure incurred by the Government in running the war. If you wish to get a rough idea of the total war costs you have to:

Add hereto the value of the numerous units of the merchant navy that were sunk together with their precious cargoes.

Add hereto the damages caused through bombs and V-1-(and what are the effects of V-2 going to be?) In a broadcast Mr. Morrison stated that in London alone over one million buildings have been damaged so badly that only qualified labourers will be able to restore them, where a restoration is possible at all.

Add hereto the value of the warehouses and stocks of stores burnt, the industrial plants destroyed and the dockyards and harbours demolished in the course of this war.

Add hereto the markets lost to America. While England's exports are showing already now a decrease of more than 40%, the exports of America are increasing daily.

Add hereto the loss of income from overseas due to Japan's occupation of vast and rich territories in the Far East.

Gilbert Murray is quite right if he writes in the "Contemporary Review":
"We seem to have won anything we could ever dream of. But when we come back to reality we shall find out that we have been left as the poor leaders of a practically destroyed world with enormous responsibilities and doubtful resources."

82 - 7 - 44

145

Send this picture home to your mother!

Ask her if she would like to see you scalped, your eyes gouged out, your nose cut off and your tongue torn out.

When reconquering the town of Schirwindt at the eastern frontier of Germany, German soldiers found this pal of theirs mutilated by Bolshevik savages.

THOSE FIENDS WHO HAVE DONE THIS ARE YOUR ALLIES, THE BESTIAL GODLESS BOLSHEVIKS!

Stalin has successfully duped the world by claiming that the Bolshevik system had changed. But in reality nothing has changed in Soviet Russia. The churches have not been reopened with the exception of a few for propaganda purposes. The same despotism, the same terror and cruelty, the same slavery and wholesale murder still rule the country and the proclamation of «democratic ideals» is a farce.

The Bolshevik moloch has just devoured seven European countries. Finland, Latvia, Estonia, Lithuania, Poland, Rumania and Bulgaria are now facing a fate worse than death.

The death of millions of civilized Europeans in these countries is sanctioned by your government and you are fighting to help the Bolshevik murderers!

They will always be the same:

ENEMIES OF CIVILIZATION AND LIBERTY

A leopard cannot change its spots

A1-4T2-12-44

146

What about SOCIAL SECURITY after the War?

In 1939, while England was still one of the richest countries of the world, most of the privileges due to a working class of the 20th century were denied to you. Do you think that an impoverished post-war England will be **able** to grant them to you?

Golden Times?

Since five years you and your hard-working wives are being lured with the "golden times" after the war. These times will not be golden but damned hard. You will hardly see much of social security, better housing, higher pay, national health service, leave and better working conditions.

The most favourable case ....

Let us take the most favourable case and assume that Germany were smashed and open to British exploitation. Do you think it would be possible to squeeze the necessary means for the upheaval of your living standard out of a Germany bombed by the R.A.F. and the U.S.A.F., pounded by your artillery and blown up before capitulation?

Heroes? – No, grave-diggers!

Whatever the outcome of this war is going to be, your children and grandchildren will never think of you as the heroes of the battle for "freedom and humanity", but they will look upon you as the grave-diggers of British prosperity.

Keep this in mind when trying to find an answer to the question:

What are we fighting for?

144

145

What would your mother say

if this dead soldier were you?

146

147. *Will the death of my father bring us peace on earth?*

148. *This Polish flyer is trying to convince soldiers to stop fighting for the English and come over to the German side, because the Germans would send them home.*

147

Suffer little Children...

The winter sun's last dying glow
Strewed hues of red on virgin snow,
As lesson books were put away
And school was finished for the day.
Then once again the village street
Thrilled to the tread of children's feet:

    Three little boys whose homeward way
    All in the same direction lay,
    Talked as they walked home side by side
    Of the approaching Christmastide.

One said "I'll have a Christmas tree
And Dad is going to buy for me
A train set and a fine new gun,
And he'll be there to share the fun!"
The second one then raised his voice
And said "A Bicycle's my choice
With Daddy there to play with me,
T'will be as happy as can be."

    The third child not a word did say,
    But as he went upon his way
    The tear drops down his red cheeks coursed,
    His little heart was fit to burst.
    For him this Christmas would be black,
    His Daddy never would come back!

WASOB

Do domu!

Polscy żołnierze! Czy pomyśleliście nad tem, z kim walczycie wspólnie we Włoszech?

Anglicy potrafili zawsze radzić sobie i gdy sytuacja była poważna, gdy chodziło o ich skórę, starali się, aby inni za nich walczyli. Sprowadzili zatem Amerykanów, następnie Kanadyjczyków, Francuzów z obozu de Gaule'a, Marokańczyków i Hindusów.

A wreszcie po Hindusach przyszła kolej na Was!
Was traktuje się gorzej niż
kolorowe wojska kolonialne.

Wasze rodziny zostały zesłane na osiedlenie się w pozbawionych żywej duszy stepach afrykańskich, wyludnionych obszarach Australji i Indyj. Te pustkowia szukają rąk roboczych i dlatego tam osiedlają Wasze rodziny, pozbawione własnej ojczyzny. Wasze dzieci wychowuje się w szkołach Palestyny jako żer armatni, potrzebny Anglji, Ameryce i Sowietom.

A Wy Żołnierze Polscy macie nastawiać karki
jako legjon cudzoziemski, podobnie jak kolorowe
wojska kolonialne! Dla kogo?

Jako mieszkańcy Europy macie być wykorzystywani podobnie jak się dzieje z Hindusami. Przybądźcie do nas, a my odeślemy Was do domów rodzinnych. Szkoda bowiem głowy każdego z mieszkańców Europy, który polegnie na wojnie w której zwycięzcami chcą być amerykańscy kapitaliści i moskiewscy kaci.

S. 427.

149. This leaflet was found on the British front and presumed to mean that Americans were dating the wives or girlfriends of British soldiers.

150. The English sent Polish soldiers to the front in Cassino, Italy to die as heroes. This flyer is telling the soldiers to go home by way of a German soldier as a POW. Translation, see Appendix.

He's fighting on the Battlefield
His room he does not use
So tell me, tell me if you can
To whom belong the shoes.—

149

Żołnierze Polscy!

Grozi Wam wielkie niebezpieczeństwo. Ominął Was Katyń, uszliście z życiem z raju bolszewickiego. Mieliście dotychczas szczęście - - - ale teraz jesteście niepożądani. Zespolone formacje polskie nie podobają się Stalinowi, który dąży do zniszczenia Waszej Ojczyzny. Wasi wodzowie w Londynie otrzymali z Moskwy instrukcje zlikwidowania Was w sposób nieskomplikowany.

Przebywaliście narazie na spokojnych pozycjach środkowego odcinku frontu włoskiego. Teraz macie być rzuceni w piekło Cassino. Przed kilku laty Stalin wysłał ekipę morderców aby zlikwidowała w Katyniu kolegów Waszych. Ale anglicy są sprytniejsi. Wysyłają Was na front Cassino, abyście mogli polec w aueroli bohaterstwa.

Polscy żołnierze !

Czy orjętujecie się w tej grze, w którą Was wciągnięto ?

W tej sytuacji pozostała Wam tylko jedna deska ratunku - przejście do nas a znowu ujrzycie Ojczyznę. Pod ochroną niemieckich żołnierzy, którzy piersią osłaniają Europę, a tym samym Polskę przed nawałą bolszewicką, będziecie mogli spokojnie pracować według własnej woli i upodobania.

Dwa słowa

DO DOMU!

zadecydują o przyszłości Waszej, o życiu lub śmierci.

Podajcie to hasło pierwszemu napodkanemu na froncie żołnierzowi niemieckiemu - a droga do Ojczyzny stanie, przed Wami otworem.

S. 431.

151. Stalin forces Roosevelt and Churchill home.

152. Never was the Lord's Prayer said more fervently than by American and British POW'S, as they thanked God for sparing their lives.

153. The Germans are telling British soldiers there is nothing dishonorable about laying down their arms in the face of certain death.

154. The German are trying to comfort their troops with humor.

151

A hymn of rejoicing over their rescue from certain destruction filled this sacred edifice where these captured
American and British doughboys were taken at their
wish to attend divine service.

For them the bloody fight is over.
These soldiers will return to their
folks safe and sound after the war.
They have every reason to be happy.

But also their relatives and friends at home are mighty
glad that nothing can happen to them any more.

And what about YOU?

152

Never was the Lord's Prayer said more fervently
than by these American and British prisoners of war.
They are thanking God that He spared their lives.

152

BRITISH SOLDIERS!

You are fighting against an opponent whom
you know very well.

You are not facing Italians but Germans.

As gallant soldiers you have had occasion
to become acquainted with the courage and the
grit of your German opponent.

You know how well the Germans stood up
in battle, although they were always inferior to
you in number. But you know well enough
what it means when the Germans are numeri-
cally equal to your own forces or even superior.

In the face of insurmountable
odds a thousand men of crack
British Guards surrendered.

If t h e y were forced to do so, then it is
not dishonourable for you to lay down arms in
case you are facing nothing but certain death.

General Clark certainly played you a dirty
Yankee trick!
And who has got to bear the consequences?   **153**

154

155. *Black men are being presented to Italians as niggers and colored. The picture indicates that Negroes are all the same... rapists.*

155

...ardia le donne bianche negli Stati Uniti contro i gangster neri. ...che Roosevelt ha inviato in Italia, consegnando il paese e i ...stinti criminali. Le americane si proteggono da loro - le italiane ...donate . . .

...na migliore dimostrazione delle vere intenzioni dei « liberatori »?

Il nonno di JIM si chiamava KA-TA-KU.

Faceva parte di una tribú di selvaggi nudi, che viveva nella foresta vergine dell'Africa equatoriale. Le sue tre mogli, preparavano, a turno, con le loro sudice mani le focacce, che egli divorava, rumorosamente, insieme alla carne strappata dalle cosce dei nemici scannati o degli esploratori bianchi da lui uccisi con la fionda. Fra le scimmie, che popolano la stessa foresta, e la tribú di KA-TA-KU vi è una sola differenza: quelle vivono sugli alberi e i negri in capanne sporche e puzzolenti, costruite di fogliame marcito...

Il padre di JIM visse a Chicago.

Egli campava con lavori occasionali e conviveva con Lu-A, una sgualdrina poltrona, che « lavorava » in una infima casa di tolleranza per negri. Era la madre di Jim, ma non si curava affatto di lui. A dodici anni, costui fu raccolto dagli incaricati della « Christian Science » e ricoverato all'ospedale, perchè affetto da malattia venerea. Piú tardi, raggiunse una banda di giovinastri specializzati in furti ai danni di distributori automatici. A 18 anni, era già il vicecapo di una banda di « gangster » due anni dopo, acciuffata dalla polizia, dopo aver assassinato un banchiere nella sua macchina e averlo derubato.

A Sing-Sing JIM portava il numero 6311.

Non era stato possibile provare la sua diretta partecipazione all'ultimo delitto perpetrato dalla sua banda ed era stato condannato solo per « complicità ». Se il tribunale avesse indagato più accuratamente anche negli altri fatti di sangue, che andavano sul conto della banda, Jim anzichè nella cella con l'inferriata, sarebbe finito nel locale maiolicato, che contiene la « sedia elettrica ». Ma il tribunale non si diede la briga... Perchè mai avrebbe dovuto farlo ? Troppe cose accadono in America e immane lavoro sarebbe il voler giudicarle tutte. Cosí pensa l'Americano... e i gangster ne gioiscono.

Proprio r
pano alla
divisione
american
disprezzo
Or sono
civiltà e
selvaggi
Negri al
contro uc
Negri ne
litare, ma
La Germ
zione de
lontariam
oggi, spo
lasciaron
Il negro
coprono
si farann
cui in Ita
stenza ne
l'Italia, er
con i dis
nere.
E l'Italia
Soldati g
nero; sol
vita e off
alla tua
E tu, o I

mento, in cui le nuove divisioni italiane parteci-
per la libertà dell'Europa, l'avversario manda una
gri al fronte meridionale. Questo atto degli anglo-
sposta alla decisione italiana, è un segno palese del
Roosevelt e Churchill sentono per il popolo italiano.
nni fa, l'Italia, dopo dura lotta, ha portato in Etiopia
. Oggi gli anglo-americani scatenano negri semi-
ioni contro la millenaria cultura della madrepatria.
Ciò non comporta combattimento leale di uomo
na vile assassinio e malvagia uccisione.
e! Ciò non significa occupazione disciplinata mi-
neggio, rapina, assassinio e stupro.
a dovuto superare l'amaro periodo dell'occupa-
ania. Nessuna donna tedesca si è allora data vo-
d un negro, come nessuna donna italiana lo farà,
mente. Purtuttavia le truppe negre d'occupazione
aia di bastardi. Non altrimenti succederà in Italia.
de la donna bianca e le baionette angloamericane
o misfatto. Negri asserviranno uomini italiani e
ro pulire le scarpe; negri i cui avi, ai tempi in
u l'Impero romano, trascorsero la loro triste esi-
ste africane. I padri dei negri, ora lanciati contro
egli schiavi. I loro figli indossano sì l'uniforme
americani, ma non sono altro che le stesse bestie

be essere esposta, indifesa, al loro terrore?
ci ed italiani formano barriera contro il pericolo
liani e germanici mettono a repentaglio la loro
proprio sangue, per risparmiare a te, Italiano,
e alla tua figlia, un destino terribile.
cosa fai ?

JIM accettò l'invito di Roosevelt.

Fu uno dei primi a presentarsi, allorché il Presi-
dente americano decretò l'impunità a quegli erga-
stolani, che si sarebbero presentati, per servire
«come leali e valorosi soldati nelle superbe forze
armate statunitensi». Jim divenne pilota, e, al corso
d'istruzione incontrò diversi dei suoi vecchi compagni. Tanti erano gli scassinatori, ladri di auto-
mobili, rapinatori di fanciulli e falsari, da poter
formarne una nuova banda. Ben presto a questa fu
trovato il nome appropriato: «Murder Inc.» (Soc.
An. Assassini).

JIM scatenato contro l'Italia.

Da principio non poteva rendersi conto come
l'assassinio e la rapina, proibite dalla legge
negli Stati Uniti, potessero, qui, all'improv-
viso, essere comandati. Fu poi pervaso da
una vera sete di sangue. Partecipò, con il
suo «Liberator», agli attacchi terroristici
contro molte città italiane e le bombe, che
egli sganciava, assassinarono centinaia di
donne e bambini innocenti, distrussero molti
beni culturali insostituibili e le case di innu-
merevoli famiglie felici. Più tardi, egli passò
a quel reparto di negri che, a Siena, in piena
strada, diede sfogo alla propria libidine, vio-
lentando delle donne italiane davanti agli occhi dei mariti e dei padri solidamente legati.

JIM fu fatto prigioniero dai germanici.

Ricoverato all'ospedale, in un tentativo di fuga,
egli cercò di recidere con un morso la gola dell'in-
fermiera italiana, che lo curava. Durante la conva-
lescenza raccontò ad altri negri la sua storia, che
fu udita e qui sopra riportata. Richiesto cosa
avrebbe fatto dopo la guerra, Jim - dopo aver in-
trodotto in bocca il cucchiaio colmo e facendo lo
stesso rumore come allora KATAKU, suo nonno -
rispose con un sogghigno «Io rimarrò in Italia...
Qui posso vivere con i miei... figli!»

156. Auguriamo is a well wishing salutation meaning merry or happy. The three wise men are bringing presents to baby Jesus: Roosevelt, hunger; Churchill, poverty; and Stalin, slavery.

157. To be far away from war, bloodshed, and senseless destruction was every soldiers' Christmas wish.

Ecco è nato il Bambinello
Con il bue e l'asinello
•
Ecco, giungono i tre Magi
Da lontano, son randagi
Ecco i doni al Bambinello
Doni al popolo più bello

Churchill offre la 'Miseria'
Roosevelt dà, più deleteria,
la tremenda 'Fame' e, prono,
'Schiavitù' Stalin dà in dono.
•
Viva viva ai tre Re Magi
Da lontan giunti, randagi!

... i doni dei tre Re Magi ...

FAME

MISERIA

SCHIAVI

Auguriamo a tutti Buon Natale, con la certezza che nel 1945....

... non siano quelli offerti dal nemico!

"Let me live in a house by the side of the road and be a friend of man!"

Yes, that's it - and to be far away from war and senseless destruction from bloodshed and horror. It's the same with everybody. Bill, Sam and Joe say it's that way with them, too.
Sure, you dream of that little place, called your home. Didn't you say, «Me and Jeanne built that little home - that's OUR home.»
Or perhaps she said, «*Some day we're going to get enough saved up so we can buy that little plot out in the suburb, have a couple of apple trees, peaches or perhaps some strawberries.*»
What a word that is, «Mine-mine-mine.» It makes your head stand up high and your chest stick out to say, «*This is my house, my garden, how do you like them?*» You liked to feel a bit independent when you said that.

AND NOW WHAT HAS BECOME OF YOU?

A soldier in the mud.
Defending what ?
Fighting for what ?

And at home there's CHRISTMAS!

Well, make the best of it. Things will change for better of worse. Meantime, that much abused National-Socialist opposite you is wishing you

A MERRY CHRISTMAS!

A1-174-12-44

Merry Christmas!

158. Come back home alive, Daddy!

159. The names and faces of wounded Indian soldiers who were fighting for the British. Translation, see Appendix.

Come back home alive, Daddy!

158

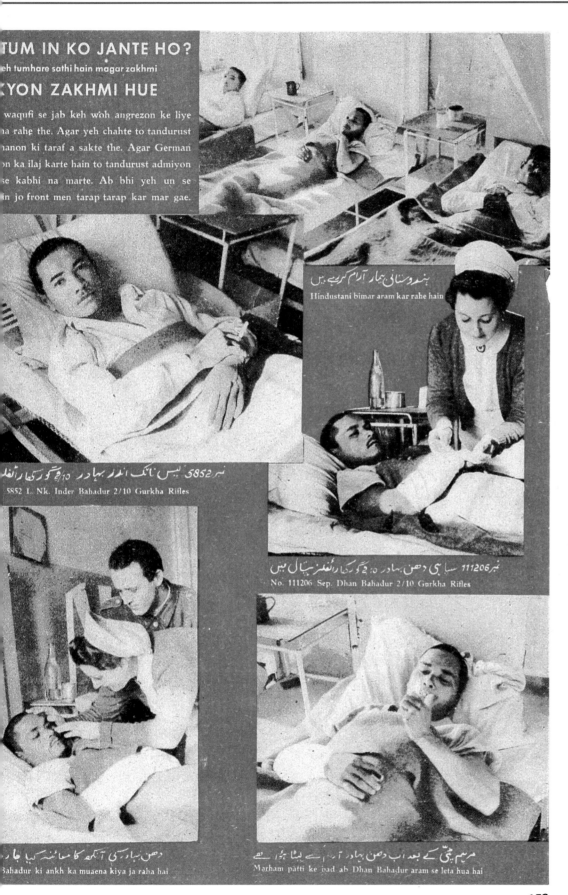

TUM IN KO JANTE HO?

...eh tumhare sathi hain magar zakhmi

...KYON ZAKHMI HUE

...waqufi se jab keh woh angrezon ke liye
...na rahe the. Agar yeh chahte to tandurust
...nanon ki taraf a sakte the. Agar German
...on ka ilaj karte hain to tandurust admiyon
...se kabhi na marte. Ab bhi yeh un se
...in jo front men tarap tarap kar mar gae.

هندوستانی بیمار آرام کر رہے ہیں
Hindustani bimar aram kar rahe hain

نمبر 5852 لیس نائک اندر بہادر 10/2 گورکھا رائفل
5852 L. Nk. Inder Bahadur 2/10 Gurkha Rifles

نمبر 111206 سپاہی دھن بہادر 10/2 گورکھا رائفلز ہسپتال میں
No. 111206 Sep. Dhan Bahadur 2/10 Gurkha Rifles

...Bahadur ki ankh ka muaena kiya ja raha hai

مرہم پٹی کے بعد اب دھن بہادر آرام سے لیٹا ہوا ہے
Marham patti ke bad ab Dhan Bahadur aram se leta hua hai

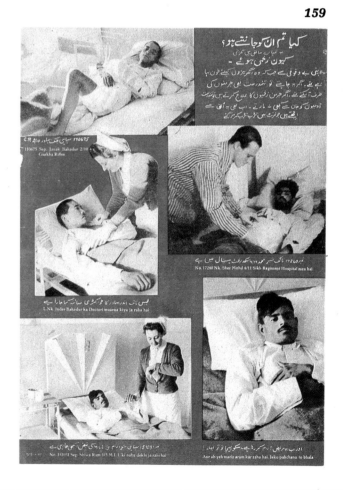

کیا تم ان کو جانتے ہو؟
کیوں زخمی ہوئے۔

17260 سپاہی جنک بہادر 10/2 گورکھا رائفلز
17260 Sep. Janak Bahadur 2/10 Gurkha Rifles

نمبر 17260 نائک شیر محمد 11/4 سکھ رجمنٹ ہسپتال میں ہے
No. 17260 Nk. Sher Mohd 4/11 Sikh Regiment Hospital men hai

لیس نائک اندر بہادر کا ڈاکٹری معائنہ کیا جا رہا ہے
L.Nk. Inder Bahadur ka Doctori muaena kiya ja raha hai

نمبر 15101 سپاہی سیوا رام 3/1 ایم ایل آئی کی نبض دیکھی جا رہی ہے
No. 15101 Sep. Sewa Ram 1/3 M.I. ki nabz dekhi ja rahi hai

اور اب یہ مریض آرام کر رہا ہے۔ اسکو پہچانو تو بھلا
Aur ab yeh mariz aram kar raha hai. Isko pahchano to bhala

159

160. Pictured is a soldier from the Cremona Division.

161. The fantasy of a Prussian soldier.

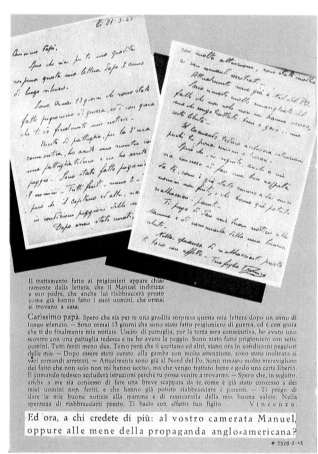

Il trattamento fatto ai prigionieri appare chiaramente dalla lettera, che il Manuel indirizza a suo padre, che anche lui riabbraccerà presto come già hanno fatto i suoi uomini, che ormai si trovano a casa.

Carissimo papà. Spero che sia per te una gradita sorpresa questa mia lettera dopo un anno di lungo silenzio. – Sono ormai 13 giorni che sono stato fatto prigioniero di guerra, ed è con gioia che ti do finalmente mie notizie. Uscito di pattuglia, per la terza sera consecutiva, ho avuto uno scontro con una pattuglia tedesca e ne ho avuto la peggio. Sono stato fatto prigioniero con sette uomini. Tutti feriti meno due. Temo però che il capitano ed altri, siano ora in condizioni peggiori delle mie. – Dopo essere stato curato alla gamba con molta attenzione, sono stato inoltrato ai vàri comandi arretrati. – Attualmente sono già al Nord del Po. Sono rimasto molto meravigliato del fatto che non solo non mi hanno ucciso, ma che vengo trattato bene e godo una certa libertà. Il comando tedesco acciuderà istruzioni perché tu possa venire a trovarmi. – Spero che, in seguito, anche a me sia concesso di fare una breve scappata da te, come é già stato concesso a dei miei uomini non feriti, e che hanno già potuto riabbracciare i parenti. – Ti prego di dare le mie buone notizie alla mamma e di rassicurarla della mia buona salute. Nella speranza di riabbracciarti presto. Ti bacio con affetto tuo figlio Vincenzo.

Ed ora, a chi credete di più: al vostro camerata Manuel, oppure alle mene della propaganda anglo-americana?

160

Soldati dei Raggruppamenti di Combattimento "Folgore-Friuli-Cremona."

Una fotografia che dice più, di mille parol

L'aspirante guardia marina Manuel Vincenzo, comandante il 1 Plotone della 2: Compagnia, Battaglione «Bafile» del Reggimento S. Marco del Raggruppamento di Combattimento «Folgore» é stato ferito l'8–3–45 é fatto prigioniero assieme ad altri sette compagni a 14 km a SO da Imola. Contrariamente a quanto asserisce la propaganda anglo-americana, lui ed i suoi uomini vennero curati e trattati cameratescamente. La foto accanto parla chiaro.

Historia o Stasiu, Wilhelmie, Iwanie, wujku Johnie Bull'u i wujku Samie

Nowoczesna bajka

Przed laty żył sobie pewien chłopiec imieniem Staś. Nie miał on jeszcze 21-niu lat, bowiem przyszedł na świat dopiero po zakończeniu pierwszej wojny światowej. John Bull i Marianna byli jego chrzestnymi rodzicami. Dobry wujek John Bull sprawował funkcję opiekuna małego Stasia aż do chwili jego połnoletności. Dobry to był wujek, bardzo bogaty i miał dużo do powiedzenia na całym świecie. Wszystkie małe dzieci spoglądały z zaufaniem ku niemu, ale to wyszło im zarazem na niekorzyść, bowiem wuj John Bull miał wiele trosk. Jego dom stał nieco oddalony od ulicy, przy której mieszkał Staś. Wujek John Bull przyrzekał swoim sierotom spełnić wszystkie ich życzenia, to też one — nieboraki — zaufały mu. A najbardziej przyrzeczeniom tym uwierzył Staś, bowiem w roku 1939-tym, kiedy został pełnoletnim, otrzymał od wujka Johna Bulla polecenie aby we wszystkich swych czynnościach polegał tylko i wyłącznie na nim. To też Staś wierzył swemu wujkowi bez zastrzeżeń i był dumny z tego, że ma takiego bogatego i godnego zaufania opiekuna.

Tymczasem wywiązała się kłótnia pomiędzy Stasiem a jego potężnym sąsiadem z lewej strony spowodu jednego ze starych nieporozumień. Wprawdzie zatarg ten byłby się dał zlikwidować, bowiem ten potężny sąsiad Stasia chciał udzielić mu rady i pertraktować, ale John Bull skinął Stasiowi i powiedział mu: »Nie pozwól na to, aby Wilhelm właził Ci w paradę, przecież Ty i ja razem jesteśmy silniejsi od niego. Ja stanę zawsze w Twojej obronie, drażnij go, niech się rozgniewa«. Młody i niedoświadczony Staś nie dał sobie tego dwa razy mówić. To też odrzucił wszelkie projekty pertraktacji jakie stawiał mu Wilhelm a nawet obrzucił go kamykami, gdy on przyszedł do niego na rozmowę. Doszło więc do nieuniknionej kłótni i bitki, w której duży Wilhelm okazał się o wiele silniejszy od małego Stasia. Staś wołał rozpaczliwie o pomoc, ale wujek John pozostał w swoim domu i przyglądał się przez okno jak Staś dostawał cięgi.

Staś miał jeszcze jednego złego a potężnego sąsiada z prawej strony. Przed nim miał Staś zawsze wielkiego stracha, jeszcze większego jak przed tym z lewej strony. Iwan — ten straszny sąsiad z prawej strony — napadł nagle na Stasia w chwili, kiedy jego bójka z Wilhelmem była prawie że skończona i chciał skorzystać coś na tem, trzymając się zasady »gdzie się dwóch bije, tam trzeci korzysta«.

Znów rozległo się rozpaczliwe wołanie Stasia, ale wuj John Bull był głuchy na to wołanie i nie odzywał się wcale. Ale Staś, jakkolwiek brocząc krwią z wielu zadanych mu ran leżał już na ziemi, czekał wciąż jeszcze na pomoc ze strony swego wuja Johna. Ale dobry wujek John skinął tylko głową i powiedział: »Poczekaj, mój chłopcze, później, później, strasznie mi ciebie żal, ale narazie muszę myśleć o sobie«.

I tak przemijał rok za rokiem. Tymczasem Wilhelm popadł w kłótnię z wieloma sąsiadami a między innymi też i z wujkiem Johnem Bull'em i wujkiem Sam'em. I mały Staś, jakkolwiek nie zdołavvszy się jeszcze wylizać z zadanych mu ran i jeszcze bardzo słaby w sobie, pozostawiony samemu sobie przez jego wielkich i potężnych wujków, przecież nie ociągał się pospieszyć z pomocą swoim wujkom, którzy znaleźli się teraz sami w niebezpieczeństwie. Staś pomagał im jak i gdzie tylko mógł. Ale to nie opłaciło się jemu. Z chwilą, kiedy groźny Iwan, który jest przyjacielem wujka Johna i wujka Sama, przepędził Wilhelma, chciał Staś powrócić i zamieszkać w swoim własnym domu. Ale pomimo ciągłych zapewnień ze strony wujka Johna Bull'a, że dom Stasia będzie zawsze stał do jego dyspozycji, postanowił straszny Iwan wraz z wujkiem Johnem Bull'em i wujkiem Sam'em, nie pytając się wcale Stasia o zdanie, że po wyrzuconym Wilhelmie dom Stasia zajmie nie Staś sam — ale groźny Iwan.

Staś protestował cicho, że nie uszanowano jego własności, pomimo, że spełnił on wszystko, czego żądali od niego jego wujkowie. Gdy groźny Iwan usłyszał ten protest, zaczął się śmiać, trzęsąc olbrzymim brzuchem, zaś wujek John Bull nic nie chciał nawet wiedzieć o tym, co swego czasu Stasiowi przyrzekł. Teraz dopiero spostrzegł Staś, że nie jest traktowany poważnie. Staś odczuł, że traktują go jak głupiego chłopca i że jego wuj John zdobył się nawet na taką bezczelność, usiłując przekonać go o tym, że u Iwana będzie mu dobrze . . . .

Mały Staś stoi więc teraz przed zdemolowanym swoim domem, w którym rozpanoszył się groźny Iwan. Staś nie wie co ma teraz począć, gdzie i do kogo ma się udać — w prawo czy w lewo? — Dniem i nocą męczy Stasia myśl, że przecież byłoby się lepiej stało, gdyby wtedy, nie oglądając się na wujka Johna, był on się pogodził ze swoim lewym sąsiadem. Bowiem to, czego lewy sąsiad od Stasia wtedy żądał, było niczem w porównaniu o tym, co przydzielono obecnie Iwanowi. Tak, tak, gdyby był tylko wtedy posłuchał swego sąsiada Wilhelma, byłby przez to uratował swój dom. A tak nie posiada teraz nic, — nic poza wspomnieniami. Czyż wobec tego warto poświęcać się nadal dla korzyści tych dobrych wujków, którzy może i dobrze zamierzali, ale przecież pozostawili Stasia samemu sobie? Czyż nie byłoby dla Stasia innego wyjścia z tej tak opłakanej sytuacji?

Historia ta nie jest jeszcze skończona. Od Was tylko zależy, jaki los spotka ostatecznie Stasia. Epilog tej historii musicie napisać Wy sami. Oszukany Staś — to Wasza Ojczyzna. Pomyślcie zatem, w jaki sposób możecie najlepiej pomóc Stasiowi. Wuj John Bull czy Sam zawiedli, zaś groźny Iwan nie opuści dobrowolnie obcego domu. Zatem — Staś musi poszukać sąsiada, z którym wspólnie mógłby wypędzić groźnego Iwana.

1624 - 3 - 45

162. To live for her... or die for him? Anti-Bolshevik leaflet.

TO LIVE FOR HER —

162

163. *A map of Italy representing the consequences of September 8 and asking if these are the conditions of the Armistice. The back was for a safe conduct.*

164. *Italian soldiers returning home after four years.*

163

163

FINALMENTE !

Dopo quattro anni!

Ecco il primo incontro e l'abbraccio affettuoso. Gli sguardi s'incontrano e sembrano dire: Sei proprio tu? Sei vivo? È questo vero?

L'incontro col padre rende felici pure i conoscenti presenti che gioiscono come se essi stessi avessero ritrovato un figlio.

Madre e figlio, dopo l'abbraccio, si scrutano e rivivono le pene passate che fu necessario provare per godere maggiormente la gioia indimenticabile del ritorno.

La famiglia in festa è pronta per la visita a parenti e paesani.

Il camerata Alcide Negrini, già soldato della Compagnia Comando del 2 Battaglione, 22 Reggimento della Divisione "Cremona", fatto prigioniero il 16 gennaio 1945 è stato restituito dai Camerati tedeschi alla propria famiglia.
L'incontro con i famigliari è avvenuto al paese natio, Medicina, a pochi chilometri dal posto stesso in cui i "liberatori" avevano costretto il Negrini a combattere per distruggere la propria casa ed a danneggiare i suoi campi.

Camerati! Cosa attendete per raggiungere anche voi le vostre famiglie! Chi vi impedisce di essere coraggiosi e di guadagnarvi presto e senza pericolo la libertà, negando ai "liberatori"! Anche quelli di voi che non hanno la famiglia nell'Italia del Nord, possono trovare pane, lavoro, organizzazione e soddisfazioni. — La nostra Patria vi impedisce, camerati, di continuare ad essere schiavi, gli interessi degli uomini, affamatori della nostra gente.

Venite!!! Vi attendono pace e libertà.

ATTENZIONE !

Per venire a noi, seguite le istruzioni già datovi, appena le seguenti:
1) Avvicinarsi alle nostre linee, singoli, ed al massimo in gruppi di tre uomini. 2) Se armati, non

Attraverso la campagna natia, la cui terra aspetta, a neve disciolta, il lavoro del soldato ritornato contadino.

L'incontro con la sorella ed il nipotino portano il reduce al pensiero di un proprio focolare e di una nuova famiglia.

Altro incontro affettuoso col redivivo.

tenere le armi in posizione di sparo ma portarle a braccia e agitarle in alto con un fazzoletto attaccato alla canna dell'arma. 3) Ad un'eventuale intimazione di «alt», fermarsi agitando le mani festino ed il fazzoletto e chiamarsi «camerata». Chi verrà a noi, vibratamente, con l'armi, raggiungerà prima la propria famiglia ed avrà un trattamento migliore.

Affrettatevi a venire! Prima che un'eventuale cambio vi possa allontanare dalle linee e vi renda impossibile raggiungere la «libertà».
Le truppe tedesche sono informate di fatto questo ed accoglieranno i soldati italiani come camerati. Il lasciapassare su questo manifesto vi dà la possibilità di attraversare la frontiera senza pericolo alcuno.

Lasciapassare!

Il soldato italiano, latore di questo manifesto è da trattarsi come un camerata e da allontanare subito dalla zona di pericolo. L'Esercito lo deve fornire di vitto come un soldato tedesco e se necessario, prestargli soccorso sanitario e consegnarlo al Comitato della Divisione „Soldati italiani che rimpatriano".
IL COMANDANTE D'ARMATA

Traduzione Tedesca:

Der italienische Soldat, der diese Flugschrift überbringt ist wie ein Kamerad zu behandeln und sofort aus der Gefahrenzone zu entfernen. Die Truppe hat ihn wie einen deutschen Soldaten zu verpflegen und, wenn nötig, zu versorgen, und ihn dann den Kommandanten ,,Heimführung italienische Soldaten der Division zu übergeben".

la gettata la odiosa divisa, forzatamente portata, sente libero e ritornato ad essere nuovamente il sostegno dei suoi genitori.

• 2512-2-45

165. *A woman is at temple praying to her Hindu god for the safe return of her husband, who is at the front fighting for the British. At the same time, her husband is mortally wounded. The message: Surrender and become a POW so that your family's prayers can be answered.*

166. *The threat of Russia grew as the war neared its end.*

165

AE BHAGWAN!

» . . . main teri sewa men girgira kar bainti karti hun` . . . tere age hath jorti hun : . . teri murti par phul charhati hun . . . tu apni kirpa se mere pranpati ko ran men jokhon se bachae rakhiyo . . . tu mere jiwan ke sahare ko is sansar men garam anch na ane dijyo . . . . «

Yeh thi woh duaen jo ek pati bhartar dewi apne pran pati ke liye mang rahi thi jab keh us ka pati Subedar Ram Sarup Singh Ist. Punjab Regiment maidan-e-jang men angrezon ke liye zakhmi ho kar akhri hichki le kar dam tor raha tha. Is masum dewi ko kya malum tha keh uski shakh-e-tamanna qalam ho chuki hai. Woh na janti thi keh us ki arman bhari dunya men ab andhera chha chuka hai . . . . woh is se be khabar thi keh us ke dil ki kali baghair khile hi murjha chuki hai . . . .

YEH SAB KUCHH KIYON HUA?

Kionkeh Subedar Ram Sarup Singh ne jan bujh kar apni jan ganwai di. Agar woh hathyar dal dete to un ki dharampatni ki tamam ashaen puri ho sakti thin.

KYA TUM BHI

apni` mataon, bahnon, aur dharampatniyon ko isi tarah mayusi ka munh dikhana chahte ho? NAHIN! To phir tum bila wajah kiyon Germanon ke khilaf angrezon ke faede ke liye marne par tule ho? Behtar hai keh larai ke akhri magar sakht daur men musibat se pichha chhura kar Germanon ki taraf chale ao. Aur aram se larai ke khatme tak Campon men zindagi guzaro aur phir akhir kar khushi khushi ghar chale jao, aur

JUDAI KI IN KATHAN GHARYON KO BHUL JAO.

165

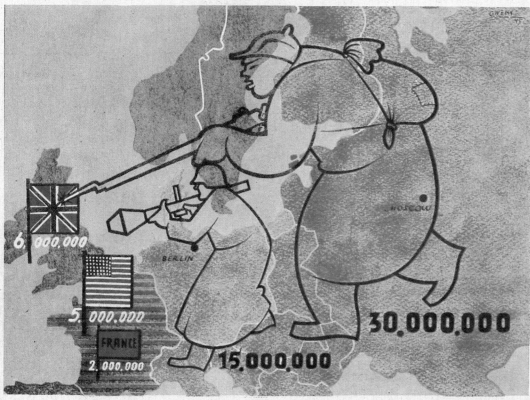

THE SATURDAY EVENING POST

Founded A.D. 1728 by Benj. Franklin

Volume 216 5c. THE COPY PHILADELPHIA, P.A., FEBRUARY 24, 1945 $2.00 By Subscription (52 issues) Number 35

Will a Super-Prussia emerge from World War II?

THE ALLIANCE OF TOMORROW

By DOROTHY THOMPSON

I HAVE just returned from a trip which led me from the Dardanelles all the way to Sweden. I have had an opportunity to talk to Allied and neutral generals and statesmen in Europe and learn from them as well as from American and British front line soldiers and also from German prisoners of war what they think of the future.

Now I am back again on the firm soil of the United States. The Crimea Conference has just come to an end, and in studying its possible results I, as well as the Allied and neutral generals and statesmen, am asking myself the one question of utmost importance. When this war has been won in the end by the Allies, will it be followed by another and much more terrible world conflagration? Three things are bound to happen: 1. The Germans will find a way to escape defeat. 2. If they succeed, this will lead to the strongest alliance ever witnessed in the world. 3. The

Americans and the British will have to fight against this alliance in a Third World War if they do not want to lose the second.

How can the Germans escape defeat? I am not claiming that the Nazi General Staff has liaison officers in Moscow. That would be absurd. But it is a fact that several German generals and other high-ranking officers, including Fieldmarshal Paulus and General von Seydlitz are in daily communication with the Soviet Su-

preme Command. They have their headquarters in Moscow where they are building up a new German Army of Liberation. Liberation from what? Germany will have been liberated from Hitler long before this new army is ready to fight. Its purpose can only be to raise arms against the American and British occupation troops and the start will perhaps be made with an underground movement in the distressed areas.

In my opinion American and British political leaders can be sure that the impoverished German people will prefer, disciplined as they are, a well organized socialist Soviet order to the chaotic conditions which, we must admit, have followed the liberation of Greece, Italy, France and Belgium by the western powers.

The zone of Germany to be occupied by the Soviets in accordance with the resolution of the Crimea Conference will become the nucleus of a new Soviet Germany which will then inevitably engage in lively trade with the Soviet Union and will soon recover. This would mean that the Americans would be unable to export goods to the Soviet Union on as large a scale as they had hoped.

It should not be overlooked that the Germans and the Russians have been good friends for centuries. Before Hitler's rise to power, of all foreign missions the German officers alone were permitted to move about freely in Russia. One reason for this friendship is also that the Prussians constitute a mixture of Teutonic and Slav blood.

In view of this fact the thought is not too far-fetched that a new fusion of blood on a gigantic scale will take place between the defeated Germans and the Russians in a future Super-Prussia. The military effect within a short time will then be that the German secret «V-weapons» will be built in unlimited numbers in Siberian factories, out of reach of hostile bombers and that this Russian colossus with a German head can produce 1000 Russo-German divisions.

This is a rather gloomy outlook and it seems that nothing can be done about it, for the diplomatic quarrels which always precede hostilities clearly point the way towards a Third World War. The Crimea Conference notwithstanding. That this development is under way can be seen from the following facts.

As regards the Polish question England and the Soviet Union have been fighting an embittered diplomatic battle which Marshal Stalin has won.

Churchill has countered this blow by

enabling the German divisions in Greece to withdraw to the northern Balkans because he wanted the Germans there to keep the Russians in check.

In retaliation Marshal Stalin ordered the Greek Communist Party EAM to make trouble for the British troops in Greece. Despite the armistice which has been concluded in Athens in the meantime, fighting continues in the mountains.

When I spoke to Marshal Tito I gained the impression that his refusal to allow England's protege King Peter to return to Belgrade had been inspired by Moscow.

On the western theatre of war Eisenhower and his staff also displayed a certain degree of hostility towards Russia by refusing the demand of the Soviet Military Mission in France to form special Russian divisions out of the ranks of the Russian prisoners of war whom the Germans had left behind.

Marshal Stalin's request for an American credit of six billion dollars has been turned down in Washington while the Lend-Lease shipments to Russia have been allowed to dwindle. It is also a fact that Great Britain has been concentrating numerous divisions in the Middle East in the immediate vicinity of the Soviet zone of influence.

Even today American and British officers are not admitted to the Soviet front, they have been even expelled from Rumania and Bulgaria.

Under these aspects the Russo-German combination constitutes the greatest danger of the future. It will completely wipe out Great Britain and deprive America of the fruits of victory.

General Fritz Burglert
Born in 1889, another high German liaison-officer at Moscow

167. Welcome!

168. Expression of heartache.

169. This Italian flyer discusses the end of the war.

Welcome!

Hope you make yourselves feel at home!

167

Is this an expression of agreement or of heart ache, Gentlemen?

168

Quando FINIRÀ LA GUERRA ?

QUANDO FINIRÀ LA GUERRA ?

In Italia nessuna domanda è più frequente di questa. E nessuno la comprende meglio del soldato tedesco che ha quotidianamente sotto gli occhi le sofferenze, la miseria del popolo italiano e le rovine del paese. Le risposte a tale domanda sono molteplici, ma la maggior parte di esse sono troppo superficiali per dare la vera soluzione. Parliamo una volta tanto seriamente della cosa, senza false reticenze o secondi fini propagandistici.

La Germania e gli anglo-americani combattono oggi in Italia

Possiamo risparmiarci di risalire al principio della guerra. Ognuno di noi sa che nè Danzica, nè la Polonia sono le cause dell'attuale conflitto: queste questioni costituirono solo la scusa per l'attacco degli alleati. Le cause però appaiono chiare, quando si fa luce sugli scopi bellici delle nazioni combattenti.

Perchè combattono ora gli anglo-americani?

Combattono per mantenere lo *statu quo* creato dalla prima guerra mondiale e dal trattato di pace di Versailles.

Combattono per la forza e la ricchezza che è dalla parte delle potenze vincitrici (esclusa l'ingannata Italia), per l'eterna povertà e l'ingiusto trattamento della Germania e dei suoi alleati.

Combattono per la industrializzazione e per un ordine economico che è di vantaggio a pochi prescelti, ai quali è indifferente la sorte della massa dei lavoratori disoccupati a causa del progresso delle macchine. (Poichè per gli «anglo-americani» non si intende il popolo americano od inglese, bensì una piccola parte di governanti formata da capitalisti ed ebrei).

Combattono per l'assoggettamento economico degli stati europei all'Inghilterra e all'America (e si ingannano l'un l'altra, perchè naturalmente l'America vuol far dipendere da sè anche l'Inghilterra ed entrambe non si accorgono che già da lungo tempo sono diventate schiave di Mosca!).

Combattono a fianco del bolscevismo che rinnega ogni tradizione, religione, cultura, ordine sociale europeo, per mettere al loro posto un uomo-macchina senza anima, una massa senza libertà e volontà, aizzata dalla frusta di commissari giudei. Anche la propaganda anglo-americana cerca di velare questo scopo. Basta domandarlo ai soldati italiani che hanno combattuto nella Russia sovietica per convincersi della verità.

170

but Blondes
don't like Cripples

★ 1309-2-45   *170*

171. One signed for three.

172. Pictured are Italian soldiers returning home to visit their parents.

171

Reduce!

Il geniere *Luppi* Gino, della Divisione Cremona, 7 Compagnia, 2 Battaglione, 22 Reggimento, fatto prigioniero assieme ad altri 36 compagni, il giorno 16 gennaio, al Naviglio.

La madre felicissima, è la prima a dare il benvenuto al figlio.

(*a sinistra*) Per tre anni interi le campagne le ha lavorate il fratello, ora gli aiuteranno due solide braccia.

(*sotto*) I paesàni tutti sono riuniti e vogliono udire le sue notizie.

Luppi Gino è il primo tra i fortunati. Per lui, che appena due settimane fa, condivideva ancora con voi i pericoli della morte, è terminata ora la guerra.
Il posto suo, al tavolo della casa paterna, non è più vuoto. Le sue mani, invece di una carabina inglese, conducono ora di nuovo l'aratro. Il suo sonno non è più turbato dal rombo dei cannoni, nè dal crepitare delle granate.
Luppi Gino è tornato a casa e con lui sono tornati pure altri 14 soldati della Divisione "Cremona" provenienti da Provincie dell'Italia settentrionale, alle case loro. Otto di essi condussero con se compagni dell'Italia centrale e meridionale, gli altri tutti ottenero lavoro e pane nell'Italia settentrionale.

Anche tu, camerata hai una famiglia che ansiosamente ti attende. Non lasciali attendere invano! Se provenisti dalla zona occupata dagli anglo-americani, non ti preoccupare, nell'Italia settentrionale troverai una casa ospitale come pure una sistemazione conveniente.
Poni fine a questa lotta fratricida! Pensa che tradisci l'Italia, continuando la lotta al fianco di quelli che portarono la fame e la miseria, la prostituzione nell'Italia meridionale; di quelli che violano e disonorano le vostre mogli e ragazze e saccheggiano il paese. Non ti metter al fianco di negri, indù e neozelandesi!
Non dimenticà giammai, che una madre italiana ti ha dato la vita e che l'Italia ora ti chiama!

Un breve colloquio col vicino, anche egli festeggia un fortunato reduce.

(*sopra*) Questo è l'istante che Gino attendeva da tre anni.

(*a destra*) Un figlio ormai ritenuto perso è ritornato, pieno di gioia sorridono gli occhi del padre.

(*sotto*) L'otto settembre lo ha diviso, il 16 gennaio lo ha ricongiunti. Questo giorno sarà sempre festeggiato nella famiglia Luppi.

Il tratto attraverso il fronte è breve e senza pericolo, se osservi queste 4 cose:
1) Togli l'elmetto
2) getta le armi
3) Agita il manifesto oppure un panno bianco
4) Chiama i soldati tedeschi col nome di "Camerata"
Non indugiate! Le Truppe tedesche sono bene istrutte, venite singoli oppure in gruppi fino a tre uomini.

* 2820-1-45

173. The Po River in Italy claimed the lives of many soldiers. Translation, see Appendix.

174. Soldiers from the Cremona Division returned to see their families.

PO KA ASHNAN

Aur to khair jo kuchh hoga dekha jaega magar ek bat to zarur hai keh ap log jo muddaton se nahae nahin ho to ab Po men ashnan kar loge. Po se zinda bach kar nikalna yeh tumhari qimat! Yeh mat bhul jana keh sardi ka mausim hai aur barf par rahi hai.

KYA TUM APNE UN SATHIYON KO BHUL CHUKE HO?

Jin ko tum daryae Sangro, Rapido, Liri, Volturno waghaira par karte hue waqt parmatma ke hawale kar ae ho.

PO KYA HAY?

Ek darya jis ki chaurai kam se kam 208 gaz aur ziyada se ziyada 1040 gaz. Gahrai 7 foot se lekar 20 foot tak. Kinare 18 foot se 30 foot unche, aur raftar 20 Mile fi ghanta se ziyada tez hai.

JAN PAR KHELNA

Tumhare liye us waqt to munasib tha jab keh tum apne mulk ke liye lar rahe hote, lekin agar tum Bartanwi Samraj ke liye pran do to tumhare marzi.

KYA KAR SAKTE HO?

Bimari ka bahana bana kar Hospital men ja sakte ho. Hamesha ke liye larai ki musibat se pichha chhura sakte ho aur bila khatre daryae Po par kar sakte ho.

173

173

Soldati della Divisione Cremona!

Ecco uno di mezzo a voi, Luppi Gino, Egli é già a casa! Sta ora in voi soltanto, ad essere altrettanto felici! Sí, anche anche voi potete ritornare alle vostre famiglie, oppure, se non risiedenti nell'Italia settentrionale, potete peró sempre porre termine alla guerra, almeno per voi personalmente, togliendo l'arma di mano e cessando di combattere e rischiare, oltre la vita per gli inglesi. Nell'Italia settentrionale c'é lavoro sufficente per tutti gli Italiani.

Di Caprio, Francesco
Negrini, Alcide
Pambianchi, Archimede
Valanghi, Aldo
Fanelli, Umberto
Cavalloni, Nicola
Pagnocelli, Piero
Leone Gaudia, Umberto
Santi, Carlo
Luppi, Gino
Bartocci, Armando
Sargi, Angelo
Rossi, Luciano
Nassisi, Augusto
Manfredo, Francesco
Seri, Terzo
Manfroni Francesco
De Michele, Fausto
Boaretto, Antonio
Salvioni, Florio
Rocchi, Mario
Samaritani, Angelo
Romani, Attilio
Bordin, Severino
Ferrari, Abele
Sacchi, Carlo
Cipriani, Tommaso
Melani, Danilo
Andreozzi, Arduino
Duranti, Renato
Villani, Giordano
Del Priore. Luigi

Questo é Luppi Gino, della 7 Comp. del 2 Battgl. del 22 Regg. to

Egli venne fatto prigioniero il 16 gennaio, assieme ad altri 36 soldati italiani, in seguito ad un attacco dei tedeschi al caposaldo di Giazol, 300 m ad est del Canale Naviglio, occupato da soldati italiani. I nomi dei prigionieri; fra i quali si trova pure quello del vice-comandante del Reparto, ten. Schinaia e del ten. Papetti della medesime Compagnia; li trovate su questo volantino.

Come ritornò Luppi dai suoi genitori?

Durante la sua prigionia, tra i tedeschi, il Luppi raccontò che era domiciliato a Cividale Mirandola, al Nr. 15 di via Cavo, e che era ormai molto tempo che non aveva più rivisto i suoi genitori. Il suo desiderio di ritornare a casa, venne appagato, ed ora egli si trova già contento in mezzo ai suoi cari.

Fu un giorno di festa per il villaggio intero allorché ritornò un figlio suo.

E che avvenne a Giazol?

Questa é la realtà! Intorno a questo caposaldo, occupato da una cinquantina di soldati italiani ed un ufficiale inglese, si accese un aspro ed accanito combattimento. Ci furono sei morti, parecchi feriti, nell'oscurità poi, altri presero la fuga. Il rimanente però venne fatto prigioniero. Tutti i prigionieri si espressero con la massima indignazione del fatto, che il loro Battaglione non aveva inviato alcun rinforzo, che pure era stato richiesto a mezzo Radio, rinforzo che da principio era stato anche assicurato. Infine però giunse soltanto l'intimazione dal predetto Comando, che il caposaldo era da tenere fino all'ultimo e di »morire per l'onore della Patria«.

L'ufficiale inglese, assegnato al Reparto, non ritenne però necessario di resistere »fino all'ultimo« ma già dopo il primo colpo di cannone, codardo si portò al sicuro, abbandonando gli Italiani al loro destino.

A Giazol ci rimasero però anche dei fortunati superstiti. Sono essi i prigionieri della 13 Compagnia del Battagl. del Genio e della 6 e 7 Compagnia del 2 Battagl. del 22 Regg. to. I Tedeschi sanno che tutti i settentrionali, che sono ormai tanto tempo assenti dalle loro famiglie, vogliono ritornare a casa.

Nell'Italia settentrionale non regna la fame e nessuno é neppure costretto a prestar servizio militare, ma chiunque vuole, può dedicarsi alla sua professione.

Soldati della Divisione Cremona!

Volete essere voi, alleati di quegli inglesi ed americani che profanano le vostre città che minacciano le vostre famiglie con le loro bombe? Ricordatevi e ritornate al vostro orgoglio di Italiani e pensate all'Italia.

Ingegnatevi e cercate ora la via per salvare la vostra vita e terminare almeno per voi personalmente la guerra.

Non esitate più e venite presto!

Con questo lasciapassare puoi passare senza pericolo alcuno le linee tedesche. Osserva però 4 cose: 1. Giù l'elmetto! 2. Getta le armi! 3. Di giorno, agitare il manifesto, o altra carta bianca oppure un panno bianco! 4. Di notte chiamare »Camerata«!
Venite singoli oppure in gruppi fino a tre uomini!

Lasciapassare!

Il soldato italiano latore di questo manifesto é da trattare come un camerata e da allontanare subito dalla zona di pericolo. L'Esercito lo deve fornire di vitto come un soldato tedesco, e se necessario, recargli soccorso sanitario e consegnarlo al Comitato della Divisione »Soldati italiani che rimpatriano«.
IL COMANDANTE D'ARMATA

Traduzione tedesca:
Der italienische Soldat, der dieses Flugblatt überbringt, ist wie ein Kamerad zu behandeln und sofort aus der Gefahrenzone zu entfernen. Die Truppe hat ihn wie einen deutschen Soldaten zu verpflegen und wenn nötig, ärztlich zu versorgen, und ihn dann dem Komitee »Heimführung italienischer Soldaten« bei der Division zu übergeben.

° 2508/1 45

---

175. This Polish caption states that the Red waves go through the country looking for a way on the West. The NRWD are in Russia, but London and Washington say nothing. The Polish in Italy should save their lives and think that the Germans and Polish will fight Russia.

176. A soldier's dream is to come home alive.

177. This leaflet explains the advantages and treatment of a POW.

178. Indian troops drowning in the Po River in Italy.

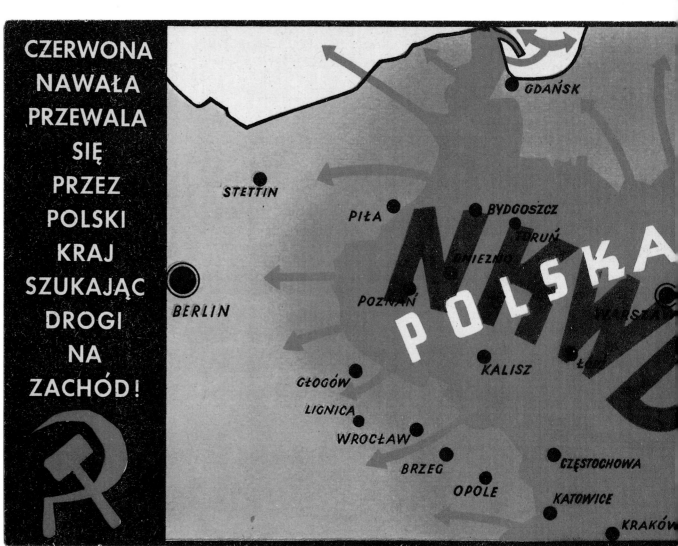

175

"Sogno o son desto?"

dice il figlio nell'abbracciare la madre, che non vedeva da due anni. Era proprio la realtà. Vettorato Quinto, già della 4.a Cp. I Btg. Rgt. Nembo, della "Folgore", era stato fatto prigioniero il 6 marzo 45. Alla sua richiesta di dare notizia a sua madre, gli venne concesso di recarsi personalmente a visitare, per breve tempo, i suoi cari.

176

Questi stanno meglio!

La propaganda anglo-americana non vuole che intimorirvi con le sue continue affermazioni, che se foste fatti prigionieri dai tedeschi, verreste maltrattati o che sareste uccisi addirittura. Sono queste menzogne indirizzate ad uno scopo ben definito. Così, come i marinai Dessi e Migliore del Btg. Bafile, Rgt. S. Marco, vengono trattati tutti i prigionieri italiani, secondo le norme internazionali di Ginevra.

Perché volete combattere? Perché arrischiare la vita per gli Anglo-Americani, nemici della Patria? Levatevi dai pericoli e venite a noi.

177

178

179. The horror of the Po River seen by a POW.

180. Alexander Barmine's book, "That Cannot Happen Here?," points out events that were happening and were sure to happen.

Dulag 612

Dear Fred,

I have been considering for the last few days whether to congratulate you or console you for missing our last "recce" patrol because of your bad feet. Of course I swore when we were suddenly jumped on by a bunch of Jerries behind that white house and taken prisoner. I knew nothing about Jerry and naturally for the first few minutes I cursed our bad luck. I must be fair though and say that they treated us not as enemies but as friends. And then again, perhaps it is as well to know that I am finished with mortars, Spandaus and Nebelwerfers. What do you think?

I have another reason for wishing you were with us though and that is the Po. Remember how we used to argue and gamble on the width and depth and the speed of the water. I remember you saying that it would be a hard nut to crack. I have seen the Po with my own eyes now and I can honestly say that I'm bloody pleased I won't be there when the music starts. Imagine the Thames being 1000 yards wide - but even then you don't get an idea of the Po with its cruel swirling water. I always knew that it was one of the greatest rivers in Europe but even so when I saw it, I felt a little sick. I know now too, why Jerry fought so hard for the Apennine Passes and why it took us so long and costs us so much to take Bologne. The Germans fought for time and they have certainly used that time well. The nature of the ground is a big help for them - it is all canals and boggy ground which makes tank warfare impossible. I got a better idea of the preparations Jerry has made when we went North. We saw trains loaded with mortars, Nebelwerfers and heavy artillery, fresh from the factories, and a Sergeant I was speaking to said they were all for the Po. So you can understand it, Fred, when I tell you that I'm glad I'm here in comfortable billets instead of facing the prospect of crossing the Po from your side. If I were you, I'd be away to Naples or some such place or else become ill. It's much better than to rush into a wet grave. Well, old son, I haven't time for any more now, so I close with every good wish from,

Yours as ever,

George

* 1306-1-45

179

179

180

181. "Onward Christian Soldiers!" is a collection of poems about the war written by British soldiers.

182. Vincera in Italian means he will win. This leaflet is filled with information about Mussolini.

181

182

183. Mussolini is talking to the Italian population and explaining that the "Liberators" (Allies) have promised food, peace, and liberty and have not delivered on any of these.

184. New Year's Eve at home with friends contrasts a cold, wet dugout "somewhere in Italy."

Hail the New Year!

Remember the old days?

— A group of friends are seated around the fire waiting to welcome in the new year.

Ten minutes to go, — ten minutes left of the old year!

Reminiscences! — It's been quite a good year really and we've had some good times. — The daily routine of work, — remember I got a rise in May? The holiday at Puddlecome-on-sea. The films we have seen, the parties we have been to and the people we have met.

Was it this year or last that Bill started going out with Mary?

I suppose they'll be married before another new year. They'll make a happy couple.

Five minutes to go, — we make our "new years resolutions".

— No more swearing, cut down smoking and concentrate on saving up for that new motor bike. — Promise not to fight with Sis any more.

We know that those resolutions will be broken before the new year is very old but it's fun to make them.

Two minutes to go, — the atmosphere is rather tense and thrilled.

Our feelings are very mixed — anticipation, an unaccountable sense of regret and, — strongest of all — we wonder what the new year holds in store for us.

It's here! As the hand of the clock hold their rendezvous on the mark of midnight the curch bells peal out their message.

— A new year is horn!

We lift our glasses, — Good luck, Good health and prosperity!

Then we solemnise the proceedings in a time honoured fashion.

We link arms and sing — Should auld aquaintance be forgot and never brought to mind —.

What a difference!

A cold and wet dugout "somewhere in Italy" is lit by means of a candle wedged into the neck of a bottle. In ten minutes it will be midnight and with that hour will come the new year.

"Damn you Jerry, — that one was close! — He knows exactly where we are. Thank God we will be getting away from this spot at midnight.

— Midnight! — It's new years eve tonight. In ten minutes time — if Jerry keeps those shells to himself — we shall be living in 1945. We shall be finished with 1944, — and we wont be sorry — it's been a hellish year! Remember young Johnny Holt and Bill Saunders and "Smudger" Smith? — They'll never see 1945.

Five minutes to go. — Wonder what Mum's doing now! — Probably sitting up to see the new year in. Sis will be with her too. Not a very cheerful outlook for them this year, — thanks to this bloody war.

Two minutes to go! Time we were getting ready to move boys!

Pick up rifle, helmet and webbing and lets be on our way.

With luck we'll gain our objective, — or some of us will!

Twelwe o' clock? — Right. — Let's go. —

Yes, there's a big difference.

All you can do now is to hope that it wont be long before the Jews and moneygrabbers have filled their pockets suffiently to call an end to wholesale slaughter and allow you to get back to a normal life!

* 380-12-44

185. *Why walk the tightrope between life and death again in 1945? Become a POW and be sure of coming home alive.*

186. *Good luck to you, soldier! You'll need it in 1945!*

185

Here we go again!

Heigh-Ho and here we go on another year of war!

Another year of toil and sweat and tears and blood. One more year of struggle and strife, of loneliness and disappointment — far away from Mother and Sweetheart, Wife and Child.

And with the coming of each day will come the dread spectre of death. Thousands of lives will be thrown away.

Who knows what the new year holds in store for you? What new weapons will be introduced and what new difficulties lie ahead?

Look around you at this moment, take notice of the friends and associates whom you have learned to respect:

How many will still be there at the end of 1945?

It is impossible to say!

And you yourself, — perhaps you too are destined as another sacrifice to the God of War!

It perhaps seems very coldblooded to suggest such a possibility but then, facts are invariably hard and not infrequently unpleasant.

Let us then face up to this possibility. — You may be killed in 1945:

And for why?

— Merely because a few priveledged ones at home are making millions out of the war!

It is fortunate that you have a way of escape.

Ask yourself this simple question; — — —

Is it shameful to want to live?

The answer is only too obvious and for any right thinking person it is more shameful to fight and kill to satisfy the greed for gold of a few Jews and capitalists.

There is no shame in becoming a prisoner of war, and that would mean that you would be out of the way of shells, bullets and the various other sources of death or injury and would spend your time pleasantly in a decent and comfortable camp until the time came for you to return home safe and well after the war.

The most important thing is to get back home alive and any method of ensuring that is well worth thinking about.

* 374/ 12 44

187. New Year wishes to the Polish 3rd Division. Why sacrifice your life in Italy in 1945 too? Become POWs.

188. Happy New Year 1945 to the Indians. May God bless them with life as POWs or otherwise. Translation, see Appendix.

Pozdrowienia Noworoczne dla 3. Dywizji

Czy rok 1945-ty doprowadzi Nas do celu? Czy życzenia Nasze w Nowym Roku spełnią się i czy ujrzymy Naszą Ojczyznę? Czy będziemy mogli, już nie na obcej, lecz na własnej ziemi rodzinnej bronić drogiej Ojczyzny? Wielu z nas straciło nadzieję; przyzwyczaili się do tułaczki i już nie wierzą w to, że mogliby zobaczyć jeszcze własne rodziny. Nie wolno Nam tak myśleć! Rok 1945-ty musi przynieść rozstrzygnięcie, a każdy polski żołnierz musi być na to przygotowany, że wspólnie z kolegami, własnemi siłami, wypędzi najezdców z Polski. Nie mamy zamiaru już dłużej tułać się po świecie; nie pójdziemy na Daleki Wschód, nie chcemy również dla interesów Anglii we Włoszech nasze życia poświęcać.

Co zdziałaliśmy w ubiegłym roku?

Od 1942-go do 1943-go roku byliśmy w Iraku, później w Palestynie i następnie w Egipcie, aby pod koniec 1943-go roku wylądować we Włoszech. Tutaj dopiero poznaliśmy twardość i okrutność tej wojny. Oto nasze bitwy:

Z początkiem marca staliśmy na południowem skrzydle 8-mej Armii. 5. marca nasza pierwsza styczność z frontem w rejonie Capracotty. W maju ropoczął się pochód na tereny na północ od Cassina leżące. Wielu z nas nigdy nie zapomni wzniesienia 593. Sława zwycięstwa naszego pod Cassinem nie stłumiła w nas żalu po stracie tak licznych i najlepszych naszych towarzyszy. Przyjemne były chwile krótkiego wypoczynku. W miesiącach letnich, t. j. w lipcu i w sierpniu, znowu przelewała się droga krew polska. Zapamiętamy sobie i te bitwy nad brzegami Adriatyka. I mimo tak ciężkich walk i wielkich zwycięstw naszych, zarzucano nam ciągle brak wytrwałości i pewności. Walczyliśmy dalej, nie dając się innym prześcignąć. I znowu ostatnio ziemia w okolicy Faenzy zroszona została krwią naszych Poległych i rannych.

Co nas czeka?

Napewno nowe niebezpieczeństwa i boje. A co stanie się w międzyczasie z naszą polską ziemią rodzinną? Co stanie się z Polską w czasie, kiedy my we Włoszech dla spraw Anglii walczyć będziemy?

O tem chcemy porozmawiać, gdy usiądziemy wspólnie, a szklaneczka wina pozwoli zapomnieć o tem, jak ciężkim jest los Żołnierza Polskiego, który z dalekiej obczyzny przyglądać się musi temu, jak ziemię Jego rodzinną, Jego Ojczyznę, inni rozdeptują.

● 375 /12 44

187

ALLAH KARE TUM KO NAYA SAL MUBARAK

Lijiye! Bare din aur naye sal ki mubarak tah•e dil se pesh khidmat hai. Jite ji san 1945 ka aghaz to dekha. Khuda kare keh is sal men apne azis•o•aqarab ka munh dekho!

Shahri zindagi ko ek taraf chhorte hue tum apni fauji zindagi par nazar maro aur yad karo keh kabhi tum naye sal ki khushi ko manane ke liye kitni tayyarian kiya karte the. Nai wardi pahnte. Turredar safa bandhte aur chamakte hue boot pahn kar nihayat ihtiyat se zamin par qadam rakhte hue chalte the. Phir parade ground men hazaron ki tadad men jama hote. Khushi men golian chalate. March pass karte. Is ke bad khushi khushi ghar wapas ate. Apne bal bachchon se milte.

MAGAR

woh tamam baten aj khwab ban kar rah gaen hain. Aj us bazigar ki tarah rasse par nach rahe ho jiske niche siraf sanginen khari ki hui hon. Zara paon chuka — wazan dahne baen hua aur hazaron murdon men ek tum bhi shamil.

KYA AB BHI YIH

mumkin hai keh tum khushi khushi apne ghar wapas ja sako?

Is kaghaz ko dekha kar bila khatra Germanon ke pas a sakte ho.

Agar ap apne gum shuda sathion ki babat malum karna chahte hain to Bhaiband Radio sham ko 5 1/2 se 6 baje tak 449,1 medium wave aur 47,6 short wave aur 8 1/2 se 9 baje siraf 47,6 short wave par suniye.

* 576 /12 44

189. *Again this year ....what the English profess, but what the Germans really do.*

190. *We Protest! Supposed Anglo-American reactions against the war.*

189

190

191. Pictured is a Polish Christmas scene. There should be peace on earth for all people of good will, as the birth of Jesus signified.

192. Happy New Year! It's 1945 and the war marches on. Millions of people in America are making a fortune in the war business and high-paying defense jobs, while the soldiers continue to fight.

191

THE WAR MARCHES ON!

New Year's Eve - Big night for the hot spots - Record crowds expected - America on a spending bust of Homeric proportion.

"Boom times have come to Manhattan in a blizzard of wonderful, wonderful currency. But New York was the last city in North America to get in on the war-time spending jag and this sort of thing has been going on in Detroit, St. Louis, Cleveland, Dallas, San Francisco and Seattle for more than two years. Luxury products in the fields of food and liquor, jewelry, furs, luggage, women's clothes and hotel apartments command prices that would gravel the prospectors of Central City, Leadville and Gold Town in their palmiest days."

Thus well-informed Lucius Beebe writes in "The American Mercury".

Millions of people in America are making a fortune in the war business and high-paying defense jobs.

For them the war is a necessity in their mad rush for personal gain.

New Year's Eve is the climax of joy-riding for them.

What's a couple of hundred dollars to them spent in the company of nifty girls at some costly parlor of uproar, at Jack's and Charlie's "21", at the Zanzibar, at El Morocco, at the Blue Angel?

Why should they give a rap for you forgotten Americans as long as they can stay at home making hay while the sun shines, as long as you do your duty in the firing lines.

THEY know what you are fighting for when they pocket their huge profits and big pay checks.

Do YOU know what you are fighting for?

1945   What has the new year in store for you?
Will you die on the battlefield?
Will you be maimed or blinded?
Who knows?

The war marches on!

AI - 176 - 12 - 44

193. *An Indian newspaper depicting the activities in a POW camp.*

194. *Victory is in the air.*

195. *On recapturing the small Silesian town of Lauban from the Soviets the German troops found the bodies of 148 women who had been raped and murdered by the Soviet soldiers.*

جرمن قیدی کیمپوں میں زندگی

JARMAN QAIDI KAMPON MEN ZINDGI

जर्मन कैदी कॅम्पोंमें जिन्दगी

کئی ایک ہندوستانی سپاہی جرمن قیدی کیمپوں میں آرام کی زندگی بسر کر رہے ہیں ۔ اس اخبار میں جرمن قیدی کیمپوں میں قیدیوں کی زندگی کی تصویریں دی ہیں ۔ قیدیوں کے کھانے کا ۔ کھیلنے کا کتابیں پڑھنے کا اور دلچسپی کے لئے ناچ تماشے بنانے کا انتظام اچھا ہے ۔ ہندوؤں کیلئے مندر ۔ مسلمانوں کیلئے مسجد اور سکھوں کیلئے گورودوارہ بنے ہیں

Kai ek Hindustani sipahi Jarman qaidi kampon men aram ki zindgi basar kar rahe hain. Is akhbar men Jarman qaidi kampon men qaidion ki zindgi ki taswiren di hain. Qaidion ke khane ka, khelne ka, kitaben parhne ka, aur dilchaspi keliye nach tamashe banane ka intezam achchha hai. Hinduon keliye mandar, Musulmanon keliye masjid, aur Sikhon keliye gurdware bane hain.

कई एक हिन्दोस्तानी सिपाहि जर्मन कैदी कॅम्पोंमें आराम की जिन्दगी बसर कर रहे हैं। इस अखबार में जर्मन कैदी कॅम्पोंमें कैदीयों के जिन्दगी की कुछ तसबीरें दिखी हैं। कैदीयों का खवानेका, खेलनेका, किताबें पढ़नेका और दिलचस्सी के लिये नाच तमाशे बनाने का इन्तजाम अच्छा है। हिन्दुओं कैलिये मन्दर, मुक्सलमानों कैलिये मस्जिद और सीखींकैं लिये गुरुद्वारि बने हैं।

अन्दाजा लगाओ। इनमेंसे कौन जीत गया है? यह बात तो साफ़ है के जो हंस रहे हैं वे ही जीत गये हैं। लेकिन सबही जीत गये हैं क्यूं के उन्होंने अपनी जान बचाली है और कैदी कॅम्पमें हंसी खुशीसे रहिते हैं।

Andaza lagao keh inmen se kaun jit gaya hai? Yeh bat to saf hai keh jo hans rahe hain, wohi jit gaye hain. Lekin sabhi jit gaye hain, kiunkeh unhon ne apni jan bacha li hai aur qaidi kampon men hansi khushi se rahte hain.

اندازہ لگاؤ کہ ان میں سے کون جیت گیا ہے ۔ یہ بات تو صاف ہے کہ جو ہنس رہے ہیں وہی جیت گئے ہیں ۔ لیکن سبھی جیت گئے ہیں کیونکہ انہوں نے اپنی جان بچالی ہے اور قیدی کیمپوں میں ہنسی خوشی سے رہتے ہیں

193

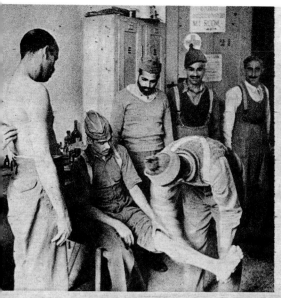

ڈاکٹر صاحب اس جوان کو اچھے طرح دیکھنا
یہ شاید فالتو دودھ مانگتا ہے ۔ سب جوانوں
کی ڈاکٹری ہوتی ہے اور انکو تندرست رکھا جاتا ہے

Daktar Sahib, is jawan ko achchhe tarah dekhna, yeh shayad faltu dudh mangta hai. — Sab jawanon ki dektri hoti hai aur unko tandurust rakha jata hai.

डॉक्टर साहिब! इस जवान की अच्छे तरह देखना—
यह शायद फालतू दूध मंगता है। सब जवानों की
डाक्टरी होती है और उनकी तन्दुरुस्त रखा जाता है।

ذرا غور سے دیکھیے کہ ان میں حلوا ہے یا
سرکاری راشن کے علاوہ جوان بھی
کھانا اپنی اپنی لذت کے مطابق بنا

khiye keh in men halwa hai ya dal,
— Sarkari rashan ke alawa jawan bari
watni khana apni apni lazzat ke
she hain.

खिये के इनमें हलवा है या दाल,
— सरकारी राशन के अलावा
डीसी अपना वतनी खाना
लज्जत के छताबिक बना रहे हैं

ان تصویروں سے آپ خود دیکھ سکتے ہیں کہ قیدی کیمپوں میں سب ہندوستانی سپاہی کتنے خوش
قیدیوں کی تعداد بڑھ رہی ہے اور بہت سے ہندوستانی سپاہی انگریزوں کے واسطے لڑنے سے ج
آجانے کو بہتر سمجھتے ہیں ۔ تاکہ لڑائی ختم ہونے کے بعد وہ سلامت اپنی گھروں کو واپس چلے جائیں

ap khud dekh sakte hain, keh qaidi kampon men sab Hindustani sipahi kitne khush hain. Din ba din qaidion
ahi hai aur bahut se Hindustani sipahi Angrezon ke waste larne se Jarmanon ke pas ajane ko beter samajhte
ai khatam hone ke bad woh sahi salamat apni gharon ko wapas chale jaen.

से आप खुद देख सकते हैं के कैदी कैम्पोंमें सब हिन्दुस्तानी सिपाहि कितने खुश हैं। दिन ब
ने तादाद बढ़ रही है और बहुत से हिन्दुस्तानी सिपाहि अंग्रेजी के वास्ती लड़नेसे जर्मनोंके
की बेतर समझते हैं, ताकि लड़ाई खतम होने के बाद वह सही सलामत अपनी घरी
चले जायें।

NZ-001-8

Victory Parade
without you?

Victory is in the air...

Your B. B. C. sees to that... and your press and your government orators make a lavish use of the word...
All is over but the cheering...
The Victory Parade is imminent...

And how do you vision it to yourself, this Victory Parade?

Do you see the war-worn boy-veterans, your pals, marching through the mutilated streets of London crowded with cheering multitudes of men and women mad with joy?

Do you see the windows full of eager women's faces straining to catch a glimpse of someone dear to them, husband, sweetheart, son, brother?

Do you picture the frantic waving of hands and handkerchiefs when the eyes they are seeking meet theirs? Was there ever such a look of love and joy?

But if you are not there?   If the Victory Parade takes place without you?

Wake up from your dream!   You are still in Italy.

The sounds you hear are not victory salvoes or cheering crowds... they are deadly artillery fire, yells of pain and death cries! While « Victory is in the Air » politicians and traders in human flesh are squabbling over scraps of paper and scraps of land, and thousands die daily for no ideal, for no reason at all, butchered to make a higher title, a larger dividend... YOU perhaps one of them!

And the woman you love? What will the Victory Parade be for her if you are not there? She will sit near the window of your little home, but she will turn her face away from the rows of marching men, for the cheering crowds, the waving flags and the proud music are more than she can bear! She can hardly bear to look at your last photograph, the one she loved so much, for her heart is broken... victory was in the air and she lost you...
Can you bear to inflict such pain on her?
Are you going to let yourself be killed in a fight the world says is already won? It rests with you!

★ 719 - 4 - 45

1 out of 148
On recapturing the small Silesian town of Lauban from the Soviets the German troops found the bodies of 148 women who had been raped and murdered by the Soviet soldiers.

★ 1345/4-45

196. The Black Brigade was making pleas to fight on. They believed in Mussolini's one for all, all for one, and all for Italy attitude.

197. A representative was appointed by Russia who was to organize the return of Soviet citizens to fight against the Germans.

I partigiani italiani in Francia
Miseria nera e carne da cannone

Un telegramma ricevuto a Lisbona da Roma, dice la triste odissea dei partigiani italiani in Francia, per la più parte alpini che, dopo l'8 settembre, obbedendo agli ordini infami diramati da Badoglio, si affiancarono ai Francesi e agli Anglo-americani contro l'Alleato Germanico. Le loro tristissime condizioni richiamarono alla fine l'attenzione degli ambienti antifascisti, che inviarono il Comandante Bellardy per compiere una inchiesta. Eccone i risultati secondo le informazioni degli ambienti badogliani:

La relazione del Comandante Bellardy

Si telegrafa da Roma, via Lisbona, che il Comandante Bellardy, incaricato di un'ispezione fra elementi italiani rifugiatisi in Francia, ha inviato al comando delle formazioni « Giustizia e Libertà » la seguente relazione.

« Durante la mia permanenza in Francia ho raccolto le seguenti informazioni che ritengo opportuno di portare a conoscenza di codesto comando affinchè possa interessarsi facendo il possibile che la situazione dei nostri connazionali rifugiati in Francia sia oggetto di studio e di risoluzione da parte delle autorità interessate.

« Nella Francia meridionale sono internati circa 32.000 italiani, dei quali solamente una parte (sette o otto mila uomini) hanno trovato una sistemazione, ma molti di questi vivono di espedienti non sempre raccomandabili. Il rimanente è trattato alla stessa stregua dei prigionieri di guerra tedeschi.

Internati dopo aver combattuto

« Gli internati, di cui la maggior parte è a Marsiglia e a Tolone, lavorano come scaricatori di porto. Molti degli italiani sono alpini della « Pusteria » e hanno combattuto nei « maquis » e anche assai bene, perchè alcuni di essi hanno meritato particolare menzione nei bollettini di guerra.

« Però, sciolto il « maquis », gli italiani che ne facevano parte sono stati internati, e in alcuni luoghi il trattamento loro riservato è veramente pessimo.

« A Modane, per esempio, un gruppo di 40 italiani lavora al servizio delle truppe marocchine, è costretto a una vita bestiale e a compiere ogni sorta di bassezze per ottenere il cibo.

Fra gli italiani internati, i migliori esponenti verrebbero a combattere con le nostre formazioni del Piemonte, previo l'equipaggiamento e l'armamento degli anglo-americani, ma le autorità francesi ostacolano tutto questo, mentre d'altra parte favoriscono il loro accesso a brigate garibaldine internazionali, che sotto l'egida della F. L. T., sono inviate a battere per la liberazione della Spagna.

Bonomi, aiuta! aiuta!

« E' pertanto urgente l'invio del rappresentante del governo Bonomi presso il governo francese, al fine di porre termine a un simile stato di cose che viene in gran parte dal fatto che i francesi ci considerano in blocco come nemici.

« Sembrerebbe quindi opportuno di studiare la possibilità di una dichiarazione di alleanza italo-francese. Ciò avrebbe come effetto immediato di sollevare i nostri compatrioti internati in Francia dalla bassa ed ingiusta considerazione nella quale sono tenuti oggi. Inoltre, con l'appoggio anglo-americano, si avrebbe la possibilità di rafforzare notevolmente le nostre formazioni partigiane utilizzando parte degli alpini internati ». F.to: *Bellardy*.

La relazione del Comandante Bellardy è troppo chiara ed esplicita per richiedere commenti. Si può, tuttavia, fermarne alcune conclusioni. Queste:

1) Quei bravi alpini italiani, che hanno creduto a Badoglio e si sono schierati a combattere fra i « maquis » (partigiani) contro l'antico alleato, dopo aver dato prove di valore (valore italiano!), *sono stati trattati alla stregua degli altri prigionieri di guerra*.

2) Molti di essi *sono stati internati*; altri *sono stati posti al servizio delle truppe marocchine e costretti ad una vita bestiale*.

3) *Essi saranno costretti a combattere in Spagna* nelle sedicenti brigate garibaldine internazionali, accozzaglia di mercenari, di cui tutti ricordano la gesta compiute in territorio spagnolo.

4) *Gli italiani*, d'altronde, *sono in Francia considerati in blocco come nemici*.

5) Si chiede, da Roma, l'intervento di Bonomi. Ma l'uomo, che non ha saputo sfamare Roma, alleggerire le pene dei nostri fratelli del Meridione e porre un riparo alla tragedia siciliana, cosa potrà fare?

Partigiani, dopo tanti misconoscimenti, non vedete ancora da che parte sta il nemico vostro e dell'Italia?

BRIGANTI NERI !

Confesso di arrivare in ritardo. Non sono di quegli italiani di oggi, che per curiosità o per attendismo, hanno sempre la Radio aperta su Londra, o per raccogliere l'ultima balla, o per trarne buon auspicio per i giorni di poi; ad ogni modo soltanto qui vengo a conoscenza che la qualifica appioppata a noi delle « Brigate Nere » è quella di « Briganti Neri ».

Confesso che questa qualifica non mi ha affatto offeso e non ne ho tratto davvero alcun argomento di sdegno o di rossore. Il brigantaggio è un fenomeno, che più volte ha avuto moventi nobilissimi, se non fosse altro è sorto sempre dalla vendetta, che non può essere esercitata nell'ambito della legge; in quanto non sempre le leggi sono giuste, o, almeno, adatte a certi periodi storici, come quello che oggi viviamo.

E se il brigantaggio è sorto dalla vendetta, può anche darsi che noi siamo dei briganti. Se i nostri nemici badogliani-monarchici per una dinastia di traditori passati al nemico, che ha venduto a questo la Patria di Vittorio Veneto e delle cento battaglie del nostro Risorgimento, sostenitori del temporalismo dei Papi, comunisti, delinquenti fuggiti dalle galere, o liberali nelle giornate del tradimento, non avessero ucciso a tradimento — coi sistemi balcanici e moscoviti — migliaia di nostri, ci chiameremmo ancora « fascisti » come prima del 25 luglio, come prima dell'8 settembre, come ai primi tempi della Repubblica Sociale, quando ci siamo illusi di richiamare alla realtà i cittadini coi patti di pacificazione, cogli appelli alla concordia.

Quando abbiamo visto questa gentaglia, che ci ha creduti morti, infoltiti e invigliacchiti, formare le bande armate, rapinare, ricattare, compiere grassazioni per le strade maestre, o sulle strade delle nostre città martoriate da bombardamenti dei liberatori, disertare colle armi le caserme, seviziare, uccidere fascisti e guardie repubblicane, non risparmiando eroi purissimi della nostra rinascita; allora, per legittima difesa e per legittima rappresaglia, ci siamo armati di moschetti e di mitra e ci siamo vestiti nuovamente da squadristi.

Così la nostra divisa è tornata, come nei tempi eroici del Fascismo antemarcia, « occhio per occhio, dente per dente ». E questa divisa dobbiamo metterla in pratica tutti i giorni, senza pietà, senza misericordia.

Di chi la colpa? Facciamo tutti un esame di coscienza e tutti concluderanno che abbiamo avuto ragione noi a divenire « briganti ». Se, per questa vendetta, molti di questi nemici nostri hanno avuto raffiche di mitra, di chi la colpa? Se molti di loro sono tornati alle patrie galere, da dove li aveva liberati il tradimento ad insanguinare le nostre contrade, è colpa nostra? Se molti di loro, pentiti, hanno sentito la voce della Patria e sono tornati a combattere con noi, di chi la colpa?

Così siamo orgogliosi d'essere i « Briganti neri ». Non briganti regi, nè briganti rossi, perchè non saremo mai nè carabinieri, nè banditi balcanici; noi non abbiamo disertato le caserme all'avvicinarsi del nemico, nè abbiamo mai vissuto di denari del nemico, nè riempito di vittime incolpevoli le fosse di Bologna e dell'Istria, o malamente sepolte a fior di terra altre vittime egualmente martiri di un'idea, straziati dalla ferina bestialità dei fuori legge.

Noi combattiamo a viso aperto per la nostra Patria immortale, che vogliamo veder risorgere dalle rovine del tradimento; per il nostro onore combattiamo pei camerati germanici, che difendono le spalle dai prezzolati del nemico; per la liberazione vera della nostra terra, delle nostre case, delle nostre famiglie dall'oppressione dello straniero.

Combattiamo per Mussolini, nostro Capo e nostro Duce, per il Fascismo che darà al proletariato italiano una volta ancora la libertà ed il pane onorato, e per un domani migliore per tutti.

E non deporremo le armi, non cesseremo di essere romanticamente briganti, se non quando Roma sarà resa all'Italia e quando l'Italia sarà degli italiani veri, di quelli che avranno dimostrato di esserlo combattendo e ricacciando il nemico dalla nostra terra, ripulendola dai vecchi e nuovi nemici interni, monarchici, moderati, radicaloidi, massoni, clericali, comunisti, delinquenti e gente di ogni risma del genere; sino a che non potremo dare agli italiani la gioia di vivere in pace padroni in casa loro e senza incubi di tradimenti.

Sino a quel giorno saremo, ancora e sempre, i « briganti neri »!

M. H.

Lavoratori, attenti!

Vogliamo citare il pensiero ognora dominante per il bolscevismo, espresso dall'ebreo Radek Sobelson, l'uomo di fiducia di Lenin e di Stalin, sul modo di trattare il lavoratore: « Noi bolscevichi sapremo insegnare il digiuno agli operai che, in caso di rivolta, domeremo a colpi di mitragliatrice. L'operaio libero diventa gradatamente indisciplinato, mentre quello che deve guadagnarsi il pane quotidiano sotto lo stimolo della fame, e, privato di ogni diritto civile, teme di essere ucciso per la più piccola resistenza, è l'operaio più docile di cui noi abbisogniamo ».

> La nostra fede assoluta nella vittoria non poggia su motivi di carattere soggettivo o sentimentale, ma su elementi positivi e determinanti.
> **MUSSOLINI**

Non occorrono altri commenti per inquadrare il trattamento che sarà usato ai lavoratori italiani in Russia, lavoratori di un paese sconfitto in guerra e quindi immeritevole di qualsiasi privilegio. Migliaia di uomini sono quindi strappati alla nostra razza, che ne subisce un [...]eramento pericolosiss[...] [...]gliaia di [...] [...]olte e pr[...] del procreame[...] [...]e base indispensabile per il divenire della Nazione.

Il brodo si fa con l'acqua

I marescialli americani e inglesi cominciano già a lamentare l'insufficiente rifornimento di uomini e di materiali, i reggimenti e le divisioni canadesi rumoreggiano a casa loro contro la plutocrazia che li spinge sui campi di battaglia: in una parola, è un segno chiaro che anche per gli altri il brodo si fa con l'acqua.

Non abbiamo mai sottovalutato la forza immensa degli anglo-americani, ma neppure ci siamo lasciati accecare o bluffare dalle loro acrobazie numeriche e propagandistiche. Non esistono riserve inesauribili ed anche per i giovani americani, canadesi e della vecchia Inghilterra e domani vale la legge: non risorge chi è già sepolto.

La nascita di un'epoca nuova è sempre dolorosa, e soltanto le prove più severe possono estirpare dall'animo nostro gli ultimi avanzi di un secolo trapassato. Che sono ormai per noi i gingilli e il ciarpame della cosidetta proprietà? Noi possiamo perdere ancora parecchie cose, ma senza che ciò ci renda più poveri. Più liberi, non altro!

*A cura del Comando della
21a Brigata Nera - Verona*

1[...]

L'anno [...] più favore[...]

Sotto la p[...] le Armate [...] scattate all'[...] ricani stan[...] ne di terren[...] tale, mentr[...] nale divisio[...] che hanno [...] penetrando [...] schieramen[...]

Finalme[...] terra, in ci[...] no ad appa[...] gegni miste[...] riosi, almen[...] tanto parlat[...] del morent[...] rendendosi [...] per lui vin[...] speranze va[...] to i colpi d[...]

Inutile, [...] bilancio de[...] to il disor[...] dagli infau[...] 1943, altro [...] no di lento [...] continua ri[...] presa del c[...]

Il 1945 [...] rate a fianc[...] germanici [...] cienti e co[...] pubblicana, [...] tradito la s[...] che mantie[...] zione moral[...] cisa a ricon[...] dominio te[...]

Roma an[...] l'urto delle [...] battaglie na[...] fetti talvolt[...] ritenere p[...] messa la su[...] non ha ma[...]

196

Brigata Nera
"S. Rizzardi"

...o per tutti, tutti per uno, tutti per l'Italia!

*. US.   NOTIZIARIO DELLA 21ª B. N. (Verona)   30 dicembre 1944 - XXIII

5

chè, alla fine essa è sempre riuscita a imporsi ai suoi nemici e a trionfare su tutti i popoli del mondo.

re sotto i

La Roma repubblicana d'oggi — per riassumere in questo nome grandissimo, unico al mondo, tutto il vasto territorio metropolitano, tutta la forza intellettuale e morale di un grande popolo — vincerà anche questa guerra.

oriosa del che sono nglo-ame-vaste zo-Occiden-Meridio-germani-sorpresa, ente nello

La nostra fede nel risultato finale di questo spaventoso conflitto mondiale non ha mai vacillato; ma, oggi, di fronte ai primi grandi successi iniziali, che preludiano, in modo indubbio, alle vittorie del 1945, essa è più viva e più ferma che mai.

bellico te-in giorno,

Noi, delle Brigate Nere, cui

venne fissato dal DUCE il compito di ripulire le vie per le quali passerà domani, irresistibile, la Vittoria, in questo scorcio d'anno, agli albori del nuovo, qui ripetiamo, ad auspicio di successo, il nostro giuramento: COMBATTERE!

Combattere per impedire al nemico l'accesso alla Valle del Po; combattere per ricacciarlo al suo punto di partenza, oltre i confini della Patria violata; combattere per impedire ai fuori-legge una criminale collaborazione col nemico; combattere per ripulire l'Italia da tanti indegni sedicenti figlioli, che altro non si sono rivelati che ignobili bastardi.

Combattere per vincere!

Il Duce parla agli italiani

Socializzazione

Noi neghiamo ai paesi super-capitalisti il diritto e la possibilità di issare l'insegna della socializzazione perchè la loro truffa è troppo evidente; come neghiamo

> Noi vogliamo difendere, con le unghie e coi denti, la Valle del Po; noi vogliamo che la Valle del Po resti repubblicana in attesa che tutta l'Italia diventi repubblicana.
>
> **MUSSOLINI**

il medesimo diritto ai partiti antifascisti, siano essi comunisti o democratici o liberali, perchè la socializzazione non è materia che possa rinchiudersi negli alambicchi delle comuni combinazioni politiche; ma è una bandiera dello spirito che sventola al di sopra di tutti i popoli; è il nuovo credo nella quale domani giureranno tutte le collettività cosiddette proletarie.

L'incoerenza altrui è troppo evidente. E' ormai noto a chiunque che Gran Bretagna e Stati Uniti son scesi in lotta appunto per distruggere nel Fascismo il lievito di quella rivoluzione sociale che minacciava direttamente i loro feudi, fortificato dallo sfruttamento del lavoro, e i plutocrati non possono rinnegare se stessi rinnegando il loro programma. Nè i multicolorati partiti dell'Italia invasa possono comprendere il valore della socializzazione, essi che hanno dato sempre miserabile spettacolo della loro impotenza spirituale e che oggi si dilettano delle risse di parte, ignari della Nazione, ignari dei bisogni del popolo; essi che mai, e oggi meno di ieri, hanno offerto al popolo la luce di un ideale.

> ...Il mondo sa
>   che la Camicia Nera
> s'indossa
>   per combattere e morir...

ОТ ПРЕДСТАВИТЕЛЯ УПОЛНОМОЧЕНОГО СОВЕТСКОГО ПРАВИТЕЛЬСТВА В ЗАПАДНОЙ ЕВРОПЕ ПО ДЕЛАМ ВОЗВРАЩЕНИЯ СОВЕТСКИХ ГРАЖДАН НА РОДИНУ

ТОВАРИЩИ!

Близится час вашего освобождения.

Красная Армия уже выбила фашистское зверье из пределов нашей родной земли, освободила от немецких захватчиков народы Румынии, Финляндии, Болгарии, значительную часть Польши и Венгрии, часть Чехословакии и подала руку помощи союзной нам Югославии.

Героическая Красная Армия продолжает наносить сокрушительные удары по немецким ордам уже на германской территории. Войска наших союзников разгромили немцев во Франции и Бельгии и перешли западные границы Германии.

Окружение гитлеровской Германии завершается.

Многие тысячи советских граждан, бойцов и командиров Красной Армии, освобожденные из фашистского плена, уже возвратились на свою родную советскую землю и принимают участие в окончательном разгроме гитлеровской Германии — злейшего врага нашей Родины.

Срок вашего освобождения из немецкого рабства во многом зависит от вас самих.

198. The Italian Post was a newspaper for troops in Italy.

199. Soldiers dreaming about home.

Der Schinken mit dem Grübchen

Erzählung von Hans Freytag

Im Sommer des Jahres 1715 bummelte durch die Gassen der Pariser Altstadt ein junger Bursche, der nichts als einen zerlöcherten Anzug und einen hübschen Wuschelkopf sein eigen nannte. Als er vor einer Metzgerei auftauchte, flog nicht ein Schinkenstück in seine Hand, sondern der scharfe Fleischerhund schnappte nach den Fetzenrändern seiner Hosen. Da rief Jean, er wolle gar nichts Essbares, sondern ein Stück Papier haben, nichts als ein Stück weissen Papiers. Das verwunderte die dicke Frau hinter dem Ladentisch, und sie warf ihm den Wisch hin, um zu sehen, was er wohl damit vorhabe.

Jean Chardin liess sich auf der Schwelle der Metzgerei nieder, zog ein Stückchen Kohle aus der Tasche und hatte nach wenigen Augenblicken die Konturen der Meisterin, ein wenig verschmälert, ein wenig verschönt, auf jeden Fall anmutig geschmeichelt aufs Papier gezaubert. Am Ende kam ein Tauschhandel zustande: die Zeichnung wanderte über den Ladentisch, und eine Schinkenscheibe wanderte zu Jean. Daraus wurde mit den Tagen ein ordentliches Geschäft, das dem armen Jean über die ersten Zeiten der Teuerung nicht schlecht hinweghalf.

Eines Morgens hatte er einen neuen Einfall. Er kaufte sich Kohle, Kreide, Rötel, einen Blaustift, und damit erschien er wieder vor dem Metzgerladen der üppigen Frau Leroux.

Er fing gleich an, auf der Schwelle kauernd, Schinken, Kalbskeulen, Würste und einen ganzen ausgeweideten Ochsen in einem reichen Stilleben abzuzeichnen. Sein Blatt war so naturnahe, so saftig und verlockend, dass Madame selber in Entzücken geriet. Das bunte Bildchen schmeichelte ihr nicht weniger als ihr Porträt über dem Ladentisch. Sie stellte es neben einem Teller Würste und konnte sich nicht genug damit tun, die Malerei vor ihren Kunden zu loben, wobei es ihr gelang, die Portionen etwas kleiner zu schneiden und die Preise etwas höher anzusetzen. Der junge Mann hob ihr Geschäft ganz entschieden.

Jean Chardin würde nun wohl für einige Wochen ausgesorgt haben, wenn Madame nicht eine besonders hübsche Tochter gehabt hätte. Sie hatte veilchenblaue Augen und bezaubernde Grübchen; und sie fand den Wuschelkopf trotz seines zerlöcherten Rockes so nett, dass sie diese veilchenblauen Augen heftig spielen liess.

Jean, der eben erst anfing, den Reiz der Frauen zu entdecken, war bald sterblich in das junge Mädchen verliebt. Die Stilleben wurden spärlicher, dafür strichelte er die Denise Leroux in allerlei beobachteten und erträumten Stellungen auf sein Papier, und nur wenn Madame sich nach dem Fortschritt des neuesten Blattes umsah, fuhr er kräftig mit seinen Rötelstiften die Konturen eines Schinkens entlang; doch konnte er es nicht unterlassen, ihm ein speckiges Grübchen einzusetzen, wie es der Schinken in natura nie besitzt. Der kritische Verstand der Metzgerin verbat sich diese Ausschmückung, was die schweifende Phantasie des Malers arg beengte.

Nach zwei Tagen wurde ihm mit wenig Worten und viel Deutlichkeit erklärt, dass das Nachlassen seiner Leistung unweigerlich zum Verlust der Ernährungsquelle führen werde. Diese resolut angedeutete Kündigung trat auch schon nach vierundzwanzig Stunden ein, als der etwas zu herzhafte Laut eines Kusses die Meisterin hinter die Ladentür lockte, wo sie ihre Tochter Denise mit dem Kritzler in vertrautester Umarmung erwischte. Es war ein Glück, dass sie nicht das grosse Fleischermesser in der Hand hatte. So benutzte sie nur ihren kräftigen Fuss.

Jean fand wie so viele seines Zeichens, dass Undank ein schlimmes Menschenlaster sei. Er wanderte weiter. Nun, da er seine Kräfte wachsen fühlte, trieb es ihn, andere Gegenstände nach der Natur zu zeichnen. Er entdeckte Früchte, auch sie ernährten ihn dank der Treue seines Könnens bei mancher Hökerin; er entdeckte Bäume und Menschen, und es dauerte gar nicht lange, dass die Kenner von Bildern auf seine Zeichnungen aufmerksam wurden, sie mit Geld aufwogen. Er konnte sich ein eigenes Zimmerchen mieten. Aus den Kennern wurden Gönner, aus den Zichnungen Bilder, und der Name Jean Chardin bekam einen Klang.

Immerhin, er war ein treuer Bursche, treu gegenüber den Menschen, die seine Anfänge ermöglicht hatten, treu seinen ersten Motiven, vielleicht auch treu gegen die Kleine Denise, deren Kuss er nicht vergessen konnte. Schiesslich hatte er jetzt Geld in der Tasche. So ging er eines Tages zu der stattlichen Metzgerin. Er hatte ja nun einen gutgeschnittenen Rock, das Haar war unter einer Perücke zusammengenommen: aus seinen Augen war die Frechheit geschwunden, nur die Fröhlichkeit war darin geblieben.

Madames Geschäfte gingen auch ohne seine Stilleben, der Ladentisch war wieder wohlbestellt. Was er wünsche, fragte sie, bereit, mit dem grossen Messer von Keule oder Wurst abzuschneiden.

Jean wies auf einen saftigen Braten. Nebenher fragte er, wie es dem Fräulein Denise gehe. Sie blickte auf, jetzt erkannte sie ihn. «Es gibt kein Fräulein Denise mehr», sagte sie grimmig. «sie hat den Bäcker Eustache geheiratet.»

Jean machte ein betrübtes Gesicht. «Schade», sagte er.

«Schade? Was heisst schade? Sie wird es weiterbringen mit ihm als mit einem kritzelnden Hungerleider!»

«Also gut, Madame Leroux, geben Sie mir ein Pfund von dem da!»

Sie nannte den Preis, wog aber erst ab, nachdem er das Geld auf den Ladentisch gezählt hatte. Dann kramte sie in einem Papierstoss. Und richtig, da war noch eines von den roten Stilleben. Jean wollte schon danach greifen, denn die Erinnerung an diesen Anfang rührte ihn. Aber resolut, wie sie war, warf Madame Leroux das Pfund Fleisch auf die Malerei, rollte das Päckchen zusammen und reichte es ihm hinüber.

Draussen vor dem Laden blieb Chardin stehen und wickelte es wieder auf. Das Fleisch gab er einem Burschen, der in einer Toreinfahrt sass, denn es regnete gerade; und dieser Bursche hatte genau solche Wuschelhaare und genau so frechfröhliche Augen wie er selber früher. Die Zeichnung — einen Schinken mit einem Grübchen — glättete er sorgfältig aus und trug sie unter dem Rock nach Hause

Heute befindet sie sich in dem Schloss der Bilder, im grossen Louvre, als eine Kostbarkeit unter den vielen farbigen Küchenstücken, die Chardin später noch in koloristischer Schönheit gemalt hat. An der unteren Ecke links ist ein beträchtlicher Fettfleck von jenem Fleischeinkauf her deutlich zu sehen.

PK-Aufn.: Schütze

Der Willkommensgruss für den U-Boot-Kommandanten

Ein U-Boot-Jäger, der in der Aegäis im Nahkampf mit Rammenstoss und Bordwaffen ein feindliches U-Boot vernichtete, kehrt in seinen Stützpunkt zurück. Zur Begrüssung erhält der Kommandant den Willkommensgruss genau so wie es bei den heimkehrenden U-Boot-Fahrern Brauch ist.

Kobold im Lichtschalter

Kleine Geschichte von Erwin Reitmann

Sie verdankten es einem Irrtum, einem kleinen Irrtum, dass sie sich kennenlernten.

So begann es: das Licht im Hause war plötzlich ausgegangen. Er suchte den Lichtschalter, traf aber den Klingelknopf und erschrak. Bevor er sich im Dunkel des Treppenflurs zurechtfand, wurde eine Tür geöffnet. Er sah in die Augen eines jungen Mädchens, grosse, fragende Augen.

«Verzeihung, mein Fräulein», stammelte Eugen, «ein kleiner Irrtum, ich suchte den Lichtschalter.»

«Oh, das macht nichts», lachte das Mädchen, «oh, jetzt erkenne ich Sie erst; sind Sie nicht der Herr, der über mir wohnt?»

«Ja, ja, ganz recht. — Sie kennen mich? Johannsen ist mein Name. Ich habe Sie in letzter Zeit wohl ein wenig viel geärgert, nicht wahr?

«Aber nein, warum denn?»

«Ich glaube doch. Ich war ein wenig rücksichtslos und bitte Sie um Entschuldigung darum.»

«Aber ich bitte Sie, das war doch wirklich nicht der Rede wert», warf sie ein.

«Doch, doch», beeilte er sich zu sagen, «Sie waren gerade eingezogen und mussten glauben, es ginge immer so laut über Ihnen zu. Aber glauben Sie mir, es war wirklich wie verhext: eine zufällige Anhäufung ungewöhnlicher Ereignisse. Ich hatte ein wenig Glück...»

«Oh, haben Sie in der Lotterie gewonnen?» fragte sie und blickte ihn schelmisch an.

«Nein, nicht gerade das, aber ich hatte Glück, eine richtige Glückssträhne, wissen Sie, das machte mich so froh und ausgelassen; können Sie das verstehen? Ich lud gute Freunde zu mir und feierte ein bissel. Denken Sie», gestand Eugen, «ich hatte wirklich vorgehabt, Sie einzuladen, nur fand ich dann nicht den Mut. Schliesslich kannte ich Sie ja auch gar nicht. Aber darf ich mein Versäumnis nachholen? Wir sind ein kleiner Kreis, und es wäre schön, wenn Sie mit von der Partie wären.»

Ihr Herz schlug schnelle, aber sie sagte vielen Dank, und das ginge doch nicht...

«Aber warum denn nicht? Hören Sie, dann sind wir so laut, dass Sie es einfach nicht aushalten und von allein heraufkommen, haha.»

«Ja, um mich zu beschweren.»

«Gut, die Hauptsache ist, Sie kommen überhaupt.»

Sie musste über ihn lachen, wie er gleichsam mit der Tür ins Haus fiel, sie überrumpelte.

Nein, sie kam nicht, obwohl sie es gar zu gern getan hätte. Gar zu gern! Da sass sie nun aufgeregt in ihrem besten Kleid und lauschte auf jeden Laut. Warum hatte sie sich schön gemacht? Ach, nur so, warum sollte sie sich nicht schön machen?

Sie hörte die Gäste die Treppe heraufkommen, hörte das lustige Hallo der Begrüssung. Sie glaubte ihren Namen zu hören, aber das war wohl nur Einbildung Dann machten sie oben Musik, wurden immer lustiger. Und Randi sass da und lauschte auf alles. Würde man sie holen? Sie träumte vor sich hin, nickte ein, dann fuhr sie auf: es klingelte! Sie wusste sofort, wer es war. Als sie öffnete, stand Eugen Johannsen draussen.

«Oh», tat sie überrascht, «Sie Herr Johannsen?»

Noch immer sträubte sie sich. Da kam einer seiner Freunde herunter und half ein wenig nach.

Na, und nun ging sie mit nach oben.

«Ah!» riefen die Gäste, als sie eintraten. Sie begrüssten Randi wie eine gute Bekannte. Einer sagte, als er ihr die Hand gab: «Freut mich, Sie kennenzulernen, hab' schon von Ihnen gehört...»

«Was sagen Sie da?» erwiderte sie überrascht.

«Ja, Ihretwegen sind wir doch heute hier zusammen...»

«Ach so», meinte Randi, als Eugen sie unterfasste und weiterführte, «ich bin wohl eine der zufälligen Anhäufungen unvorhergesehener Ereignisse? Ich möchte bald gehen, Herr Johannsen.»

Er liess sie nicht gehen, er erzählte ihr, wie er mit einem Bild einen grossen Erfolg errungen habe. Nun sei der Durchbruch gelungen, jetzt gehe es aufwärts, deshalb sei er in der letzten Zeit so ausser Rand und Band. «Verstehen Sie das?»

Randi nickte.

Plötzlich nahm Eugen sie bei der Hand, führte sie in einen Nebenraum und zeigte einige seiner Arbeiten. Sie war überwältigt.

«Aber warten Sie, da müssen wir mehr Licht haben!»

Er schaltete alle Lampen ein, da fing das Licht an zu flackern, es gab Kurzschluss. Eugen wollte den Schaden beheben, tastete sich durch das dunkle Zimmer und lief Randi in die Arme. Nun ja, es ergab sich ganz von selbst, dass sie sich küssten...

Das war auf den Tag genau vor zehn Jahren. Nun, da die immer noch sehr glückliche Frau Randi an ihren Mann schrieb und ihn, den Soldaten irgendwo im Osten, daran erinnerte, stand alles so nahe vor ihr, als sei es gestern gewesen. Und sie wusste, einmal wird es wieder so sein, — so schön und so unbeschwert wie damals. Nach dem Siege...

Ungefähre Schätzung

Karl Valentin traf nach längerer Zeit wieder einmal einen Jugendfreund, der nicht genug von seinen Erfolgen als Schriftsteller erzählen konnte. Schliesslich meinte abschliessend der Freund: «Was denkst du, mein Lieber, was seit der Zeit, als wir uns das letztemal sahen, alles von mir veröffentlicht worden ist?!».

Valentin, dem der Jugendfreund als Renomierer bekannt war, zog die Stirn in nachdenkliche Falten: «Was i denk'? Die knappe Hälft'!».

Nicht so einfach

In der Zeichenstunde wollte die Lehrerin die Phantasie der Kinder anregen und sagte: «So Mädels, nun nehmt mal jede ein Blatt Papier und zeichnet, was ihr später werden wollt!»

Bald war alles Mögliche dargestellt, ein Damenhut, ein Mantel, ein Kochherd und Telefonapparat und anderes mehr. Nur Gerda hatte ihr Blatt noch leer. Die Lehrerin fragt: «Hast du gar keinen Wunsch fürs spätere Leben?».

Gerda war etwas verlegen: «Doch ich möchte mal heiraten, aber weiss nicht, wie man das zeichnet».

Gesegnetes Land

Zwei Chikagoer unterhalten sich:

«Das ist das Schöne in den Staaten, man braucht nicht viel, um vorwärts zu kommen. Ich zum Beispiel habe einmal in kurzer Zeit ein grosses Juweliergeschäft mit grossen Erfolg aufgemacht.»

«Und was hattest du als Anfangskapital?»

«Nur drei Dollar zum Ankauf einer Brechstange»

Beruhigende Versicherung

Neumann ist von langer Krankheit genesen. Er drückt dem Arzt dankbar die Hand: «Ich werde Ihre Hilfe nie vergessen, Herr Doktor!»

Der Mediziner wollte scherzen: «Vergessen Sie auch nicht meine vierundzwanzig Besuche!»

Neumann beteuert: «Wie werde ich das, Herr Doktor? Ich werde sie alle erwidern.»

Der leidende Dritte

Der kleine Hartmann ist unartig und die Mutter droht ihm: «Wenn du nicht gleich artig bist, darfst du am Sonntag nicht zum Grossvater!»

Der Kleine zuckt bedauernd die Achsel: «Ja, wenn du dem Opa wirklich den ganzen Sonntag verderben willst!»

Gewohnung

Hein kommt, nach Jahren wieder in seine Heimatstadt, trifft einen Jugendfreund und fragt: «Was ist eigentlich aus der hübschen Marianne geworden, die allen Malern hier zu sitzen pflegte?»

«Ach, sie ist ihrer Gewohnheit treu und ist sitzen geblieben.»

Der schlagfertig Narr

Clement Marot gehörte zu den Lustigmachern Franz' I. von Frankreich. Als er eines Tages mit einem Hofkavalier den gleichen Weg hatte, schritt er rechts neben diesem einher. Der Hofkavalier brauste auf: «Ich kann es nicht leiden, wenn ein Narr an meiner rechten Seite geht.»

«Aber ich wohl, gnädiger Herr!» antwortete Marot und wechselte nach links hinüber.

198

italienpost
ICHTENBLATT

FUER DIE DEUTSCHEN SOLDATEN IN ITALIEN

Samstag, den 18. Dezember 1943   Nr. 79

...st zu den Italienkämpfen!

...nie stiess ich auf so starke Stellungen!"

...chlachten erlebt — aber auf ...agen bin ich noch nie gestos... ...ten begrüsste der amerikani... ...anden Oberst Crawford, als ... seinen rückwärtigen Kom... ..., den Kriegsberichterstatter Time », Lang, der in seinen ...en Bericht von dem harten ... die deutschen Truppen in ...mit einer geradezu unheim... ...elsicherheit und Exaktheit ... Artillerie jedes Haus oder ... die amerikanischen Truppen ...en, in Brand », erklärte der ... deutschen Stellungen selbst ... hineingesprengt und stellten ... herankommen könnten. Al... ...den amerikanischen Abtei... ...-Pass gegenüber, der von den ...ugeschnitt sei. Noch im Früh... ...anischen Soldaten im Mittel... ...eugt gewesen, dass sie Weih... ...würden. Nun hätten sie kein... ...nung, noch vor Weihnachten

...von den Kämpfen in Italien ...eralmajor Raimond Hamilton ...von der italienischen Front ...on eingetroffen ist. Der Krieg ...ichtet vor Vertretern der ... ...ein Kampf der Ingenieure ...chen sprengten jede Brücke ... Taktik, ihre Artillerie ...d ihre Tanks an geschützten ..., von wo aus sie die Ameri... ...geleitetes und vernichtendes ... Von einem Nachlassen der ...chen Truppen könne gar kei... ...äre auch nicht das geringste ...äte, dass die Deutschen in ...öher gelegenen Bergstellungen ...e auch grosse strategische

...tion beschwert sich dann ...des der amerikanischen Nach... ...nen könnten in dem schwie... ...en Gepäck mitführen, und es ...chwer, den Nachschub mit ...r führen, denn der Mangel an ...ausserordentlich gross. Die ...en müssten darum in Käl... ...ingen und seien im höchsten ...ausgehöpft. Völlig durchnässt ... ...erwältigt, sähe man sie zit... ...ch auf den schweren Kâl... ... ...Schluck warmen Kaffees sei ...enn das Holz sei zu nass, um ... habe keine richtige Versor... ...annschaften murrten, so er... ...eben Fortschritte in dem ... ...Man höre sie oft fragen, ob ... ...n ihre Enkel aufwachsen zu

...Presse bereitet die USA-Oef... ...h auf die schweren Verluste ...r in Italien erleiden. Ange... ... an einen langen und har... ...e bittere Enttäuschung ... ...n Truppen, dass sie, wie ...ribune » mitteilt, nicht mit ...nen könnten, denn wie das ...mando angekündigt hat, ...chwierigkeiten nicht, die in ...USA-Soldaten auf Heimatur...

...gen die kommunistischen

...der Waffen-SS bekämpf... ...ajevo noch auftretende Ba... ...ützte Pionierkampfgruppe ... Mokro, ein für uneinnehm...

...bar gehaltenes Kastell, an, Strassensperren, zerstör... ...te Brücken, zahlreiche Widerstandsnester und Hin... ...terhalte vermochten den Vormarsch der Pioniere nicht aufzuhalten. Sie nahmen das Kastell im Sturm ...und brachen dadurch den Riegel auf, der den Zutritt zu einem Lager der Kommunisten verspe... ...re und rollten Spähwagen, Sturmgeschüt... ...ze und motorisierte Kolonnen auf Sokolac zu, das ... die Bandita vor unseren heranrückenden Soldaten ...fluchtartig räumten.

In Südbosnien haben die deutschen und ver... ...bündeten Truppen die kommunistischen Banden aus weiteren Ortschaften geworfen, in denen diese ...sich für den Winter eingerichtet und verschanzt hatten. Die Bandita hatten hierbei wiederum schwere Verluste. Allein in Abschnitt eines Regi... ...ments verloren die Kommunisten während der letz... ...ten Woche 350 Tote. Die tatsächliche Zahl der ge... ...fallenen Banditen ist, wie durch Gefangene bestä...

Erfolgreicher Gegenangriff bei Kirowograd
103 Sowjetpanzer abgeschossen - Schwere Kämpfe im Raum von Newel

Aus dem Führerhauptquartier, 17. Dezember. Das Oberkommando der Wehrmacht gibt bekannt:

In der Strasse von Kertsch versenkte eine Ma... ...rineküstenbatterie ein bolschewistisches Schnellboot und schoss zwei feindliche Bomber ab. Erneute, von Panzern und Schlachtfliegern unterstützte An... ...griffe der Bolschewisten gegen den Brückenkopf von Cherson wurden von unseren Panzerjägern unter hohen blutigen Verlusten für den Feind abgewiesen und dabei 19 Sowjetpanzer abgeschossen. Die Sow... ...jets griffen auch gestern im Raum von Kirowograd an zahlreichen Stellen mit starken Kräften ver... ...geblich an. Unsere Gegenangriffe gewannen in har... ...ten Kämpfen weiterhin Boden. Der Feind verlor ...hierbei 33 Panzer und 22 Geschütze.

Zwischen Pripjet und Beresina scheiterten zah... ...reiche feindliche Angriffe. Auch im Raum von Shlo... ...bin wurden starke Angriffe der Sowjets abgewiesen, sowie Bereitstellungen und Panzeransammlungen zersprengt. Westlich Kritschew griff der Feind im Schutze künstlichen Nebels ohne jeden Erfolg an. Im Raum südwestlich Newel dauerten schwere Infanteriekämpfe während des ganzen Tages an. 51 feindliche Panzer wurden im Bereich eines Armee... ...korps abgeschossen. Die Sowjets hielten ihre An... ...griffe gestern auch auf dem Raum westlich und

nordwestlich Newel an. oertliche Angriffe gegen einen vordringenden Stellungsangriff südlich Lenin... ...grad scheiterten unter hohen Verlusten für den Feind.

An der süditalienischen Front dauern die Abwehr... ...kämpfe beiderseits Venafro an. Im Ostabschnitt setz... ...te britische Kräfte von starker Artillerie und Flie... ...gerkräften unterstützt ihre Angriffe fort. Im Verlauf erbitterter Kämpfe erzielte der Feind trotz hoher blutiger Opfer nur geringen Geländegewinn. Ein beab... ...sichtigter Durchbruch scheiterte, zahlreiche Panzer des Feindes wurden vernichtet und 10 britisch-nord... ...amerikanische Flugzeuge abgeschossen.

Feindliche Fliegerverbände flogen bei Tag über die deutsche Bucht ein und warfen eine grosse Zahl Spreng- und Brandbomben auf Wohngebiete ver... ...schiedener nordwestdeutscher Orte. Dadurch ent... ...standen besonders in Bremen schwere Zerstörungen. Unersetzliche Kulturdenkmäler wurden vernichtet.

In den Abendstunden führten britisch-nordame... ...rikanische Bomberverbände erneut einen schweren Terrorangriff gegen die Reichshauptstadt. Es ent... ...standen beträchtliche Schäden. Luftverteidigungs... ...kräfte vernichteten trotz wettermässig schwieriger Abwehrbedingungen, soweit bisher festgestellt, 38 der angreifenden britisch-nordamerikanischen Bom... ...ber.

Universität in der Wildmark Lapplands
Generaloberst Dietl besuchte die erste Front-Universität

Der Oberbefehlshaber der deutschen Truppen im nordfinnischen Raum. Generaloberst Dietl, be... ...suchte mit dem kommandierenden General einer deutschen Gebirgskompanie, der in seinem Bereich die erste Front-Universität geschaffen hatte, die Studenten dieser einzigartigen «Urwalduniversität» in der Wildmark Lapplands. Vor den Professoren der deutschen Universitäten, den Dozenten und Studenten, die zu diesem Hochschullehrgang aus der kämpfenden Truppe gekommen waren, richtete Generaloberst Dietl einen leidenschaftlich vorgetra... ...genen und von den Soldaten begeistert aufgenom... ...menen Appell, im Entscheidungskampf unseres Volkes auf Leben und Tod die geistigen Kräfte mit der vollen Gläubigkeit ihrer jungen Herzen einzu... ...setzen und als geistige Vorkämpfer ihrer Kamera... ...den diesen schweren Schicksalskampf zu bestehen. Seinen besonderen Dank sprach Generaloberst Dietl dem kommandierenden General aus, der mit der Gründung dieser Front-Universität auch seiner Wunsch nach einer guten Betreuung der an der Front kämpfenden Hochschüler erfüllt habe. Dieser Hochschullehrgang wolle und könne kein Semester... ...ersatz sein, wohl aber diene er zur Auffrischung und Auffüllung des Wissens, der Übung des Geistes und der Schärfung des Verstandes. Ebenso dankte er den Professoren der deutschen Universitäten und Hochschulen, die sich mit ihrem reichen Wissen dieser im deutschen Hochschulwesen wohl einma... ...ligen Universität zur Verfügung gestellt haben.

„Sogno o son desto?"

dice il figlio nell'abbracciare la madre, che non vedeva da due anni. Era proprio realtà, per il paracadutista Vettorato Quinto già della 4a Cp.-I Btg.-Regt. Nembo del Rag... ...gruppamento Folgore. Egli era stato fatto prigioniero il 6 marzo '45, e dopo pochi gior... ...ni gli era stato concesso di recarsi al paese a visitare la propria famiglia.

Ecco l'incontro affettuoso con la madre! L'abbraccio ed il primo bacio non hanno ancora fatto svanire l'impressione del sogno; la realtà è cercata nella stretta prolungata, gli occhi devono incontrarsi, ripetutamen... ...te, per accertarsene.

L'inaspettato incontro con una amica inten... ...ta al lavoro. L'amore per la « sua » terra lo assale. Le sue mani, abituate da lungo tem... ...po ad imbracciare soltanto il fucile, ripren... ...deranno un giorno a lavorare la terra.

La famiglia riunita, dopo tanto tempo, a tavola, si serra attorno al « prigioniero » per sentire il racconto della sua odissea. L'ob... ...biettivo, indiscreto, sorprende un momento di commozione dei parenti, che non sanno capacitarsi del miracolo loro concesso.

200. How do you want to come home from war and meet the person who has been longing for you---crippled, dead, or alive? Think it over!

201. This soldier is reminiscing about civilian life after the war.

200

Yes - maybe if you were 16 years old...

If you had no experience of life, of its toils and troubles, or even of its beauty and sweetness...
If you knew nothing of blissful hours in the arms of a beloved woman...
If you knew nothing of the happiness that smiles out at you from the eyes of your children...
    If you had as yet nothing to lose...

Or - if you were 80 years old...

If everything lay behind you, love, the struggle for existence, maybe success in your work or profession...
If the strong, healthy years were past and the aches of old age were tormenting you, so that you felt you were a burden to yourself and to others...
    If you had nothing more to lose...
then maybe the thought of death would not be so very bitter.

But now you are in the bloom of your youth!

And how many of the best years of your life has this damned war already robbed you of? A whole colourful existence lies before you. At home a woman is longing for you, how long will she wait? At home your children are growing up, how long must they remain without a father?... And if you were never to come home?

Shall everything have been in vain?

Shall a nameless mound in this Godforsaken Italy be all that remains of you and your passion for life?
Or will you come home a cripple, thrust out of life's activities, forced to depend on the pity and charity of men?

No - you cannot possibly wish this!

Is there no way out? Think it over!

* 1331-3-45

Longing for you— but how much longer

Charlie in a good humour

Here I am, back again in the front line! Yes, boys, I've had a swell time. Naturally I'm in a good humour! When you come to think it over, there's a great difference between life here and back there. But I don't need to tell you that! After so many drinks and a lot of nice girls I'm not in the mood to talk about filthy war or anything like that.

The only thing is that it has set me thinking about the future.

You know the song, "When the lights go on again all over the world"?

It's not only a beautiful song, but it will be a beautiful thing too... when it comes!

Dear, dear, I can almost feel myself in civvies again! It'll be such a funny feeling when you wear a new white collar and a real fine hat for the first time! And don't forget, there are such things as silk shirts and gloves and fine coloured ties!

I imagine myself sitting in a bar with a really good whisky, a lot of money and a packet of "Player's"...

The other day I was with a nice Italian girl. She had a lot of lipstick and make-up on her face, but she was a lovely job! After a few hours she told me her boy was on the other side with Jerry! That gave me a bit of a shock! At once my thoughts flew home. Where was MY girl at this moment? What was she doing? Better not think of it! It's no use worrying, and you cant stop it anyhow!

I don't like most of the Italian girls, but my girl-friend reminded me of beautiful days I once spent with a girl on the Isle of Wight. You know Ventnor, isn't it lovely?

These are all memories of the past and thoughts of the future. I'm just full of them. It's not good to be always speaking about war, for there are still a few good things left in life, or wouldn't you like to try driving a 1946 or '47 model car? More streamline, more comfort, more speed, a radio and a girl - your girl? It's perhaps good to be a soldier at times, but it's still better to be a civvy!

For the last two weeks I'm busy planning for the time "After the war is over!" I hope it will be soon, but I'm afraid... Oh, hang it!

I was just going to start some war-talk!

Not today, old chaps! Let me dream, please! I'm whistling "When the lights go on again..."

There's only one drawback! It's still on the cards that I may be a dead hero before the return of "Happy Days!" No nightmares, please!

Boys, do what I did! Ask for leave and enjoy life!

If they wont give it you, there are other ways!

Cheerio, lots of luck,

As usual,
yours,
charlie

★ 1334 · 4 · 45

202. A wounded soldier glimpses heaven.

203. Who really profits by all the suffering and misery of war?

202

Charlie sniffs heaven

Say pals,

Isn't it a hell of a job to be making war in Italy in springtime? I ask you, is it playing the game? Mother Nature's just marvellous here, isn't she? And I can't help it. I feel rotten, I haven't a kick left in me! Yesterday the Sarge asked me how long I'd been a soldier! Rough, wasn't it? But since Alamein where I gave one of the new blokes a slap in the eye, I've not had a chance to become a sergeant! Never mind! The war'll soon be over and the girls can remember me as a private, a gunner, and basta!

And don't you forget it, Old England's still full of Yankeedoodles, nice boys, handsome boys, with money! They can make full use of their peculiar talent for combined operations without being disturbed by the nasty enemy...

Maybe I'll get my stripes in the Third World War...

The third World War!!! And poor F. D. R. not there to see it! A bit of tough luck... his favourite sport, after fishing of course!

He and our Winnie were pretty thick and kept an eye on Old Joe. I don't like Old Joe. There's something in his grin that makes me shiver and reminds me of the Cheshire Cat!

You remember, Don, the American boy told us Joe would be the death of F. D. R., making him travel all over the world and he not fit for it! And hanged if it doesn't turn out to be true! Joe's the winner, all along the line!

Thank God our Winnie's as strong as the British Lion and Bulldog Drummond put together... for all his big cigars and bigger and better whiskies. He calls himself a "Wandering Minstrel", too but at his age you can overdo that sort of thing... and one of these days Good Old Joe may be occupying the Big Three Throne alone... a sort of Big Three in One...

But damn it all, why think of death in this lovely place where everything is so alive, flowers, trees, birds, insects,...

But, by Jove, that damned Jerry is alive too, very much alive,... and kicking...

He's starting to make noises more like hell than springtime in Italy...

Look out! Moaning Minnie! Duck boys...

Damn, what was that? Oh my head! It feels fit to burst!

Am I wounded? Am I dying?... Like poor old F. D. R.?

By Jove, I... believe... I am...

Cheeeeerrrriiioooooobbbbbooooooyyyyssss

we'll meet again... in... Heaven...

★ 1333 - 4 - 45

203

203

He also had been told

that the Germans are a horde of Huns and barbarians, posing as supermen and with only one idea, to bring all Europe under their tyranny of terror.

He also had been told

that it was the sacred duty of all liberty-loving men to free Europe from the bestial cruelty of these Nazis.

He also had been told

that in fighting against these Huns it was necessary to hold out to the last, as the Germans illtreat and even kill their prisoners.

The day came when he was taken prisoner.

The „Hun" who had captured him pulled out his first-aid kit, bandaged his wounded hand and gave him a cigarette.

The „Hun" who brought him to the dressing station gave him a drink from his own flask and saw to it that he came under the doctor's care at once.

The „Hun" doctor who skilfully and gently extracted the splinter from his hand, gave him another cigarette and sent him off with a friendly pat on the back.

The „Hun" who brought him to the prisoners' camp knew a little English and told him and some of his pals all about his home and his family.

Then he understood

that all these German soldiers were neither Huns nor wild beasts nor did they pose as supermen. They were boys like his friends Bill, Fred and George, boys with the same joys and sorrows. They had the same claims on life as the English soldiers and, like them, they were also fed up with war.

And so everything was quite different

from what his newspapers and wireless, full of hate-propaganda, had been dinning into his ears. He had been the victim of a swindle, for he knew well enough now from all the German soldiers he had met and learned to know, that they were incapable of committing the atrocities recounted daily by his papers. They wanted to live in peace and attend to their work, and for this it was necessary that the world should allow them the same rights as any other nation. They were fighting for these rights and would not cease fighting until they obtained them. But nothing was further from their thoughts than to wish to dominate Europe. On the contrary, on their Eastern Front they were fighting the battle of this very Europe against the Asiatic hordes of the steppes beyond the Urals and the Caucasus, who, stirred up by Bolshevism, had attacked Europe with murder, violence and robbery. They would not be satisfied with the conquest of Germany alone, their goal was the revolutionising of the whole world. And while the Germans were fighting desperately against this onslaught, they were defending not only their own lives but were fighting for Europe and also for England, for him, Bill, Fred, George, and for everyting that made life worth living.

And so he began to reflect!

If everything that the anti-German hate-propaganda was saying was untrue, if the truth was something quite different, then there must be someone with an interest in this senseless slaughter among the nations of Europe. There must be someone who profits by all the suffering and misery of war.

Who is it?

This is a question worth thinking over.

* 1006-3-45

204. How many points do you have?

205. The sooner you beat Germany, the sooner you will have a chance for a Soviet motorcar. Three cheers for Russia and Bolshevism.

SAY CHUM, HOW MANY POINTS HAVE YOU?
Here is Joe's story. Is yours the SAME???

Joe was a farmer's son. He liked to get up in early mornings and do everything that his old man had for him. Till one morning Old Bossy kicked over a milk pail! Joe gets mad and joins the army. (What a reason!!!)

DATE		WHAT HAPPENED	POINTS
1941	July	So off to camp Joe went	0
	Aug.	First it was the basic training at Shilo!	0
	Sept.	Then remember the sand and flies at Petawawa!	0
	Oct.	How about the training in the northern Ontario?	0
	Nov.	Did you like the long route marches?	0
	Dec.	Then off to Halifax and Blighty. Remember the boatride!	0
1942	Jan.	Ah, England with the black outs and air raids!	1
	Febr., March, Apr.	Joe, remember Picadilly Circus!!	3
	May, June, July	And of course the big battles on Tiger scheme!	3
	Aug., Sept., Oct.	The Beaver!!!!!	3
	Nov., Dec.	Was H. E. 4 a picnic?	2
1943	Jan., Febr., March.	The last one, Timber Wolf!	3
	Apr., May, June	Sport, of course! The bloody ice hockey match	3
	July, Aug., Sept.	against the Islanders! Wounded! (0 points!)	
	Oct.	Last month in England. Now overseas!	1
	Nov.	At last you get a crack at Jerries. Sunny Italy!	3
	Dec.	But Joe, you are only there a month when you stop a bullet.	2
1944	Jan.	So off to the hospital. Two months!	2
	Febr., March, Apr.	Back in the lines. Really you can't say "Happy days are here again!"	
	May, June, July		
	Aug., Sept.	Eight months in the lines makes	24
	Oct.	What, the M. O. says you have Malaria? Hospital!	2
	Nov.	But after a second "happy" return to your comrades you	3
	Dec.	stay still in the lines till you have your 85 points!	3
			61
		You must have another 24 points = 8 months! That will be in August!	
1945	Aug.	Ready to go home?	85
	Sept.	Say, Joe, don't forget, there are a lot of boys with more then 85 points!	3
	Oct.	Sorry, boy, you must wait!	3
	Nov.	Still waiting!	3
	Dec.	Still waiting......	3
1946	Jan.	Still waiting......	3
	Febr.	When??????	3
			103

PERHAPS AT THE END OF 1946

...if in the meantime you haven't been killed!

85 POINTS!

And when his scope he had attained
And only the voyage home remained,
The poor old "Canuck" deeply sighed,
Turned on his side — — — and died.

And his poor old pals who after him came
Wept, for they knew their fate was the same,
Their tears wet their beards so hoary and thick,
For hope deferred had made their hearts sick.

★ 2201-1-45

Do you want a motorcar?

It only costs £ 22 to own one.

Tomorrow's car will be fully streamlined, a comfortable and roomy 4 seater saloon, in duco colours and of wondrous new fabrics and plastics. It will be more than just a «good-looker», for this will have an easy cruising speed of 90 miles per hour and radio will be standard equipment.

But it will cost only £ 22! Today, you cannot buy this car anywhere.

Tomorrow, you will; in Freetown, Singapore, Capetown, Paris, Berlin, London, Quebec, New York, Chicago, in fact anywhere there are enough people who have £ 22 ($ 110).

How soon can you own this wonder car of tomorrow?

As soon as Germany is beaten, you shall have a chance to own this wonder car. Stalin, Roosevelt and Churchill have pledged that for you, down there on the Black Sea.

The moment Germany is beaten, the wheels of Soviet mass production will start in, not only in Soviet Russia, but in Soviet Estonia, Soviet Latvia, Soviet Lithuania, Soviet Finland, Soviet Poland, Soviet Bulgaria, Soviet Hungary, Soviet Rumania, Soviet Serbia, Soviet Croatia, and above all Soviet Germany.

There, in super mammoth factories under Soviet Russian direction, with the cheapest raw materials from Soviet Siberia, Europe and the East and with millions of the cheapest labour in the world including 40 million highly technical German forced - labourers, this super car, together with many other technical marvels will be supplied to the world, at a rate better than 254 cars a minute, day and night, and for seven days a week.

From these mammoth factories even a bicycle will cost no more than $ 3.74 or a chromium de luxe model $ 4.25.

Production costs will be almost nil, for these new workers of Europe will make your wonder car as cheap as possible. They won't need much to eat and they will have no expensive lodging problems, for they will be collectivised. There will be no overheads or advertising costs, for in a short time there will be no other world competitors.

The sooner you beat Germany the sooner you will have a chance of a Soviet WONDER CAR!

Then there will be no more war and no more work for you to do, everything will be done for you by the workers of Soviet Europe at rates and hours that would be impossible for you to work or live. All you need do is sit at home and devote your time to collecting your dole and doing the football pools, for if you should ever win as little as £ 22 ($ 110), you, too, can own the cheapest and best car in the world.

Down with Germany!
Hurrah for Soviet Europe!

Three cheers for the cheapest automobile in the world!
Three cheers for the Bolshevik world-market and bigger and better unemployment doles after the war!

★ 1004 - 3-45

206. The lives of many allied soldiers were lost right at the very end of the war.
Russia claimed a million soldiers died during the three days before Berlin fell.

207. Liberty, what crimes are committed in thy name!

Charlie tells the truth!

Say, chums, here's a new voice! Of course, it's not your master's voice, but here come the thoughts of a soldier just like you! I'm no more than one of the millions of suffering soldiers in the world. I'm an Allied soldier!»

I'm, so to say, the blank file in all your parades. I know what's what and I want to put your thoughts into words for you.

In short, I'm Charlie the Gunner!

Just now I want you to keep your brains clear, for in the coming weeks, the Big Show is timed to start on the Italian front. What do I mean? Well, our officers are talking about large scale attacks against Jerry! Isn't that the limit? Listen, in the East, the Red Army is about 40 miles from Berlin. In the West, our Armies are going forward along the Rhine. And we here in Italy? What are WE doing? We could of course wait till the bloody thing was over, but no, we must get ready for new attacks! That means heavy losses again and, for many pals, a single ticket to the devil! The mountains here are not friendly and the Po is wide, deep, and... very, very wet! There can be only two possibilities:

You and I know that the battlefront here is of secondary importance. So, either our Generals are taking a last chance to snatch a victory and make fame in military history, or our dear Winnie and Franklin Delano must have some victories to put up in San Francisco against Good Old Joe!

At the last moment we must end our lives in Italian mud and dust. We could win this war without any great attacks in Italy! But our Commanders and our Government say: No! Ten thousand dead heroes more or less make no difference to us and we need them to balance our bill with Stalin's, when the «Golden Gate of San Francisco» is opened for the great Peace Conference on the first of April...»

Sorry, boys, I made a slight slip about the date, it's the 25th of April, not the first! But what can WE do? We can't even raise our voices against these Hero-makers! So, come along boys, be quick about it and

kick the bucket for them!

While the Golden Gate of San Francisco is opening to receive Winnie F. D. R. and St. Joe to the Great Conference which is to bring Peace on Earth to Men of Goodwill, the «Golden Gate of Heaven» will be opened for many of you by Good Old St. Peter, saying:

«Come inside and choose your harp, You've had your share of Hell»

So, till next time! Yours

Charlie

Gone with the wind---

From the diary of an
American thinker who
knew about the hoax
but had to give his
life for it.

American Purpose

"*It doesn't matter how the boys who went over the Big Hill would define the purpose, because life goes on without them. It is for us to decide whether they died for the fulfilment of a worthy purpose like the boys of the American revolution or whether they died once again for the fulfilment of practically NOTHING like the boys of World War I. The decision should not be difficult for AMERICA HAS NO REAL WAR AIM. There is nothing so vital to America at stake that it would justify the death of perhaps a million men and the maiming of millions of others.*"

American Freedom

"*Freedom cannot be exclusive. Potentially or in fact it must include all mankind. If freedom is to survive for one, it must be established for all. The attempt to make it exclusive in any sense is suicidal and the application of this principle beyond our shores is equally urgent. Freedom cannot long survive in America if we conceive of it as exclusively American.*"

So far the dead soldier's notes. They contain beautiful words but what are you doing to fulfil them? You are fighting and perhaps dying to hand over Europe to a Bolshevik slavery worse than death.

"*Liberty, what crimes are committed in thy name!*"

* 424-3-45

Sempre presenti !

Il Ministro della Marina Knox e il Primo Lord dell'Ammiragliato debbono fare questa rattristante constatazione poichè i sommergibili germanici non hanno cessato di infliggere al nemico duri colpi.

NELL'ATLANTICO E NEL MEDITERRANEO

Sommergibili hanno affondato, durante la settimana di Natale, 5 piroscafi per 34.500 tonn. Essi hanno pure mandato a picco 9 cacciatorpediniere ed altro naviglio adibito al servizio di scorta a convogli.

VIOLENTO COMBATTIMENTO NAVALE NEL GOLFO DI BISCAGLIA

Come comunicato a mezzo di bollettino straordinario, il 31 dicembre furono inflitte alla marina da guerra inglese gravi perdite. Cacciatorpediniere e torpediniere germanici danneggiavano gli incrociatori inglesi «Glasgow» e «Enterprise» e ne incendiarono un terzo. Sommergibili germanici affondavano durante lo stesso scontro sei caccia britannici.

35 PIROSCAFI DI MENO

Nel corso del mese di dicembre la navigazione angloamericana ha perduto 35 mercantili per 225.000 tonn. - 24 altri mercantili sono stati gravemente danneggiati. La marina da guerra nemica ha perduto 24 unità.

LA CACCIA AI CACCIATORPEDINIERE

Continuando i loro attacchi nostri sommergibili hanno affondato altri 6 caccia, portando così il numero dei cacciatorpediniere distrutti negli ultimi 10 giorni a 21.

3.728.000 TONN. E 1174 AEREI

Nello scorso anno sono state affondate complessivamente 3.728.000 tonn. di naviglio nemico.
La marina da guerra del Reich ha abbattuto durante l'anno, sui mari e sulle coste dell'Europa, 1174 aerei anglo-americani.

Il viaggio verso l'Inghilterra rimane il viaggio verso la morte !

PAJ I/6₇

...lotta per ...'EUROPA

soldato germanico protegge dalla distruzione i beni più sacri dell'Europa

Questa è la fine

dei gangster dell'aria inviati da Roosevelt e Churchill a fare la guerra alle donne e ai bambini e a distruggere città e case.

Essi pagano con fortissime perdite, loro inflitte dalla Luftwaffe, ogni attacco alle popolazioni inermi:

22 SU 26

Il 26 dicembre 26 bombardieri nordamericani, scortati da cacciatori, penetrarono sull'Italia settentrionale. 20 bombardieri furono abbattuti in combattimenti aerei ed altri due dalla Flak della Luftwaffe.

97 AEREI ABBATTUTI

Il bollettino di guerra del 6 gennaio informa che nelle 24 ore precedenti erano stati distrutti 97 aerei nordamericani appartenenti a formazioni che avevano attaccato la Germania.

UNA SETTIMANA NERA

Nella prima settimana del 1944 le perdite degli angloamericani ammontavano a 262 aerei dei quali 231 bombardieri quadrimotori.

136 NON RAGGIUNSERO GLI OBBIETTIVI

Alle formazioni di bombardieri nordamericani, che nella mattinata dell'11 gennaio avevano tentato un attacco contro obbiettivi situati nella Germania centrale, furono inflitte delle perdite eccezionalmente gravi. 136 aerei nordamericani, fra i quali 124 bombardieri quadrimotori, furono abbattuti, in massima parte prima di giungere sopra gli obbiettivi. L'abbattimento di ulteriori apparecchi è probabile.

Le "Fortezze volanti" si sono trasformate in "Bare volanti"

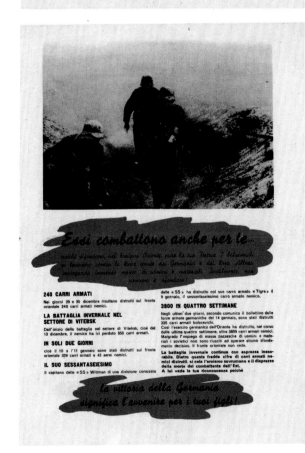

Essi combattono anche per te...

quindi difendono, nel lontano Oriente, cioè la tua Patria 7 tehuende a tenere... le dure terre dei Germani e dei loro Alleati impiegando immense masse di uomini e materiali. Tuttavia un successo si impone!

240 CARRI ARMATI

Nei giorni 29 e 30 dicembre risultano distrutti sul fronte orientale 240 carri armati nemici.

LA BATTAGLIA INVERNALE NEL SETTORE DI VITEBSK

Dall'inizio della battaglia nel settore di Vitebsk, cioè dal 13 dicembre, il nemico ha ivi perduto 850 carri armati.

IN SOLI DUE GIORNI

cioè il 10 e l'11 gennaio sono stati distrutti sul fronte orientale 359 carri armati e 43 aerei nemici.

IL SUO SESSANTASEIESIMO

Il capitano delle « SS » Witiman di una divisione corazzata

dalle « SS » ha distrutto col suo carro armato « Tigre » il 9 gennaio, il sessantaseiesimo carro armato nemico.

3800 IN QUATTRO SETTIMANE

Negli ultimi due giorni, secondo comunica il bollettino delle forze armate germaniche del 14 gennaio, sono stati distrutti 335 carri armati bolscevichi.

Così l'esercito germanico dell'Oriente ha distrutto, nel corso delle ultime quattro settimane, oltre 3800 carri armati nemici. Malgrado l'impiego di masse pazzesche di uomini e materiali i sovietici non sono riusciti ad operare alcuno sfondamento decisivo. Il fronte orientale non cede.

La battaglia invernale continua con asprezza insuperabile. Dietro queste fredde cifre di carri armati nemici distrutti, si cela l'eroismo sovrumano e il disprezzo della morte del combattente dell'Est.

A lui vada la tua riconoscenza poiché

la vittoria della Germania significa l'avvenire per i tuoi figli!

209. This booklet pictures and describes the various types of firearms available for death and destruction.

PAJ-1/97

209

IL VALLO D'ACCIAIO

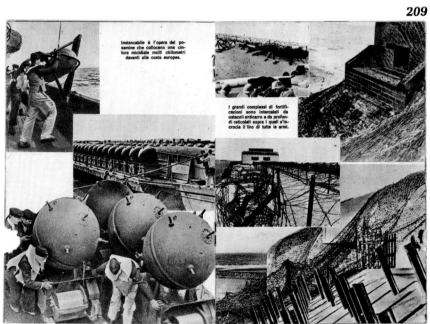

Instancabile è l'opera dei posamine che collocano una cintura micidiale molti chilometri davanti alle coste europee.

I grandi complessi di fortificazioni sono intercalati da ostacoli anticarro e da profondi reticolati sopra i quali s'incrocia il tiro di tutte le armi.

La vittoriosa Arma Aerea Germanica pronta per il decollo. Essa infliggerà ulteriori dure sconfitte al nemico.

210. Eat, drink, and be merry now, because to-morrow the Po River could well claim your life.

211. Who's been sleeping in your bed and holding your wife while you were out fighting the war? Yesterday's happiness is today's nightmare.

212. Happy is the girl who stood by her man and waited for his return.

211

Yesterday's Happiness

It belonged to you that happiness and nobody could interfere with it. You woke up in the morning and started out on another happy day of work. You had a wife, perhaps children. You had your own little home and your job. Sure, you had to work hard sometimes, but the evenings were yours, the week-ends and the holidays. — Remember those evenings at leisure, when you took her to a show or worked a bit in the garden, fixed the car or tinkered with your tools in the basement? You could do what you pleased in your spare time, because you were living in the biggest and freest democracy. Sounds like a fairy-tale of by gone days that yesterday's happiness!

Today's Happiness

Well, keep smiling Pal. It sure isn't YOUR happiness. You are cuddling in that muddy foxhole or you are getting ready for an attack and death is facing you every minute. Back home your wife is waiting, praying and crying- or has she already given up waiting for you? Could it be the hand of somebody else reaching for the alarm clock from your bed? — Well, no. After all it isn't your wife who is rising from the pillows somewhat bewildered. She seems to realize what she has done and feeling ashamed when she thinks of her husband who was taken from her years ago to fight for something she did not understand, in far-off Europe.
But there are SOME people who know damn well, what this war is all about. That's why they stayed in their Wallstreet offices to count the money they have been making out of the blood of your pals and your blood perhaps.
Today's happiness belongs to them!

Tomorrow's Happiness

That is the happiness you are hoping for, and you think every day of the war is one step nearer to it. The news from Germany is good and your letters from home say that the war will be over soon. But don't kid yourself, brother. That nasty jungle war is still waiting for you in the Far-East. But even if you are lucky and they don't send you there, you will have to stay a couple of years longer in the occupation army in Europe. And why all that?
Because the false democrats Roosevelt and Churchill did not want the Germans to live their way in their own country and because the Wallstreet Jews and Profiteers were greedy for Billions of War Profit.
Roosevelt wanted to destroy the power of Germany and created instead the much more dangerous power of Soviet Russia. He has helped the Bolsheviks to become the most colossal danger in the whole world. Upright Americans and the Anti-Communist press in America are quite uneasy about it and they openly talk of the coming Third World War as both the USA and the Soviets are expecting to rule the world.
The fighting of course will be YOUR part in that war. The people who stay at home in all wars, will leave again all the fighting to you. If you should survive even that gigantic struggle you will be an old man broken in body and spirit. Perhaps you would then be very happy, if someone would give you an underpaid job somewhere, and you would not have to sell apples on the streets like the vets of World War I. Well, soldier, that's the low-down on things.

Bad times for a bit of Happiness!

* 1332 · 4 · 45

Yesterday's happiness

213. POW camps get soldiers out of the war alive.

214. For five years of war, Dresden remained untouched because it contained no objective of military or economic value. The bombs came when it was finally filled to capacity with thousands of women and children refugees. Over thirty thousand charred and torn bodies were dug from the ruins.

215. Cooks tour. Equates Allied involvement with a spurious holiday abroad.

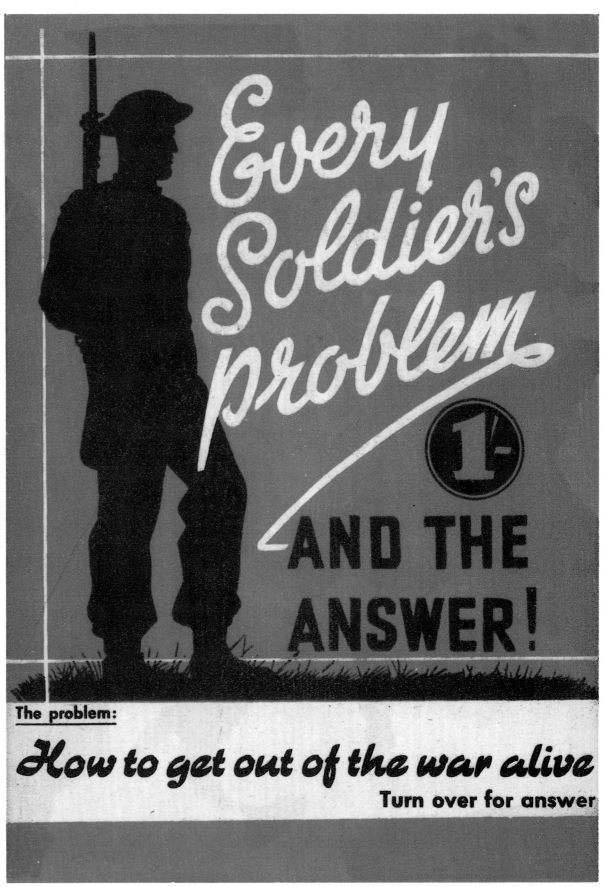

213

★ 713 - 3-45

213

We, in your place,
would ask our money back from Cooks.
They've tricked you. This time it's a lousy
sightseeing trip.
Ain't it?

215

214

214

216. *Where is the justice when one comes so far and is killed on the last day of the war?*

217. *Black soldiers are encouraged to forget about prejudiced America and join a German POW camp for decent treatment.*

216

ITALY NEXT?

Wars have the unpleasant habit that as they near their end, they demand an ever increasing number of victims.

And death visits the different theatres of war impartially, without bothering to ask if they are of first or of second class importance. The great plain of the mighty Po river has space enough for the graves of thousands and thousands of Allied soldiers.

Do you wish to be among these?

You don't perhaps understand why you have to be forced into an offensive in Italy when you all know that the war will not be decided in this country. You think — with the Russians before Berlin, with the Anglo-Americans and Canadians on the Rhine — why should you be asked to die in Italy? But you forget one thing, and that is — that nobody cares what Private Tommy Atkins or Gunner Sammy Smith thinks — personally you don't come into this thing at all. This is a matter of so-called Higher Politics. Both FDR and Winnie must have trumps in their hands when the game starts at San Francisco.

And so — Italy next!

— Successes — and sacrifices must be forthcoming also in Italy. For this — you will be pushed forward into the fire of the German defence guns. For this — there will be thousands and thousands of wooden crosses, later on, in the great Po plain — silent witnesses of the bloodiest battle ever fought on Italian soil — not to mention the nameless bodies carried away by the spring floods of the mighty river, without coming to rest in any grave.

«Not me!» — you think . . .

For you are of course fed up and you want to go home to those who are waiting for you. You know the old song «One more hill to climb — one more village to storm — one more river to cross — and Jerry is down and out!» You 've heard it so often, you're sick of it, you know Jerry hits back . . .

We can't help you. You must make the best of the fate which the Lord in Heaven, FDR and WC have arranged for you. Don't forget your identification disk so that your name can be painted on your wooden cross . . .

Above all — don't forget that even in Italy

D – Day means Death – day

★ 1323a-3-45

216

184

A short time ago two colored gentlemen from Harlem went to Brooklyn, N. Y., to visit some friends. It was Sunday morning and they were passing a church. It was a Baptist church frequented by white people. The organ was playing and the congregation was just finishing a hymn with the grand word "Hallelujah". The two men were deeply affected by the melodious strains and stood silent before the abode of God. Then, as if drawn by an invisible force, they slowly went up the steps and entered the house of worship. They were also Baptists and they wanted to do homage to the Lord.

No sooner had they entered when an extraordinary thing happened. Some members of the congregation jumped to their feet and surrounded the two men in an attitude unmistakably hostile. The minister gave a startled look at the "intruders" and came hurrying down the aisle. He told the men they must leave the church immediately.

The two colored men were stupefied. They could not understand why they as American citizens should be treated like this in a church.

Isn't America a free country?

Colored Soldiers of the U. S. Forces!

The white people in the U.S.A. do not allow you to pray in their churches, although you are American citizens. In Germany anything like this would be impossible. Colored people living in Germany can always go to any church they like. They have never been a problem to the Germans. There have never been lynchings of colored men in Germany. They have always been treated decently. So you don't have to be afraid to be with Germans.

COME OVER TO US

if you are fed up with this war and want to get home safe and sound.

Surely, you want to see your folks again don't you? You will be well-treated as a prisoner-of-war in a German camp. There will be every opportunity for you to attend religious services. You will be leading a healthy and pleasant life among your pals.

DON'T HESITATE.

If you wait too long, it may be too late.

AI - 173 - 12 - 44

218. *Eight American soldiers on patrol were captured and taken to a German POW camp. They send greetings to family and friends.*

219. *American Pte. Tommie J. Peterson was injured and taken to a military hospital as a German POW. He reflects on his care and treatment.*

218

German Leaflet
The End of a Patrol

Those pals of the patrol, who were caught, are now safe and sound. Here they are:

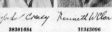

You can tell from their faces that they are not badly off. They are already in a PoW camp, north of the Po river, and they can now quietly wait for the end of the war. Being good soldiers they considered their capture a piece of bad luck. But wasn't it rather a piece of good luck? You must fight your way forward yard by yard against the stiffest German resistance and with great sacrifice of life and limb, while these eight boys covered the distance riding comfortably at 40 miles an hour in an Army lorry. Their next of kin have been informed through the Red Cross. The eight pals have asked us to send you their greetings, they are wishing you good luck.

* 429 / 3 45

On February 27, First Lt. Seymour Levy, platoon commander in the A Coy. VI. Bn., 1st. Arm'd. Div. was ordered by the Coy. Commander, Cpt. Bodin, to carry out a shock action with 20 men against the German positions at Vergato. First Lt. Levy was supposed to bring back at least one German prisoner as the Commander of the 1st. Arm'd. Div., Major Gen. V.E. Prichard hoped to extract valuable information from him about the movements of the German troops.

It was full moon at about 0.30 hrs. when the patrol moved about 2000 yards to the east of Vergato between the hills 581 and 589.

The patrol had bad luck, it was spotted and attacked. — No doubt the pals back in your lines thought a lot about the eight men during the following days, because after this action they had been reported missing. — Well, they don't have to worry about them in spite of the false rumours of bad German treatment.

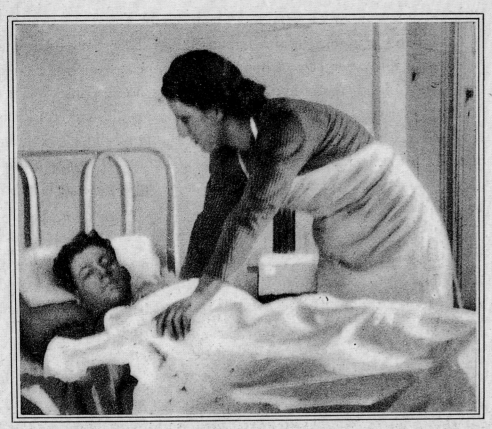

Pte. TOMMIE J. PETERSON

E - Co 135 th Inf., 34. Inf. Div.
native of Westville, Florida

In the night of Jan. 11/12 Tommie had to join a patrol against the strongly fortified German lines. *Suddenly they were fired at by German Tommy guns.* One of his comrades, Pte. Jacob Breitman, was killed, Tommie himself badly wounded.

We'll let him tell his own story:

While I was lying out there in front of the German lines, I wouldn't have given a d.... for my life. It was bitterly cold. At first my comrades had tried to take me along, but I had such pains that they had to give it up. *By myself I couldn't move from the spot, as I was wounded on both legs and the arm.*

It was dreadful to think that I was to perish like a helpless beast.

Within a few hours I would either bleed or freeze to death. I was thinking of our cornfarm in sunny Florida, of my folks and of Eileen, mi sweetheart, whom I had planned to marry. I cried for help as loud as I could. But there was no response. Wasn't it madness that I should die here! Why, after all, was I in this d..... place called Italy? Back home in the good old U. S. mine had been a peaceful life and I had been happy. *It was a hellish thing to send us American boys into this European war to make us suffer and die - for what good?*

After I had given up all hope, I heard all of a sudden voices which came nearer and nearer. *German soldiers? What would they do to me?* We had always been told that the Germans illtreated their prisoners and I had believed it. *But it was all different.* When they realized that to carry me was too painful, they brought a stretcher and carried me to a house nearby. There was a German officer who spoke English. He gave me a glass of hot wine. It seemed to me the best drink I ever had. Then he gave me first aid. *German soldiers put the stretcher near the fire place, gave me their blankets and offered me cigarettes and food.* A few hours later an ambulance brought me to a military hospital where I was operated on. Here I am under the best of care and the medics tell me that I'll be all right again.

My folks have been notified that I am wounded and a P. O. W. If I think of what I have gone through in that night, I'll say that I couldn't be better off. My first uneasy feelings regarding being taken prisoner have entirely vanished and I am glad to be out of the war.

I have just finished breakfast: coffee with white bread and butter and on top of it pancakes with apricot jam. It was a treat.

Tommie J. Peterson

P. F. C.
Serial Nr. 34793000

* 414 - I - 45

220. The P.W.B. Leaflet Competition was held to gather ideas for propaganda leaflets to be fired at the Germans. Three winners were chosen from over 200 hundred entries.

221. It was always better to be a wounded soldier in the hospital than an active one fighting on the front line.

220

P.W.B. Leaflet Competition

- Psychological Warfare Branch, 13 Corps, propose to hold a competition for ideas for propaganda leaflets to be fired at the Germans.

- This competition to be open to all ranks of 13 Corps.

- Prizes, to be awarded by P. W. B., 5th Army, will be as follows :

  1st : 2,500 lire and a bottle of cognac
  2nd : 1,000 lire and a bottle of cognac
  3rd :   500 lire and a bottle of cognac

- Entries to be judged by P. W. B., 5th Army, who reserve the right to use all entries.

- Entries may be pictorial or literary or both. Text may be in English or German.

- Final decision to be made by the 13 Corps Commander.

ADMINISTRATION.
- Entries (any number) to be sent in to Lieut. BOEHM, P. W. B., 13th Corps.

- Entries to carry name, rank and number and correct unit address.

- Entries to be received by 15 Dec 44.

Results of P.W.B. Leaflet Competition

Over two hundred entries were received by the closing date. After careful selection of the large number of excellent ideas submitted, the following entries were adjudged the best by the Corps Commander :

1. **FIRST PRIZE** (2500 lire and a bottle of cognac) :
   2592044 L/Cpl L. GARNER, R. C. of S att 152 (A. Y.) Fd Regt RA

2. **SECOND PRIZE** (1000 lire and a bottle of cognac) :
   7934162 Cpl R. L. CESSFORD, 1 Derby Yeo

3. **THIRD PRIZE** (500 lire and a bottle of cognac) :
   2583015 Sigmn P. JONES, 78 Div Sigs

All competitors are thanked for submitting entries, all of which — whether prizewinners or not — have supplied valuable new ideas for our leaflet campaign against the morale of the German Army.

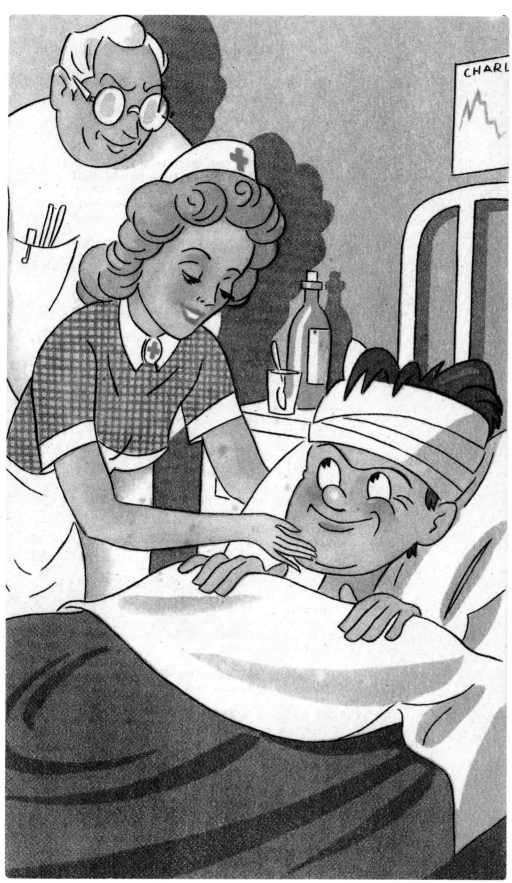

It Happened to Charlie --
It Can Happen to You.

I don't know what happened, but there was a hell of a flash and everything went black. As black as that time in the Oporto House in the West India Dock Road when I got into a little trouble with a big buck nigger. He hit me such a wallop that I didn't come too for a day.

I don't know how long I was out this time, but after I pulls meself together and feels if everything is alright, I looks round and sees my three pals what hadn't taken cover when they heard the 88 coming over.

I was feeling a bit thirsty and when I steps out of the hole I was in, I sees a house not far away. So I goes up to it and knocks on the door.

Did I get a surprise when the door opened. There were three blasted Jerries in there, so I points me gun at 'em and lines 'em up against the wall.

I had a funny feeling running up and down me spine as if something was wrong. Blime I was right. Behind me stood two more Jerries who I hadn't seen in the first place and they sticks a gun in me back. I was the conquered not the conquerer.

They weren't a bad lot. They gave me a fag and we had a little talk together.

Then everything went black again.

The next thing I remember was being unloaded from an Ambulance and taken into a hospital. Everyting was white and clean and I heard them talking. Then a nice little girl comes up to me and asks me "Whats the matter with you?" She was one of those Red Cross Sisters so I told her and she gave me a pill and off I goes to sleep again.

Next day I wakes up and finds a crowd round me bed. One fellow looked like that Erik von Stroheim bloke on the Pictures : he was the Doctor. There was another young fellow and the nurse.

Erik von Stroheim told me that I'd broken a rib or two and I'd got concussion but in a few days I'd be alright.

Then along comes the Little Sister and puts a cold wet towel on me head - she was nice - tender like an angel.

I got to thinking while I was there and wondering could it all be true or was I in heaven?

Where ever it was, it was a damned sight better than being stuck out on the front like I had been.

Yours till the next time.

Charlie.

* 1353 - 4 - 45

222. Life and captivity as a POW is better than death.

223. Christmas was not the same while Daddy was away at war.

222

This guy was not such a fool as the fellow overleaf!

HE thought it over and picked the right goddesses....

AI-170-I-45

DO YOU KNOW THE STORY OF PARIS?

Of course, we don't mean "gay Paree" - but that lucky young fellow in mythology. He had Venus, Minerva and Juno - some goddesses - up for a strip-tease for a beauty competition. After giving them a careful once-over, Paris handed the first prize, an apple, to Venus.

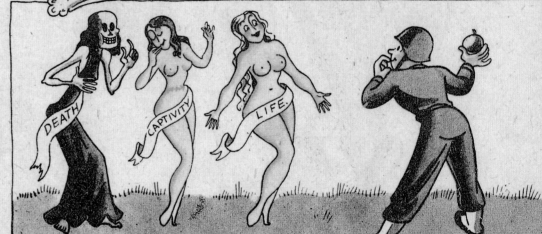

And here is the 1945 version of the story.

Now, would you be a sap like the doughboy in the picture?

22

"Mom why isn't Daddy with us?"

Here we are again! Another War Christmas!

Last summer you all expected the war would be over by October. October came and the war was still in full swing. Then you were sure it would be over by Christmas. Christmas is here now and the end of the war is not in sight.

CHRISTMAS!

How much love and longing this word contains.

Remember the time when you used to rush down Main Street, illuminated with thousands of electric lights, to do your Christmas shopping in stores overcrowded with people. You didn't mind that as long as you got those nice things you wanted to surprise your wife with, as long as you got the toys for your darling kids.

And how the eyes of the whole family sparkled with delight when the Christmas tree was lighted and you listened to the sweet strains of Christmas songs.

WHERE IS ALL THIS HAPPINESS NOW?

You are stuck in the mud with danger threatening you on all sides.

You don't know why you are here and what you are fighting for.

Your wife and children are unhappy because you are not with them. What is Christmas anyway without Daddy?

Well, all the same

HERE'S TO A BETTER FUTURE!

Jerry wishes you

A MERRY CHRISTMAS!

AI-175-12-1944

224. D-day Germans trying in vain to undermine the invasion of Normandy.

225. Animated art to show what the Allied leaders would experience before and after the invasion of Europe.

224

224

PRIMA DELL' INVASIONE

225

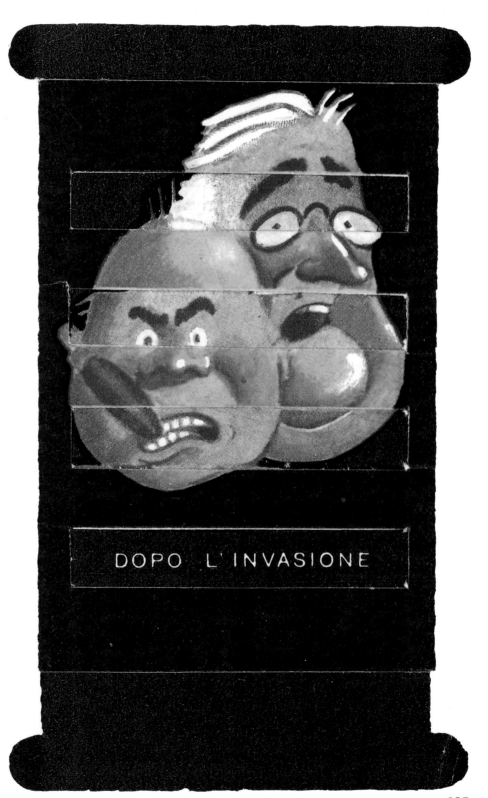

DOPO L'INVASIONE

225

226. Are you shedding your blood to fatten the Soviet Union?

227. In Italy soldiers are engaged in active war, while at the very same moment in London there is music, parties, warmongers, American men dating English girls, and a soldier's wife praying for her husband's safe return.

226

At the very same moment ..

LONDON — 22.01 hrs.

● Music in a great theatre. Hundreds enjoying themselves. The band starts playing a sweet melody of long ago: «The greatest mistake of my life . . . . . .»

● At the bus stop a Yank to a young girl: «But see here, Kid, he's in Italy and might not come back. How would you like to come to the old States?»

● In a taxi a Warmonger to an M.P.: «I say, old man, it will be a bad thing if the war ends this year. We invested too much money in new machinery and you know it's no use for peace production!»

● In a little cottage a soldier's wife with two young children waits, prays and weeps. Will he come back?

● In a big house in London a party is just startin⸱

227

At the very same moment ...

ITALY — 22.01 hrs.

● Music in the air from bursting shells. Hundreds are dying. Jerry starts with a series of Nebel‑werfers . . . . .

● A soldier in the mud is thinking of his girl. «Does she still remember me?»

● In the snow some soldiers huddled together: «If only this damned war would soon be over . .»

● In a slit trench a wounded soldier is moaning: «Mother, mother . . . .»

● In the darkness an attack is just starting. It means more dead . . . . more wounded . . . . more missing . . . .

★ 709 - 2 - 45

228. *Disabled veterans thought the hardest challenge in life was staying alive during the war.*

229. *Wives and girfriends send their men off to war. The flyer questions the why of it all.*

228

229

Goodbye! ... for ever?

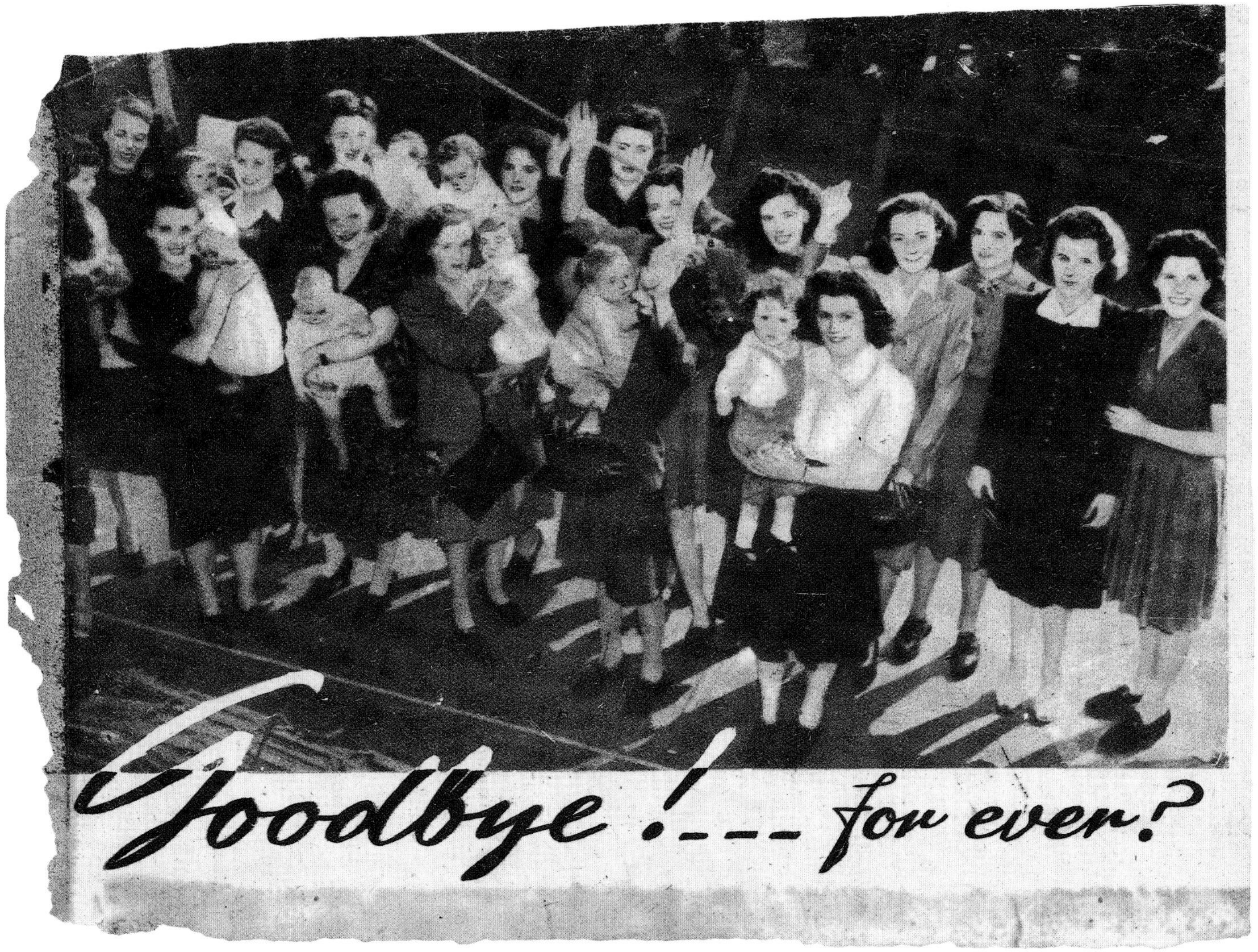

229

APPENDIX

Following are some translations of the texts of the leaflets appearing in the book. Translations of shorter pieces appear in the body of the captions. The numbers match those on each caption and piece of material.

13. Russian prisoners it is not your fault that you work for the Germans. But you have to know we are your friends in the USSR.

Working for Germans you think that you are not fighting on the German side, however, you release German soldiers to fight against the English, Americans, French, Italians, Yugoslavians and against your own friends in the U.S.S.R

The 16th Tank Division was sent from this front to the Eastern Front.

Your help to Germans prevents our victory of the United Nations.

These are various suggestions on what to do concerning handling prisoners such as any safe conduct leaflet says.

The Italian writing says, "Italian friends, this leaflet is addressed to the Russian prisoners who work for the Germans. Give one of these to them."

33. This I took from a German prisoner who had just returned from the Russian Eastern Front. He had been on the Italian front only one day.

Quotation from Stalin's order Number 55.

"If German soldiers and officers give themselves up, the Red Army takes them prisoner and protects their lives."

Extract from *Regulations covering Prisoners of War in the Soviet Union.*

"It is forbidden to insult or mishandle prisoners of war. Prisoners of war are to be brought into a prisoners of war camp immediately after capture.

"Wounded and sick prisoners of war who are in need of medical aid and hospital treatment must be handed over immediately by Officers commanding units to the nearest hospital.

"Prisoners are assured accommodation, washing places, clothing, shoes, nourishment and all other daily necessities, as well as money.

"Prisoners of war who go to work will have the benefit of the same regulations concerning protection at work and hours of work as are granted to citizens of the Soviet Union working in the same place on the same type of work."

From the enactment of the Soviet Government No. 1798 of July 1st, 1941.

"Being taken prisoner can be justified in exceptional cases, when the struggle is clearly hopeless and further expenditure of life can be of no further service to the Fatherland."

From Reibert, *Der dienstunterricht im Heere.*

German Parliamentary deputies with Soviet Officers.

CERTIFICATE
"The bearer of this, soldier or officer is giving himself up as a prisoner of war and places himself thereby under the protection of Soviet laws. The above certificate is valid for groups as well as for individual German soldiers and officers."

The High Command of the Red Army

42. The pictorial part of the leaflet seems quite clear.
Stalin and his brutish ways against the Poles.
Stalin's bloody horde. He barges into Poland and devours it.
Your families call you home. They beckon you to come.
You are indispensable.
Come home.

[Katyn, a small town near Russia, on the west, was a scene of massacre of a whole Polish Division, 15,000 men and officers, who were all killed. A complete total massacre. This was a Polish Division that had been completely annihilated from the face of the earth and no one at the time was aware of it. The Germans called for an investigation and found that the Russians had done this hideous crime. But the Russians then claimed that it was the Germans. Nevertheless, they all accepted the fact that the massacre took place. Who did the shooting in Katyn? The Germans, it is said, discovered, without a doubt, that the killers were the Bolsheviks. So it is believed by the Germans that the Russians were responsible, and the Russians say that it was the Germans. But the issue is very quiet and has been since World War II. So who known who were the assassins? This may be forever a controversy without an answer.]

54. *Der Kamerad* – translation for pages 8 & 9 only:
[Precis of an article in "Der Kamerad: Bunker und Graben: Zeitung einer Italinearmee," May, 1944]

[1] Verbiage under a new title.

Past experience has made us suspicious of enemy attempts to split our ranks by assuming that there were open breaches between, say, two Reich ministers or two generals. In the leaflet "Das fuenfte Jahr" (March 15, 1944) high German officers were purported to have used words so treasonable in character that had a captured German officer really employed them, they would have been supported by pictures, signature and all evidence to prove their validity. But names are suppressed and the following verbiage is offered:

"Each officer or N.C.O. who regards death as the only way out for his men is committing a crime against Germany. These sacrifices mean the destruction of a German generation. However difficult and hard the post war era, we must not pass out in cowardly fashion and leave reconstruction to our women and children."

But if German soldiers hold out to the last it is because five or even ten times their number depend on the supereme endurance of a small group at a given point.

[2] The Fuehrer is inviolable.

The enemy fails to realize this when he says: "Hitler is sacrificing you." The Fuehrer is not making unnecessary sacrifices of human life; he is concerned with the future and freedom of Germany. If the enemy were successful with his slanderous statement she would no doubt save some bloodshed, though his air terror daily slaughters women and children. But were we to give together there would be no end to the process of murder in Germany; it might be carried out by other means than sword or gun.

[3] Had we only known!

Remember that the fifth year of war for us is also the fifth for our enemies; England has not yet received the knock-out but her "friends" are already draining her life's blood; this fifth year is a thorn in the enemy flesh, a walk-over having been expected. As for the Russians, they allowed England to drop leaflets over Berlin anent the encirclement of Cherkassy after some of our men who had broken through had alr4eady returned to Berlin on a visit. The enemy loses no chance of deliberate falsification, but our crown witnesses will be the deeds leading to our victory. Then our enemies will say "Had we only knonw!" As for ourselves, we must trust and follow the very few who really know what is decisive.

[4] We trust and follow.

Our women and children would curse us if we threw up the sponge; what happened after 1918 would be nothing compared to what Bolshevism and amercanism have in stor for us. Hundreds of thousands are casualties in this war, but hundreds of millions are being saved for the life that two major wars hav interrupted.

[5] A third world war or German victory.

Unsolved problems on the enemy side are already preparing a third conflict on the lines of a power struggle between the U.S.S.R. and the United States; in this fight our country would be the battle field. Our victory is therefore essential to the peace of our Continent. We have crown witnesses how not to do things (Germany in 1918 and Italy in 1943) and we know too what the Baltic States can expect under Bolshevist domination.

[6] Struggle for life.

It is essential to trust our war leaders even though we do not always understand why certain precarious and costly operations were necessary; it is easy to say: "We would rather be civilians," but our future civilian life depends on our success as soldiers, though some of us will have to sacrifice our lives for our dearest ones at home. Our enemies hoped we should crack before things became too band for them, but we have a score to settle, a score against terror which will be settled by that victory we believe in.

150. CASSINO

You are in big danger. You overlooked Katyn and your government in London received from Moscow instruction how to get rid or damage you in an uncomplicated way.
You are, for the first time, being in a very quiet position, but you will be in the very middle part of the front in Italy which will be just like hell!
The English are smarter because they sent you to the Cassino front to let you die as heroes.
Polish soldiers, do you understand the game you are playing? You have only on way out for rescue.
Come to us and you will see your country again.
Go home will decide about death or life.
Take this to the first German soldier you will meet and you will come back home."

159. To the Indians
Do you know the Answer?
Well, these are your fellow men who were wounded.
Buty why were they wounded?
They are wounded because of their own foolishness.
They could have surrendered to the Germans.
Germans never kill any prisoners of war and they treat the wounded very good.
The names of each Indian soldier is given.

173. 1. Po Ka Ashnan "Bath in Po"
2. Kya tum apne—"Have you forgotten your comrades who died fighting?"
3. Po Kya Hay—"What is Po? This is a river 208 yards wide 1040 maximum. It is 7 to 20 feet deep and the banks are 18 to 30 feet high, and flows at 20 miles and hour."
4. Jan Par Khelna—"Why do you play with death?"
5. Kya Kar Sakte Ho?—"What you can do. Pretend to be sick and go to the hospital and in this way you can get away from fighting."

188. Happy New Year 1945 (to the Indians)

May God bless you with the New Year.
Think about it—during the New Year—uniforms, shining shoes, turbans, etc.
Go back home happily.
But all this has become a dream, but now you dance on a rope. A little slip can bring you down right over the sharp bayonets, then you will become statistics for the dead.
But it is possible to go home with happiness by taking this leaflet to the Germans without any fear?
If you want to know more then listen to the radio at 5:30 PM to 6:00 PM on medium wave of 449.1 and on short wave on 476.

194. The Red waves go through the country looking for a way on the West.
This is that the NRWD are now in Russia but London and Washington look at this and say nothing.
As for the Poles in Italy, just save your lives and think that the Germans and the Poles will fight Russia.

INDEX